BRICS and Development Alternatives:
Innovation Systems and Policies

BRICS and Development Alternatives: Innovation Systems and Policies

Edited by

JOSÉ EDUARDO CASSIOLATO
AND VIRGÍNIA VITORINO

ANTHEM PRESS
LONDON · NEW YORK · DELHI

Anthem Press
An imprint of Wimbledon Publishing Company
www.anthempress.com

This edition first published in UK and USA 2009
by ANTHEM PRESS
75-76 Blackfriars Road, London SE1 8HA, UK
or PO Box 9779, London SW19 7ZG, UK
and
244 Madison Ave. #116, New York, NY 10016, USA

British Library Cataloguing in Publication Data
A catalogue record for this book is available from the British Library.

Library of Congress Cataloging in Publication Data
A catalog record for this book has been requested.

ISBN-13: 978 1 84331 799 9 (Hbk)
ISBN-10: 1 84331 799 0 (Hbk)

1 3 5 7 9 10 8 6 4 2

TABLE OF CONTENTS

LIST OF CONTRIBUTORS

Dinesh Kumar ABROL

B.Tech (Electronics), Birla Institute of Technology and Science, Pilani & M.Phil (Science Policy), Jawahar Lal Nehru University, India. Director Grade Scientist, National Institute of Science, Technology & Development Studies, New Delhi, India.
Email: dinesh.abrol@gmail.com

José Eduardo CASSIOLATO

Ph.D., SPRU, University of Sussex, UK. Coordinator of RedeSist and Professor, Institute of Economics Federal University of Rio de Janeiro Brazil.
E-mail: cassio@ie.ufrj.br

Leonid GOKHBERG

Professor, First Vice-Rector, State University – Higher School of Economics (HSE), and Director, HSE Institute for Statistical Studies and Economics of Knowledge (ISSEK). Russia.
E-mail: lgokhberg@hse.ru

Natalya GORODNIKOVA

Dr., Director for Research, Centre for Science, Information and Education Programmes, Russia.
E-mail: gorodnikova@hse.ru

Priscila KOELLER

Ph.D. Candidate, Economics Institute, Federal University of Rio de Janeiro, Brazil. Adviser of Directorate of Surveys, The Brazilian Institute of Geography and Statistics, Rio de Janeiro, Brazil.
E-mail: priscilakoeller@ie.ufrj.br

Glenda KRUSS

Chief Research Specialist, Education, Research Programme on Science and Skills Development, Human Sciences Research Council, Cape Town, South Africa.
E-mail: gkruss@hsrc.ac.za

Tatyana KUZNETSOVA

Dr., Director, Centre for S&T, Innovation and Information Policies, HSE Institute for Statistical Studies and Economics of Knowledge (ISSEK), State University – Higher School of Economics (HSE), Russia.
E-mail: tkuznetzova@hse.ru

K. J. Joseph

Ph.D, Jawaharlal Nehru University, Professor, Centre for Development Studies Trivandrum Kerala India.
E-mail: kjjoseph@cds.ac.in
Centre for Development Studies Trivandrum Kerala India.
E-mail: kjjoseph@cds.ac.in

Jianbing LIU

Ph.D, Researcher, Graduate University of Chinese Academy of Science.
E-mail: liujianbing@126.com

Xielin LIU

Ph.D, Tsinghua University, Professor and associate dean School of Management, Graduate University of Chinese Academy of Science.
E-mail: liuxielin@gucas.ac.cn

Jo LONRENTZEN

Ph.D, European University Institute, Fiesole, Italy. Chief Research Specialist, Science and Innovation Unit, Research Programme on Education, Science, and Skills Development, Human Sciences Research Council, Cape Town, South Africa.
E-mail: jlorentzen@hsrc.ac.za

Bengt-Åke LUNDVALL

Professor, Aalborg University, Denmark, Special Invited Professor at Sciences-Po, Paris, France, Coordinator of worldwide research network Globelics.
E-mail: bal@business.aau.dk

Helena Maria MARTINS LASTRES

Ph.D., SPRU, University of Sussex, UK. Head of the Secretariat for Local Production and Innovation Systems and Regional Development of the Brazilian Economic and Social Development Bank (BNDES), Senior Researcher, IBICT, Brazilian Ministry for Science and Technology, Brazil.
E-mail: hlastres@redesist.ie.ufrj.br

Alexander SOKOLOV

Professor, Deputy Director, HSE Institute for Statistical Studies and Economics of Knowledge (ISSEK), and Director of the HSE/ISSEK International Foresight Centre, State University – Higher School of Economics (HSE), Russia.
E-mail: sokolov@hse.ru

Stanislav ZAICHENKO

Researcher, Centre for S&T, Innovation and Information Policies, HSE Institute for Statistical Studies and Economics of Knowledge (ISSEK), State University – Higher School of Economics (HSE), Russia.
E-mail: szaichenko@hse.ru

PREFACE

Until the end of the last century, generation of scientific knowledge was concentrated mainly in three regions of the world – Japan, the USA and Europe. The last decade has brought a marked shift towards other major players. Today the 'BRICS countries' – Brazil, Russia, India, China and South Africa – are contributing strongly to knowledge production.

This change in the global research landscape, together with the urgent need to tackle jointly key global challenges, such as climate change, energy and food security and poverty reduction, created a need for Europe to step up its international cooperation on science and technology (S&T) with other parts of the world.

The 'Strategic European Framework for International Science and Technology Cooperation' adopted by the European Commission in September 2008[1] and endorsed by the EU Member States in December 2008, was the European Union's answer to this need. The aim was to create the conditions for a more coherent and coordinated approach to international S&T cooperation based on strategic partnerships with leading countries and regions.

These strategic partnerships need to be based on an analysis of the comparative strengths of potential third-country partners and of Europe alike. Such analysis would lay the foundation for determining the scope and opportunities for cooperation and the potential mutual benefits.

This book is expected to contribute to such analysis. It presents research findings about the national innovation systems of the five BRICS countries and compares trends in their science, technology and innovation policies.

The chapters are based on papers presented and discussed at the second 'BRICS Project' workshop held in Rio de Janeiro, Brazil, from 25 to 27 April 2007.[2] The 'BRICS Project' was launched as part of the Globelics[3] network with the aim of comparing innovation systems from Brazil, Russia, India, China and South Africa.

By providing a robust analysis of the S&T environments of the BRICS countries, this book will contribute to an understanding of the rise of these new emerging S&T powers and to improving evidence-based S&T policymaking with regard to these countries.

ACKNOWLEDGEMENTS

This book presents important results of a collaborative effort. The contributions presented here were first discussed at a seminar held in Rio de Janeiro in April 2007. This seminar (IInd International Workshop of the BRICS Project), co-funded by DG RTD, marked the launching of the Comparative Study of the National Innovation Systems of Brazil, Russia, India, China and South Africa, an ongoing research project conducted under the auspices of Globelics— the Global Research Network on the Economics of Learning, Innovation and Capacity Building Systems. We are grateful to the seminar participants for their constructive criticism.

The research project as a whole has benefited from some key inputs that deserve special mention. First and foremost, we are grateful to Professor Bengt-Åke Lundvall, the coordinator of Globelics, who supported and promoted the BRICS project from the outset in 2003 and organised the Ist International Workshop of the BRICS Project in Aalborg, Denmark, in 2006. Without his leadership and enthusiasm the project could not have taken off. We owe special thanks to Helena Lastres, now at BNDES (Brazil's National Social and Economic Development Bank), and Maria Clara Couto Soares at RedeSist (part of the Economics Institute of the Federal University of Rio de Janeiro, Brazil), the organisation responsible for coordinating the project, for all their work throughout the different stages of the project. Also at RedeSist, Eliane Alves provided administrative and secretarial support and Fabiane da Costa Morais and Tatiane da Costa Morais helped with editing tasks. Max Hubert dos Santos provided the technical IT support for the research network.

None of this work would have been possible without financial support. The first phase of the BRICS project, from 2006 to August 2007, was carried out with grants from various agencies of the Brazilian Ministry of Science and Technology, especially FINEP, the Brazilian Innovation Agency and CGEE (Centre for Strategic Management and Studies in Science, Technology and Innovation). In particular, we would like to thank the General Secretary of the Ministry of Science and Technology, Dr Luiz Antonio Elias, and the President of FINEP from 2005 to 2007, Dr Odilon Marcuso do Canto, who have given enthusiastic support to the BRICS project since its inception. After September 2007, the BRICS research project could not have continued without a grant given by the International Development Research Centre of Canada. We are much obliged to IDRC and their staff for their support.

At the European Commission, we are very grateful for the support of International Cooperation Directorate from DG RTD, co-publisher of this book, and in particular of Virginia Vitorino who, with the technical assistance of Emanuela Ciavarini Azzi, has provided substantial help in the preparatory work that led to its publication. Jonathan Marten, Francis Flaherty, Ivan Buck and Douglas Jenks from Unit D/4 of DGT (Directorate-General for Translation) supplied the English revision.

José E. Cassiolato and the
BRICS project research team

Foreword

THE BRICS COUNTRIES AND EUROPE

Bengt-Åke Lundvall

Introduction

Over the past 10 years the world scene has changed and major new actors have taken the stage. It is thus interesting to note that the Lisbon strategy was mainly occupied with lessons to be drawn from the relative success of the US in the ICT-based new economy and that the strategy showed little concern with the five BRICS countries. Today it is obvious that Europe needs to recognise their role both as potential competitors in world trade and as potential partners when it comes to solving major problems of economic instability and environmental sustainability. While in 2000 it seemed adequate to regard the 'knowledge-based' economy as reigning solely in the OECD area, this report demonstrates that it is no longer the case.

As we can see from the contributions in this volume Russia and India have impressive knowledge bases in terms of their educational level while China has expanded its investments in both higher education and research at an outstanding rate. In Brazil and South Africa government bodies increasingly apply systemic approaches to policies aimed at promoting innovation. Understanding the specific dynamics linking the knowledge base to innovation and economic performance in each of the five BRICS countries is today a prerequisite for understanding the direction in which the world economy is heading. Here the BRICS project contributes with interesting insights.

The BRICS Project and the Globelics Framework

The BRICS project was initiated 2004 in the framework of Globelics and its general direction reflects the ideas behind the formation of this network. Globelics is an open and flexible network of scholars who use the concept of 'innovation and competence building systems' in order to understand what drives economic development (www.globelics.org). The intention is to strengthen the knowledge base for innovation policy through stimulating research on innovation, especially outside the OECD area. The network, established 2002 in honour of the major innovation scholars Christopher Freeman and Richard R. Nelson, has been successful both in mobilising leading scholars from the West and North and in creating links to new and growing research communities in the South and East.[1]

One of the basic ideas behind Globelics is that 'horizontal' exchange of ideas and research among less developed countries is especially important. Building strong research capacity for innovation in Africa, Asia and Latin America makes it possible for those regions to learn from each other rather than depend on imitating ideas developed in the rich part of the world.

While Globelics has been inspired by innovation scholars such as Richard Nelson (1993) and Christopher Freeman (1987), Cassiolato & Lastres (2008) remind us that important contributions to understanding the links between technology and economic development were developed by scholars with roots outside the OECD area, such as Raul Prebisch, Celso Furtado and Amartyar Sen.

In the introduction to this volume José Cassiolato, the leader of the BRICS project, and Helena Lastres present an analytical framework explaining economic performance on the basis of a broad understanding of what constitutes a national system of innovation (Lundvall 2008). This is helpful as a guide to the ensuing country-specific chapters, which have as their main focus the role played by science and technology policy in the different countries.

In the following we will relate development in the BRICS countries to global issues and not least to how it affects the role of Europe vis-à-vis these countries. We will point to unexploited development potentials in the five countries and argue that it is in the interest of Europe to see these potentials realised. But we will also point out that in order to avoid friction it is important for Europe to renew its strategy for domestic development and to upgrade production and work, especially in the south and east of Europe.

Transformation of the BRICS' Innovation Systems—China and Russia

A common feature of the five countries covered in this book is that their innovation systems have gone through radical transformations over the last couple of decades. In some cases this reflects wider system changes such as the move towards the market economy in China and Russia and the end of apartheid in South Africa, while in the case of India and Brazil changes have been driven by globalisation and by public policy responses to the globalisation process.

It is interesting to note both the similarities and the differences in the transformations that have taken place. China is unique in many respects. On the one hand, the very high rates of growth have been based on very high rates of capital accumulation in traditional manufacturing rather than on growth of new knowledge-based activities—most of the high-technology exports still emanate from foreign-owned firms. On the other hand, the rate of investment in education and research has been high and the transformation of the old Soviet model has resulted in a diversified knowledge infrastructure. Therefore there is a big gap between what has been accomplished so far in terms of knowledge-based economic growth and what may be achieved in the future in China.

If the current long-term strategy, where the 'innovation system' is used as conceptual tool, succeeds in reforming institutions and public policies so that they become more supportive to the formation of a 'learning economy' in China, we might witness a new kind of growth less oriented towards mass production and more in the form of high-quality products and services (Gu & Lundvall 2006). This requires a change in the macro-economic dynamics, with more emphasis on home market growth and income redistribution in favour of weak and poor people and less developed regions. It also requires radical reform in education and in working life, giving students and workers more opportunities to develop and implement their own ideas.

While China since 1978 has been quite successful in transforming the innovation system from a situation where inefficient centralised government-sector institutes dominated the scene, the corresponding developments in Russia have been much more problematic. One of the first steps after the old system broke down was to reduce drastically government support for science and technology. This was based on the assumption that the market would regulate the production and use of knowledge. This did not happen and the resulting discontinuity is still in evidence in a generalised weakness in the innovation system.

In Russia there is great unexploited potential in terms of human resources. The level of education is high compared with other countries at the same income level. In this context it is interesting to note that China combined strong investment in the domestic higher education system with programmes helping students to study abroad. One major challenge is to find a way to combine the opening-up of the national innovation system with a stronger focus on the most pressing problems of society. There is also a need to combine increased investments in R&D in both the private and public sectors with reforms that upgrade 'social capital' and entrepreneurship.

India, Brazil and South Africa

All these three countries have a history of colonisation that in different ways has left imprints on the current structure and working of their national innovation systems. All three have experienced how colonial powers consciously put a brake on the production, diffusion and use of knowledge in the economy. This has contributed to awareness that one important prerequisite for independence is to host institutions that promote science and technology.

After decolonisation the Indian governments placed strong emphasis on government efforts to promote certain 'key technologies' such as nuclear power and space technology. Until the middle of the 1980s the major player in science and technology was government. In fact, both science policy and industrial policy was inspired by the Soviet Union. In the 1990s the economy became less regulated and market exchange with the rest of the world was facilitated (Joseph 1997).

It is interesting to note that the opening-up of the Indian economy took place in parallel with the transformation and opening-up of China's economy. The outcome in terms of economic performance and economic structure was quite different, however. While China became 'the factory of the world', service sectors, including the film industry and software services, were much more important in India. This indicates a cultural bias in favour of theoretical and academic knowledge and it signals unexploited opportunities also in the Indian innovation system. The fact that in India the focus is on science and technology policy rather than on 'innovation policy' may be seen as another indication of such a bias. It might be reduced through changes in the education system giving greater prominence to project work and practical experience.

Brazil started from a weak position in terms of its knowledge infrastructure and most of its strong economic growth in 1950–1970 was based on exports of natural resources and production for a growing protected home market. After a prolonged period of stagnation in 1970–1990 there was a shift towards deregulation and opening up the economy both for imports and for inward flows of foreign capital. The outcome of the increased transformation pressure was less inflation but not higher economic growth. In fact, many of the domestic firms with strong technological capabilities that were created in the earlier period disappeared or were taken over by foreign owners.[2]

In the case of Brazil the most promising unexploited opportunity may be a combination of natural resources with specific technological capabilities related to process industries, including bio-fuels. Building industrialisation by combining access to natural resources with the use of the most advanced new technologies in the field of nanotechnology, biotechnology and materials may take advantage of a new window of opportunity opened up by the next technological revolution (Perez 2009).

South Africa has been able to develop its own innovation policy only after the end of apartheid and it still suffers from the transformation. Opening up reasonable opportunities for access to learning and competence-building for the black population is a major concern that is part of this policy. Also in South Africa it may be especially important to link together innovation in exploring natural and agricultural resources with innovation in processing and transforming them into high-quality products.

But for both Brazil and South Africa this needs to be combined with activities that create jobs and link supply to domestic needs of the population. South Africa faces the major challenge of defining its innovation policy both in relation to the rest of the world and in relation to the rest of Africa. Here lie important problems as well as opportunities.

The Role of Europe in Relation to the BRICS

From time to time, when specific manufacturing sectors in Europe such as footwear and clothing have been exposed to competition from China, Europe has initiated protectionist schemes. Another potential source of conflict has to do with intellectual property rights, where firms in BRICS countries from time to time copy ideas protected by international law. Finally it has been argued that China's trade surplus has fed the process that led to the current crisis.

This raises questions about how the role of Europe should be perceived in relation to the BRICS countries. Are they competitors whose efforts to exploit their full potential should be weakened? This was the classical approach among colonial powers and sometimes we see a fall-back to that kind of attitude. But today BRICS countries with or without direct colonial experience have both awareness and sufficient strength to respond to behaviour of this kind and the final outcome may be an unravelling of the world economic order.

Or should the strategy be one of opportunism, where Europe tries to exploit resources within these countries, including well-trained scientists, without offering much in return? This type of behaviour is 'legal' in the current WTO regime for global regulation of knowledge flows, where disembodied knowledge in the form of patents, mainly controlled by the North, are protected while knowledge embodied in skilled people is free for the rich countries to import from the South.

A third kind of strategy would be to regard the world economy as a positive sum game where economic growth in BRICS countries constitutes a dynamo that benefits economic well-being in the rest of the world. For Europe such a strategy would have dramatic implications both for its 'domestic' and for its 'foreign' economic policy.

Within Europe it involves upgrading skills and work in the south and east of Europe on a scale that is much bigger and more adequate than that pursued by the current regional funds and the common agricultural policy. This would be the best way to reduce friction related to sunset industries both through renovating such industries and through closing some of them down.

In terms of foreign economic policy Europe and Europeans should be willing to accept invitations to help BRICS countries to exploit the kind of opportunities that have been sketched out above. Most of the effort to tackle the problems must come from within each country but Europe should be ready to join common efforts to promote both institutional change and technical innovation.

The Role of China in the Global Economy

All the BRICS countries have an important role to play in shaping the future of the world economy—also because they have regional leadership. But perhaps what will happen in China is most important in this respect. Economic growth in China over the last couple of decades brought material progress both for Chinese and for people in the rest of the world. It reduced living costs and inflation through low-cost exports and increased the demand for raw materials from countries such as Russia and Brazil. Finally, the export-oriented economic growth model made it possible for lax monetary policy to go on for a long period.

But it is equally valid that this growth trajectory was not sustainable. This is true in terms of growing inequality, negative environmental consequences and global imbalances. The Chinese strategy left limited scope for industrialisation in Africa and Latin America. It is therefore important to follow the current search for a new growth model among the Chinese leadership. This is taking place with reference to two key concepts: 'harmonious growth' and 'independent innovation'.

While harmonious growth is linked to social and environmental considerations, independent innovation refers to a new relationship between domestic and foreign actors when it comes to developing and using new technology. A key for achieving both these goals is to link innovation to domestic needs and in general to give more priority to domestic consumption. If Chinese leaders were to succeed with this strategy it would have a major impact both for the other BRICS countries and for Europe.

For the other BRICS countries Chinese success would be seen as leading the way towards more socially and environmentally balanced strategies. Strengthening domestic technological capabilities and the capacity to use new and old technologies would become an even more highly prioritised agenda for governments and other agents.

Such a development would mean that Europe would need to move on and upgrade its production systems in order to remain competitive. The activities that would be competitive in this new context would need to combine creativity and innovation in work with advanced forms of organisation and distribution. Only workplaces where the majority of workers are educated, have space to apply their own ideas and are willing to take on responsibility will be sustainable. This requires new social contracts where workers offer a willingness to contribute to change while society offers social security as well as new forms of education where learning creativity is as important as learning mathematics.[3]

But this scenario is, of course, the most optimistic one. Others where conflict dominates the picture both domestically and abroad may be as realistic. In a world characterised by 'radical' fundamental uncertainty, the only thing we know for certain is that unforeseen radical change is ahead. But not least in such a context is a world vision likely to be useful.

References

Amsden, A. H. (1989), Asia's Next Giant: South Korea and Late Industrialization, Oxford University Press, USA.

Arundel, A., Lorenz, E., Lundvall, B.-Å. and Valeyre, A. (2007), 'How Europe's economies learn: a comparison of work organization and innovation mode for the EU-15', *Industrial and Corporate Change*, 16, (6).

Cassiolato, J. E. and Lastres, H. M. M. (2008), 'Discussing innovation and development: Converging points between the Latin American school and the Innovation Systems perspective?, *Globelics Working Paper*, No 08–02, www.globelics.org

Freeman, C. (1987), Technology policy and economic performance: Lessons from Japan, London, Pinter Publishers.

Gu, S., Lundvall, B.-Å. (2006), 'China's Innovation System and the Move Toward Harmonious Growth and Endogenous Innovation', *Innovation, Management, Policy and Practice*, 8 (1/2): 1–26.

Joseph, K. J. (1997), Industry under Economic Liberalisation: Case of Indian Electronics, New Delhi, Sage publications.

Lall, S. (1992), 'Technological capabilities and industrialization', *World Development*, 20(2): 165–186.

Lundvall, B.-A., Ed. (2007). Innovation system research: Where it came from and where it might go, *Globelics Working Paper*, No 07–01, www.globelics.org

Nelson, R., Ed. (1993), *National innovation systems. A comparative analysis*. New York, Oxford University Press.

Perez, C. (2008), 'A vision for Latin America: A resource-based strategy for technological dynamism and social inclusion', *Globelics Working Paper*, No 08–04, www.globelics.org

Wade, R. H. (2004), 'Is Globalization Reducing Poverty and Inequality?', *World Development*, 32 (4): 567–89.

BRICS and Development Alternatives: Innovation Systems and Policies

Chapter 1

SCIENCE, TECHNOLOGY AND INNOVATION POLICIES IN THE BRICS COUNTRIES: AN INTRODUCTION

José E. Cassiolato and
Helena M. M. Lastres

1. Preamble

The crisis that has hit the world economy since 2008 has lent support to suggestions put forward previously that a significant share of the growth potential of the world economy resides in a few large less developed countries. Brazil, Russia, India, China and South Africa (BRICS) have such potential. More than just that, the BRICS countries are thought to have the capacity to 'change the world' on account of both the threats and the opportunities they represent from the economic, social and political points of view.

International agencies and analysts suggest that investors should pay careful attention to the opportunities offered by these countries. In such analyses, the focus has been restricted to identifying investment possibilities in the BRICS production structures and examining the prospects offered by their consumer markets. This book is part of a study—the BRICS project—where the interest in analysing the BRICS goes much further. These countries present significant development opportunities, as well as several common characteristics and challenges. Identifying and analysing them may help to uncover possible paths for fulfilling their socio-political and economic development potential. More importantly, it can also reveal development alternatives that might help both developed and underdeveloped countries to overcome the problems brought by an exhausted production and consumption system and a malignant regulatory and financial regime.

The BRICS project is an investigation conducted by the Global Research Network for Learning, Innovation and Competence Building Systems—

Globelics[1]—and the Research Network on Local Production and Innovation Systems—RedeSist—at the Economics Institute of the Federal University of Rio de Janeiro, Brazil[2]. It is carried out by researchers from the five countries. The central focus of the study is a comparative analysis of the national systems of innovation (NSIs) of Brazil, Russia, India, China and South Africa.

Conceptually, the project is structured around the systems of innovation (SI) framework. The notion of innovation system has at its centre the industrial, S&T and education subsystems, but includes also the promotion, financial and regulation subsystem, as well as other spheres connected to the national and international contexts where knowledge is generated, used and diffused. The objective is to characterise and compare the NSIs of the five countries, pointing out convergences, divergences and synergies and identifying connections both actual and potential.

This book presents a discussion of recent science, technology and innovation (STI) policies pursued by the BRICS, using the broad understanding of the NSI approach as a general analytical framework. In this approach, delineated in section 2 of this chapter, the effectiveness of policies directed towards STI depends on a wide-ranging set of factors that includes the historic specificities of each country, its position in the world hierarchy and the existing general macroeconomic framework, context and policies. Besides stressing the importance of the innovation systems concept for an analysis of STI policies, with an emphasis on contributions by several authors from the developing world, this introductory chapter offers a general picture of the BRICS, pointing out their present relative importance and strength in section 3, and bringing forward in section 4 elements of their STI policies that will be dealt with in more detail in the country chapters. Section 5 sets out the concluding considerations of the chapter.

2. The Systems of Innovation Framework and its Importance to Development

Some of the most fruitful thinking developed in advanced countries in the last 30 years came from a resurrection and updating of earlier thinking that emphasised the role of innovation as an engine of economic growth and the long-run cyclical character of technical change. In 1982, Freeman's paper pointed out the importance that Smith, Marx and Schumpeter attached to innovation (p. 1) and accentuated its systemic and national character (p. 18). He also stressed the crucial role of government policies to cope with the uncertainties associated with the upsurge of a new techno-economic paradigm and the very limited circumstances under which free trade could promote economic development.

Since it was formulated in the 1980s, the SI approach has been increasingly used in different parts of the world to analyse processes of acquisition, use and diffusion of innovations and to guide policy recommendations[3].

Particularly relevant in the SI perspective is the fact that since the beginning of the 1970s, the innovation concept has been widened, to be understood as a systemic, non-linear process rather than an isolated occurrence. Emphasis has been given to its interactive character and to the importance of (and complementarities between) incremental and radical, technical and organisational innovations and their different and simultaneous sources. A corollary of this argument is the specific and localised character of innovation and knowledge. Innovation should then be understood as the process by which firms master and implement the design and production of goods and services that are new to them, irrespective of whether or not they are new to their competitors—domestic or foreign, is particularly important for the analysis of innovation in less developed countries (Nelson 1993, Mytelka 2000).

This understanding helps to avoid overemphasis on R&D in the innovation process, encouraging policy-makers to take a broader perspective on the opportunities for learning and innovation in small and medium-sized enterprises and in the so-called traditional industries (Mytelka & Farinelli, 2003). Understanding innovation as a localised, context-specific and socially determined process implies, for instance, that acquisition of technology abroad is not a substitute for local efforts. On the contrary, a lot of knowledge is needed to be able to interpret information, select, buy (or copy), transform and internalise technology.

Systems of innovation, defined as a set of different institutions that contribute to the development of the innovation and learning capacity of a country, region, economic sector or locality, comprise a series of elements and relations that link together the production, assimilation, use and diffusion of knowledge. In other words, innovation performance depends not only on firms' and R&D organisations' performance but also on how they interact, among themselves and with other agents. Innovation capacity derives, therefore, from the confluence of specific social, political, institutional, and cultural factors and from the environment in which economic agents operate. Different development trajectories contribute to shaping systems of innovation with quite diverse characteristics requiring specific policy support.

It is this understanding of the systemic nature of innovation that allows two crucial dimensions of the SI approach to be explicitly discussed: the emphasis on historical and national trajectories and the importance of taking into account the production, financial, social, institutional and political contexts, as well as micro, meso and macro spheres (Freeman, 2003; Lastres, Cassiolato & Maciel, 2003). Although all of these contexts are relevant for discussions about development, two in particular should be singled out that are pertinent to this paper. One is the financial context, recognised by Schumpeter (1912) in his Theory of Economic Development. For him entrepreneurs, to become the driving force in an innovation process, must be able to convince banks to provide the credit to finance innovation. In this sense, any discussion about systems of innovation has necessarily to include the financial dimension[4]. The other is the idea that space matters, that analysing systems of innovation should be done at the national (Freeman, 1982; Lundvall, 1988) and local levels (Cassiolato, Lastres & Maciel, 2003). Such territorial dimension of SI should vitally include how these systems are influenced by (and influence) their various modes of insertion in the international geo-political context.

The national character of SI was introduced by Christopher Freeman (1982, 1987) and Bengt-Ake Lundvall (1988) and has been used as an analytical tool and as a framework for policy analysis in both developed and underdeveloped countries. As a result, research and policy activities explicitly focusing on SI can be found in most countries and a rapidly growing number of studies of specific NSIs have been produced. Although some authors tend to focus on the NSI in a narrow sense, with an emphasis on research and development (R&D) efforts and science and technology organisations, a broader understanding of NSI (Freeman, 1987; Lundvall, 1985) presents a number of advances. This approach takes into account not only the role of firms, education and research organisations and STI policies, but includes government policies as a whole, financing organisations, and other actors and elements that influence the acquisition, use and diffusion of innovations. In this case emphasis is also placed on the role of historical processes—which account for differences in socio-economic capabilities and for different development trajectories and institutional evolution—creating an SI with very specific local features and dynamics. As a result, there are good reasons for examining the national character of SI.

Figure 1.1 is an attempt to show both the narrow and the broad perspectives on NSI. The broad perspective includes different, connecting subsystems that are influenced by various contexts: geopolitical, institutional, macroeconomic, social, cultural, and so on. First, there is a production and innovation subsystem, which contemplates the structure of economic activities, their sectoral distribution, degree of informality and spatial and size distribution, the level and quality of employment, the type and quality of innovation effort. Second, there is a subsystem of science and technology, which includes education (basic, technical, undergraduate and postgraduate), research, training and other elements of the scientific and technological infrastructure such as information, metrology, consulting and the intellectual property regime. Third, there is a policy, promotion, financing, representation and regulation subsystem that encompasses the different forms of public and private policies both explicitly

Figure 1.1. The Narrow and the Broad Perspectives on the National System of Innovation

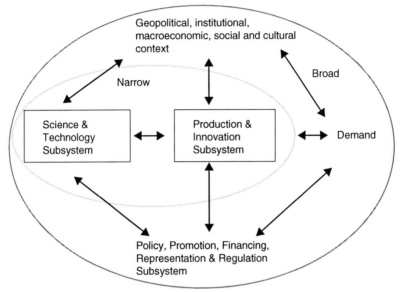

Source: Adapted from Cassiolato & Lastres, 2008.

geared towards innovation or implicit, i.e. those that, although not necessarily geared towards it, affect strategies for innovation. Finally, there is the role of demand that most of the time is surprisingly absent from most analyses of SI. This dimension includes the pattern of income distribution, the structure of consumption, social organisation and social demand (basic infrastructure, health, education).

This portrayal of the national innovation system framework is a corollary of the understanding that:

- innovation capacity derives from the confluence of specific economic, social, political, institutional and cultural factors and from the environment in which they operate, implying the need for an analytical framework broader than that offered by traditional economics (Freeman, 1982, 1987; Lundvall, 1985);
- the number of firms or organisations such as teaching, training and research institutes is far less important than the habits and practices of such actors with respect to learning, linkage formation and investment. These shape the nature and extensiveness of their interactions and their propensity to innovate (Mytelka, 2000; Johnson & Lundvall, 2003);

- the main elements of knowledge are embodied in the minds and bodies of agents or embedded in the routines of firms and in relationships between firms and organisations. Therefore, they are localised and not easily transferred from one place/context to another, as knowledge is something more than information and includes tacit elements (Lundvall, 1985);
- the focus on interactive learning and on the localised nature of the generation, assimilation and diffusion of innovation is in opposition to the idea of a supposed techno-globalism. The understanding of innovation as a context-specific process implies that the acquisition of foreign technology abroad is not a substitute for local efforts (Cassiolato & Lastres, 1999);
- the national framework matters, as development trajectories contribute to shaping specific systems of innovation. The diversity of NSIs is a product of different combinations of the main features that characterise their micro, meso and macroeconomic levels, as well as the links between these levels (Freeman, 1987; Lastres, 1994).

The particular importance of policies during the advent and diffusion of a new techno-economic paradigm is also stressed. For authors such as Freeman and Perez, development proceeds in long waves, the pivot of which lies in technological revolutions. They thus build on Schumpeter's theories of long cycles in economic development and his exploration of 'creative gales of destruction'. Chris Freeman and Carlota Perez, who developed further these ideas (Freeman, 1987; Perez, 1983; Freeman & Perez, 1988, Perez, 1988), point out that changes in the techno-economic paradigm (TEP)—pervasive transformations with a major influence on the behaviour of the entire economy and society—are essential to explain periods of economic growth and crisis. While fuelled by revolutionary technological opportunities it takes time for a new paradigm to crystallise and even longer for it to diffuse right through the economy. Crises are seen to arise when there is a mismatch between the emerging new paradigm and the old institutional framework. Public and private policies are essential to internalise the benefits of the new paradigm and minimise its costs.

In their paper to the Rio Globelics Conference, Reinert and Reinert (2003) warned against the abuse of the IS perspective in academic and policy circles. They mentioned that 'by integrating some Schumpeterian variables to mainstream economics we may not arrive at the root causes of development. We risk applying a thin Schumpeterian icing on what is essentially a profoundly neoclassical way of thinking' (p. 63). Their point was that development ideas and policy proposals that have been spreading over the last few years are just attempts to introduce the fashion around innovation and knowledge in frameworks of analysis that still emphasise that: (i) both theory and policy recommendations are independent of context; (ii) the economy is largely independent from society; and (iii) there is no distinction between the real economy and the financial economy. In other papers (Lastres & Cassiolato, 2004, 2005) we discuss some of the important policy misunderstandings that derive from such attempts.

From the specific point of view of less developed countries (LDCs) the usefulness of the SI approach resides precisely in the fact that (i) its central building blocks allow their socio-economic and political specificities to be taken into account and (ii) it does not ignore the power relations in discussing innovation and knowledge accumulation. As this book argues, these features are particularly relevant in the analysis of the BRICS' innovation systems. As the analysis of economic phenomena also takes into consideration their social, political and historical complexity, policy prescriptions are based on the assumption that the process of development is influenced by and reflects the particular environment of each country, rather than recommendations based on the reality of advanced countries.

A number of development studies have followed these ideas, arguing that technical change plays a central role in explaining the evolution of capitalism and in determining the historical process through which hierarchies of regions and countries are formed. Furtado (1961), for instance, established an express relationship between economic development and technological change, pointing out that the growth of an economy was based on the accumulation of knowledge and understood development within a systemic, historically determined, view. Although original, these contributions are in close correspondence with Myrdal's (1958) proposition that (i) contexts and institutions matter; (ii) positive and negative feedbacks have cumulative causation; and (iii) cycles may be virtuous or vicious, as well as with Hirschman's (1958) point that interdependencies among different activities are important.

The neo-schumpeterian perspective also argues that economic development is considered as a systemic phenomenon, generated and sustained not only by inter-firm relations, but most significantly by a complex inter-institutional network of relations. Innovation is eminently a social process. Therefore, development—resulting from the introduction and diffusion of new technologies—may be considered as the outcome of cumulative trajectories historically built up according to institutional specificities and specialisation patterns inherent to a given country, region or sector.

Each country follows its own development trajectory according to its specificities and possibilities, depending fundamentally on its hierarchical and power position in the world capitalist system. The more distant underdeveloped countries are from the technological frontier, the larger will be the barriers to innovative integration in the new technological paradigm. More serious than technological asymmetries are knowledge and learning asymmetries, with the implication that to access, understand, absorb, master, use and diffuse knowledge turns out to be impossible. However, even when access to new technologies becomes possible, most of the time the technologies are not appropriate to the reality of underdeveloped countries and/or these countries do not have a pool of sufficient knowledge to make adequate use of them. This occurs because the learning process depends on the existence of innovation and production capabilities that are not always available. On this aspect, Arocena and Sutz (2003) argue that there are clearly learning divides between North and South that are perhaps the main problem of underdevelopment nowadays. Additionally, Tavares (1972, p. 50) points out that 'underdeveloped countries import a kind of technology conceived by leading economies according to a constellation of resources that is totally different from ours. The need to import this technology was given by the very substitutive character of industrialisation and by the impossibility of creating new techniques more adequate to our own conditions'.

One corollary of such important and complex discussion is the argument put forward by Arocena and Sutz (2003, 2005) that a new framework of thought is fundamental to the analyses of development problems related to knowledge, innovation and learning. This book makes a contribution in that direction. By analysing the innovation systems of the BRICS we believe that we have achieved a perspective that is relevant to the study of innovation, learning and capacity-building in developing countries. This allows us to advance ideas that emphasise that:

- economic agents and processes are embedded in the economic, social and political environment;
- both theory and policy recommendations are highly context-dependent;
- constraints—internal and external—to development will always exist and should be the central concern of policies.

3. The Importance of the BRICS

The BRICS countries have a significant strategic position on their continents: the Americas, Asia, Europe and Africa[5]. Taken together, these five countries account for approximately 30 per cent of the earth's surface. The importance of this vast territory is related to the amount of their mineral, water and energy resources, the availability of fertile land for agriculture and their biodiversity. All five countries have intensively developed activities in these areas with varying degrees of success. The relative importance of agricultural and extractive activities, the transformation of mineral and energy resources and the magnitude of the BRICS' agro-industry are shown by their share in global trade in commodities and in the evolution of industrial activities. Their rich biodiversity also provides the opportunity for the development of very dynamic industries such as pharmaceuticals and biotechnology.

The total population of the BRICS is even more significant than their territory. The BRICS' percentage of global population remained constant at around 43 per cent of the world's total population over the period 1985–2005. China's share of the world population declined from 22.1 per cent in 1980 to 19.6 per cent in 2005. However, the population of all the other BRICS except Russia increased, both in absolute and in relative terms. The most significant increase in population occurred in India, which had 17.4 per cent of the world population in 2005. This large share of the population represents both a challenge and a source of opportunities. Challenges that frequently occur in large populations are those to do with the provision of water, food, energy and sanitation, as well as with the health and education systems. Other undeniable challenges associated with the population problem take the form of unemployment and the high degree of inequality in the distribution of income. These problems are common to the five countries, where a significant portion of the population lacks access to essential goods and services, and demand urgent redress. Data available from the United Nations show that Brazil and South Africa are among the countries with the worst distribution of income and that India and Russia are among those with the largest percentage of the population living below the poverty line, 28.6 per cent and 30.9 per cent respectively in the mid-2000s. Problems related to the perverse distribution of income and limited access to public services—education, health, housing and urban infrastructure, public safety, etc.—are reflected in their low human development index. However, the data show that except for South Africa and with the notable exception of India, the other countries have shown a slight tendency towards improvement in the quality of life of their populations.

Huge regional disparities in human and economic development are evident in all five countries. In general, the wealthier regions are those that are more industrialised. Practically 60 per cent of the total GDP of Brazil originates in the states of the south-east. The Chinese economic development model favours the coastal provinces, while other provinces in the interior are much less developed. There is also a large gap between the rural and urban population. In South Africa, economic activity is concentrated in Gauteng province, which contributes approximately 33 per cent of GDP, and in the western part of Cape Town, which accounts for 15 per cent of GDP. The industrial development of Russia occurred principally around cities such as Moscow, St. Petersburg, Nizhny Novgorod and Ekaterinburg, while Siberia and the regions to the east continue to have low-level industrialisation. India also shows significant inequalities between the rich regions to the south and the northern regions of the country,

Figure 1.2. Share of BRICS' GDP in World GDP in PPP, 2007

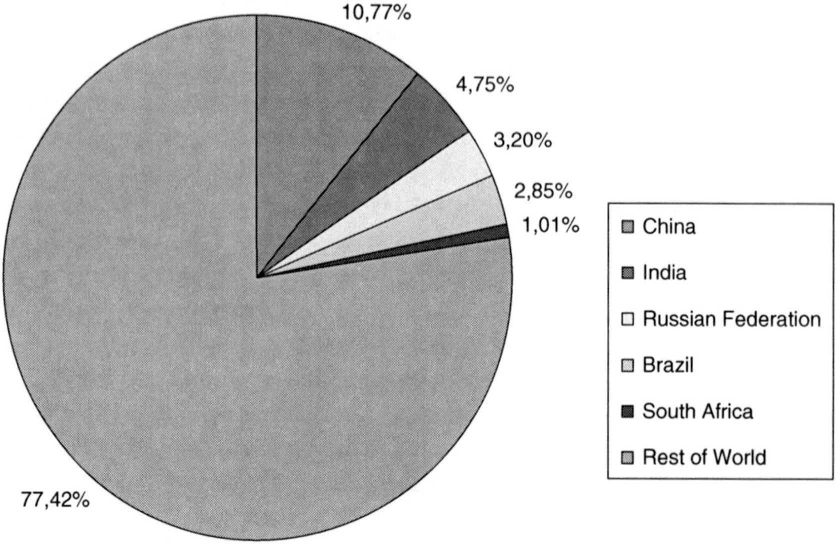

Source: World Development Indicators Database (World Bank, 2008).

as well as between the rural and urban populations. Regional redistribution of income and access to essential goods and services represent a significant challenge that these five countries have in common.

Regarding the structure and performance of production, the combined GDP of the BRICS (in terms of purchasing power parity) represented in 2007 approximately 23 per cent of world GDP (Figure 1.2), more than the United States. In that year, China and India accounted for 10.8 per cent and 4.8 per cent of world GDP respectively. Further, the BRICS have other characteristics in common that make them the focus of observation and analysis. The countries in this group have been undergoing an intense transformation process since the turn of the new millennium. But they have followed different strategies for development, reflecting various degrees and forms of integration into the world economy.

The economic performance of the BRICS has, however, varied widely in the last decades, as can be observed in Figure 1.3. China has maintained the fastest growing economy worldwide. India has grown significantly and more regularly. Russia, after experiencing a severe crisis in the 1990s (a 40 per cent decline in GDP in real terms), and being faced with significant disorganisation of the socialist economy, began a phase of significant growth in this decade propelled by the role of oil and gas in the economy. Brazil and South Africa have seen

Figure 1.3. BRICS—Average Rates of Growth of Real GDP (%), 1980–2007

	1980–1990	1990–2000	2000–2005	2006	2007	2008
Brazil	2.8	2.9	2.8	3.7	5.7	5.1
China	10.3	10.4	9.6	11.6	13.0	9.0
India	5.8	6	6.9	9.8	9.3	7.3
Russia	–	–4.7	6.2	7.4	8.1	5.6
South Africa	1.6	2.1	4.0	5.4	5.1	3.1

Source: UNCTAD Handbook of Statistics, 2008, for 1980–2005 data and IMF – World Economic Outlook, April 2009, for 2006–2008 data.

a small improvement in their economic performance, also well below their potential. These different accomplishments were accompanied by significant changes in the production structure of the five countries. The spectacular economic growth in China is mostly due to the competitiveness of its manufacturing sector. In India the manufacturing sector has grown in the same proportion as GDP, remaining relatively small (15 per cent of GDP), while in Russia, South Africa and Brazil the manufacturing sector lost relative importance. As a result, from the point of view of the share in world value added, China doubled its percentage between the beginning of the 1990s and the middle of the first decade of the new millennium, India increased its share slightly, South Africa stagnated and Russia (like Brazil) saw its share diminished.

It is important to point out that the industrial system in China has diversified to a significant degree during the last 25 years. The share of the manufacturing sector in the composition of China's GDP is unusual and growing: it was around 42 per cent in 1983 and reached more than 50 per cent by the early 2000s. The most noteworthy change, in recent years, has been the growth in the consumer durables and electronics sectors. Furthermore, in China, the share of technologically intensive sectors in industrial output during the middle of the present decade approached 35 per cent of the total value added by the manufacturing sector. This share is between 14 per cent and 17 per cent in the other four countries. In 2005 these sectors were responsible for 36 per cent of Chinese exports. Employment in these sectors represented 19 per cent of total employment in 2002. In Russia, India and South Africa this percentage is around 8.5 per cent (the same as in Brazil). However, most of the Chinese labour force remains in rural areas. The relative share of the agricultural sector, that reached 33 per cent in 1983, is constantly falling, to 14.6 per cent of GDP in 2003. The share of services grew from 22 per cent in 1983 to more than 30 per cent in 1993, remaining at this level ever since.

Even so, major differences can be seen in the characteristics of the manufacturing sector, with Russia and South Africa (as well as Brazil) having a relatively greater share of products based on natural resources and commodities. In Russia, it is important to note the contribution of the defence-related industrial complex, in addition to the oil and gas industries and to a strong production base in non-electric machines and equipment.

In India, an economy that has significant capacity in the area of services, skills in the manufacturing sector are relatively modest and are concentrated in non-durable consumer goods and in the chemical-pharmaceutical complex. More recently, significant advances have been observed in the automobile manufacturing complex and in certain basic industries such as steel, stemming from the creation of strong domestic private-sector groups. Finally, South Africa has an industrial sector heavily based on natural resources (particularly steel and non-ferrous metals), with some increases in capacity occurring in non-durable consumer goods and the automobile sector.

Although the share of the agricultural sector in India's GDP is declining, it still represented 22 per cent in 2003 (compared with 36.6 per cent in 1983) and constitutes an important determinant of overall economic growth. In the last two decades, the contribution of manufacturing industry to India's GDP has been constant, around 26 per cent. Services in India is the sector that is growing fastest, particularly those linked to ICT: the share of services in GDP has grown from 37.6 per cent in 1983 to more than 51 per cent in the mid-2000s.

In Russia, the contribution of the manufacturing sector to GDP declined from 44.6 per cent in 1983 to 34.2 per cent in 2003 and the share of services in total GDP grew from 36 per cent in 1990 to 60.6 per cent in 2003. The primary sector (agriculture and mining) of the Russian economy accounts for 13 per cent of GDP (14.8 per cent of value added). Russia's oil and gas industry alone is responsible for 10.2 per cent of gross value added. Since 1999, production activities in Russia have started to grow faster. The highest rates of growth were achieved in oil and gas extraction (6.5 per cent per year from 1999 to 2006). Also, some manufacturing activities oriented towards domestic markets grew by more than 11 per cent a year (Gokhberg, 2007).

Brazil has gone through a structural transformation since the late 1980s, with a significant reduction of the share of manufacturing industry in total GDP and rapid growth in services (19 per cent and 75 per cent respectively in 2003). It is worth emphasising that agricultural goods that have had an important role in the trade surplus were responsible for only 5.7 per cent of GDP in 2003, a significant fall from 11 per cent in 1983.

The services sector has also been playing a more important role in the South African economy. The share of value added of this sector in total GDP value added was already 51.1 per cent in 1983 and grew to 65.2 per cent in 2003. The development of the financial sector and the growth of tourism have contributed to this expansion. The share of manufacturing value added has decreased in the last 20 years, reaching 24 per cent of GDP in 2006. The metal and engineering sectors dominate the manufacturing sector. The primary sector was responsible for 11 per cent of GDP value added in 2006, with mining remaining important from the point of view of foreign trade and employment. Although the relative shares of sectoral value added have not varied much in the last few years, there have been two remarkable changes within the services sector: government services decreased from 17 per cent of total value added in 1999 to 15 per cent in 2006 while finance, real estate and business services increased from 19 per cent to 22 per cent.

All the BRICS have raised their export and import levels in the last two decades, both in volume terms and as a share of GDP. In China, Russia and South Africa, foreign trade reached, in 2002, more than 50 per cent of GDP while in Brazil and India it represented approximately 30 per cent of GDP.

Figure 1.4 shows the BRICS' exports and imports, both in current US$ and as a percentage of world exports and imports during 2000–2007. After a phase of stagnation between 2000 and 2002, world exports grew significantly, from US$ 6,481 billion in 2002 to US$ 9,123 billion in 2004 and US$ 14,056 billion in 2007. Imports also followed the same trend. The participation of the BRICS in this process has varied significantly.

The most notable fact is the well-known growth of China's participation in international trade: its exports grew from 3.9 per cent in 2000 of world exports to 6.5 per cent in 2004 and 8.8 per cent in 2007. As can be seen from the table in figure 1.4, Chinese imports more than trebled in the period (from US$ 296 billion in 2002 to US$ 955 billion in 2007), reaching 6.8 per cent of world imports in 2007. It is worth emphasising the strong role of primary goods in these imports, which benefited other BRICS significantly.

India, Russia and Brazil also experienced high, albeit smaller, growth in both exports and imports. Fostered by the Chinese and commodity booms, Brazil's and Russia's share of world exports grew rapidly. Brazil's share rose from 0.85 per cent in 2000 to 1.2 per cent in 2007, taking it back to where it stood in the early 1980s; Russia's share grew from 1.64 per cent in 2000 to 2.6 per cent in 2007. India's growth was steeper, as it reached 1.1 per cent of world exports in 2007 (from 0.66 per cent in 2000). South Africa was the only BRICS country that has not increased its share of world exports in the last ten years. The increase in Brazil's exports is marked by impressive diversification towards markets of the developing world, a unique feature among the BRICS.

On the import side, all five countries increased their share of world imports, with the exception of Brazil. Brazilian imports' relative share of world imports

Figure 1.4. BRICS—Merchandise Trade. Value (Current US$ Billion) and Share in World Total (%), 2000–2007

Exports	2000		2004		2007	
	Value	%	Value	%	Value	%
World	6,455.98	100	9,182.96	100	13,833.04	100
Brazil	55.08	0.85	96.67	1.06	160.64	1.20
China	249.20	3.87	593.32	6.50	1,218.01	8.80
India	42.38	0.66	76.64	0.80	145.43	1.10
Russia	105.57	1.64	183.20	2.01	355.46	2.60
South Africa	29.98	0.47	46.14	0.50	69.78	0.50
Imports	2000		2004		2007	
	Value	%	Value	%	Value	%
World	6,653.66	100	9,462.99	100	14,056.58	100
Brazil	59.06	0.87	66.43	0.70	126.58	0.90
China	225.09	3.40	561.22	5.90	955.80	6.80
India	51.52	0.80	99.77	1.10	215.50	1.50
Russia	49.12	0.70	107.12	1.10	245.36	1.70
South Africa	29.69	0.40	53.46	0.60	81.75	0.60

Source: WTO.

declined in the period (from 0.87 per cent to 0.70 per cent), even if their absolute value increased from US$ 59 billion to US$ 66 billion. In general terms China, Brazil and Russia managed to achieve a surplus in their merchandise trade, while India and South Africa continued to run up trade deficits.

The BRICS have been the recipients of significant amounts of foreign direct investment (FDI) in the last 50 years. Prior to 1984, Brazil received the greatest amount of FDI of all the BRICS. Although China reached the same level in 1985, Brazil continued to be a major destination for FDI during the 1990s, most notably during the process of privatisation that took place during that decade.

China became the largest recipient of FDI in the world beginning in 1993. The Chinese policy of attracting multinational companies was part of a strategy to expand their technological knowledge and later to strengthen domestic industries and companies. However, China imposed conditions—such as the

Figure 1.5. BRICS—Foreign Direct Investment (FDI): Inflows and Share in World Total, 1980–2007

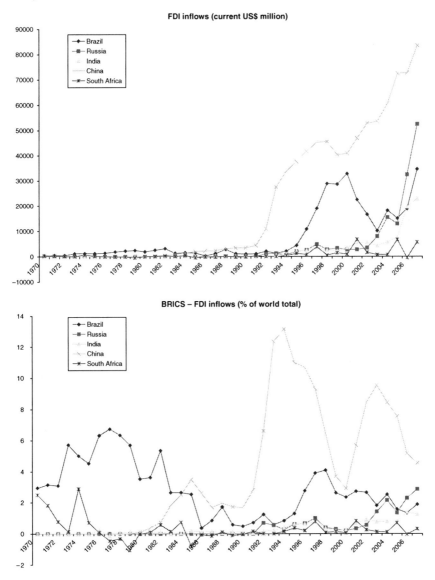

Source: UNCTAD.

establishment of joint ventures and the requirement that R&D be carried out locally—that had to be met before the subsidiaries were to operate in China or sell in its markets. Further, with respect to foreign direct investment it is important to point out that countries such as Brazil, Russia and South Africa, where the economies were liberalised with fewer restrictions, received more portfolio investment. But most of the investment received by the manufacturing sector was used to buy up local companies. In China and India, where the capital account was not liberalised, FDI seems to have been concentrated in new investments in production and innovation.

This demonstrates the economic and political importance of the BRICS. The increase in the degree of influence of these countries took place during a period marked by intense transformations in the economy and global society. One of these is the integration in the economy and society of a significant proportion of previously marginalised segments of the BRICS population. According to one estimate (Ravallion, 2009) about 1.2 billion people joined the developing world's middle class in the period 1990–2002. Fifty per cent of these people are in China. In India, similar estimates range from 120 million to 250 million (Sridharan, 2004; Shukla, 2008), while in Brazil after 2003 more than 50 million people were integrated in the market economy as the per capita income of the poorest 10 per cent of the population grew by 7 per cent per year, three times the national average (2.5 per cent) and seven times more than the income of the 10 per cent richest (IPEA, 2008).

The crisis that started to affect the world economy in 2007–2008 has repositioned the role and importance of the BRICS. In a new scenario characterised by geopolitical realignment and where the role and function of the State in the economy are being redefined, their economic weight has in fact increased. Also, their capacity to remain immune is seen as a relevant source of ideas about how to survive during the crisis and to find ways of overcoming it. True, the differentiated role of the BRICS in the configuration of global power and the global economy will in some way constrain the evolution of their domestic systems for innovation. Also, their national systems of innovation are highly dependent on their historical development and on how the different domestic actors interpret global developments as well as how they position themselves in the national and international economies. On the other hand, more room for manoeuvre for setting up new industrial and technological policies may be expected.

4. STI Policies of the BRICS

As mentioned earlier, the present condition of the national innovation systems of the BRICS countries is strongly influenced by their historical evolution. With the exception of Russia and China, colonisation plays an important role in explaining their current scientific and technological capabilities. In the case of Brazil and South Africa, such influence was more dramatic as they are, in practice, constructions of colonisation.

In Brazil, the Portuguese not only forbade the setting-up of all production activities that could be either performed in Portugal or the subject of exchange with Portuguese commercial partners, but also impeded the establishment of any academic or research institution. All training in law, medicine or technical fields of Brazilians up to 1808 necessarily had to be conducted in Portuguese institutions. Even after that, and for more than a century, domestic scientific and technological training was restricted to activities such as medicine, law, agricultural research and health and hygiene.

As for South Africa, although considered the cradle of humanity, its development trajectory was totally influenced by an aggressive colonisation that was started in 1652 by the Dutch East India Company to exploit the abundance of its natural resources. It was only in 1961 that the country officially gained independence from Britain but it can be argued that its national system of innovation only began to take shape after the end of the apartheid regime in 1994.

India suffered through colonisation in a different way. India had a well developed scientific and technological heritage, the most advanced production system in textiles and clothing, etc. However, British colonisation hampered Indian technological and industrial development by relegating the country to the status of a raw material supplier and by forcing it to adopt an educational system which focused only on the production of clerks and administrators. All of this contributed at least to slowing down Indian scientific and technological development.

China was never colonised and was already a proto-industrialised country in the 13th century. For centuries China has been a nation characterised by strong central power and governed as a political unit. Arguably, some of the most important inventions of mankind such as paper, the compass, gunpowder, ceramics and printing were Chinese.

Russia, as a nation, also has a long history. The Russian Empire became a world power for the first time only under the Romanov dynasty and Peter I the Great. In the 18th century the Russian Academy of Sciences and Arts was established, together with the Moscow State University and a system of professional schools and academies in such disciplines as engineering, medicine, navigation and military science.

Given such historical differences the recent developments of science, technology and innovation policies in these countries display several similarities and important disparities that should be taken into account in a comparative exercise. All these countries have tried to pursue strategies to enhance their domestic capacity for innovation. These strategies have, however, been implemented differently, taking into account the cultural and historical heritage of each country. China and India have had greater freedom to define and implement their policies and strategies for STI than South Africa, which emerged from the apartheid regime in 1994 with its economy in difficulty. Russia, on the other hand, was able to adopt a more independent strategy only after the arrival of the Putin government in 2000. South Africa still suffers from the profound divisions that occurred in the country during the apartheid period and the dualism of its science and technology is only now beginning to diminish. China and Russia have strong central governments, while India has to cope with a significant number of sub-national entities in the execution of policy and South Africa has to live with more than a dozen different nationalities, each with its own language. All four countries have huge regional disparities and all suffer from a perverse distribution of income. These characteristics have a significant and differentiated impact on the domestic innovation systems that cannot be minimised in a comparative analysis.

At the same time, there are significant specific differences. In general terms, the strong position of Russia in higher education is very important. This capacity is not just quantitative—in 2006 more than 72 per cent of the school-age population was enrolled in higher education (Figure 1.6)—but also qualitative, especially in the areas of mathematics and physics. The earlier levels of specialisation and training, such as those in defence and the petroleum and gas complex, should also be noted. Russia has faced significant challenges in its institutional plan, particularly with regard to the transformations necessary to make use of the more than 4 000 research institutes inherited from the Soviet period.

In the case of India, there was a significant improvement in qualitative terms in the educational and scientific infrastructure and also serious attempts to increase the foundations of the system throughout the 1990s. Even so, only 10.7 per cent of the school-age population was able to enrol in institutions of higher learning in 2000 and 11.85 per cent in 2006, the lowest percentage among the BRICS (Figure 1.6).

Figure 1.6. BRICS—Enrolments in Higher Education as a Percentage of the Total School-Age Population, 1990, 2000 and 2006 – %

Countries	1990	2000	2006	Var (%)1990–2006
Brazil	11.2	16.2	25.48	127.50
China	3.0	12.7	21.58	619.33
India	6.1	10.6	11.85	94.26
Russia	52.1	62.8	72.28	38.73
South Africa	13.2	14.6	15.41	16.74
World	16.0	23.9	23.69	48.06

Source: UNESCO.

South Africa has been working to achieve a significant increase in quality higher education but R&D and innovation activities remain relatively weak, with limited scientific training. Training programmes with technological content are confined to the areas of mining and agro-industrial sectors (namely the production of wine).

Once again it is China that is presenting the most impressive results, especially because the creation of scientific and technological training is one of the principal aspects of its development strategy. China has significantly increased the number of enrolments in higher education (especially in the areas of engineering), growing from 3 per cent of the school-age population in 1990 to 13 per cent in 2000 and 21.5 per cent in 2006, with an astonishing rate of growth of 619 per cent in the period. At the same time, the strategy is concentrated on sending a significant number of Chinese students to study abroad (approximately 150,000 in recent years). The Chinese share of scientific publications grew from 2.05 per cent in 1995 to 6.52 per cent in 2004.

Despite the difficulty in finding reliable indicators, it is fair to say that these countries are passing through a period hallmarked by a sharp increase in R&D activities. Based on data from UNESCO, Figure 1.7 shows that, between 2000 and 2008, R&D expenditure in these countries increased from US$ 88.4 billion to US$ 191.8 billion, equivalent to an increase of 70.6 per cent over the period. R&D spending in China led this growth, increasing by 113 per cent in that period, rising from US$ 45 billion (0.9 per cent of GDP) to US$ 122 billion (1.3 per cent of GDP). In all other BRICS countries, however, the increase in absolute terms has not been matched by an increase in relative terms, as the ratio between R&D expenditure and GDP hardly changed during this period.

When the agents responsible for making investments in R&D are taken into account (Figure 1.8), it can be seen that the government's share of total R&D expenditure is particularly high in India, 75 per cent of GDP in 2004. In that country, the level of firms' expenditure on R&D is persistently low. The only sectors which have relatively high R&D expenditure are the pharmaceutical, transportation materials and chemicals industries in the private sector of the economy. In the public sector, the important areas are defence and defence-related inputs industries.

In all other countries (China, Russia, Brazil and South Africa) the share of government expenditure is relatively low, fluctuating around 21 per cent and 26 per cent in 2004. However, there are some important differences in these four BRICS. In the case of China, where 68 per cent of total R&D expenditure is performed by firms, it should be borne in mind that State-owned companies still constitute the core of the Chinese entrepreneurial sector. In Russia, the large percentage share of the entrepreneurial sector's R&D expenditure (68 per cent) reflects the intense efforts devoted to the process of re-conversion of the

Figure 1.7. BRICS—R&D Expenditure, 2000–2008. US$ Billion PPP and % of GDP

Country	2000		2001	2002		2003		2004		2008	
	Value	%	value	value	%	value	%	value	%	value	%
Brazil	12,573	0.94	13,584	13,408	0.91	13,344	0.88	13,558	0.83	17,762	0.82
China	44,894	0.90	52,435	65,515	1.07	77,899	1.13	95,498	1.23	122,706	1.33
India	20,177	0.77	18,378	18,933	0.73	19,663	0.71	21,189	0.69	22,575	NA
Russia	10,760	1.05	12,983	14,655	1.25	16,517	1.28	16,360	1.15	24,127	1.07
South Africa	NA	NA	2,978	NA	0.80	3,607	0.86	4,176	0.92	4,462	NA
BRICS	88,406		100,360	112,512		131,031		150,782		191,632	
TOTAL	705,114		752,735	776,115		827,279		896,066		NA	
% BRICS	12.5		13.3	14.5		15.8		16.8		NA	

Source: UNESCO and OECD.

Figure 1.8. BRICS—R&D Expenditure 2004–2007. Total, Percentage of GDP and Distribution by Sector (2004)

Country	Gross Domestic Expenditure on R&D (GERD) as a % of GDP		GERD by Sector of Performance (%)—2004			
	2004	2007	Business Enterprise	Govern-ment	Higher Education	Private Non-Profit
Brazil	0.91	0.91	40.2	21.3	38.4	0.1
China	1.34	1.43	68.3	21.8	9.9	0
India	0.61	0.69	19.8	75.3	4.9	0
Russia	1.07	1.08	68.0	26.1	5.8	0.2
South Africa	0.87	0.92	56.3	20.9	21.1	1.7

Source: UNESCO and OECD.

manufacturing structure. In the other two BRICS, what stands out is the excessive relative participation of higher education institutions, which accounted in the case of Brazil for 38 per cent of total R&D expenditure and in the case of South Africa for 21 per cent in 2004.

Although these figures should be considered with caution, given the problems with STI statistics mentioned earlier, they nevertheless confirm some patterns that are qualitatively assessed by the different country chapters of this book. They in fact illustrate a general picture of the national system of innovation of these countries which has been affected—positively and negatively—by explicit and implicit STI policies.

Although policies directed to science and technology have been implemented in both the developed and the developing world in a systematic way only since the end of the Second World War, governments of different countries have been designing policy mechanisms that have influenced their scientific and technological development over a long period of time.

The BRICS are no exception to this rule, particularly the oldest civilisations. The Chinese inventions of the ancient world and the country's evolution into a proto-industrialised country already in the 12th century were possible only with a strong government that supported technological development extensively. This is also true of India, which had technological capabilities in metallurgy more than 500 years before the industrial revolution, and Russia, where Peter the Great set up the Russian Academy of Sciences and Arts in the early 18th century together with a system of professional schools and academies in different technical fields.

But it was only after the end of the Second World War that governments began to perceive the importance of steering scientific and technological development. One effect of the war was a generalised perception of the importance of technology and that governments should organise scientific and technological activities. But, as pointed out in the Brooks Report (OECD, 1971), up to the early 1960s STI policies were mostly of the science-push type, governed by a strong conviction that scientific development would necessarily lead to social and economic development. After that—and supported by a series of empirical studies on sources of innovation—the core of STI policies shifted significantly. The objectives moved towards fostering STI activities towards attaining national strategic achievements. In the developing world, at least up to the late 1970s, organising scientific and technological activities and controlling foreign technology that accompanied foreign direct investment were the basic objectives of STI policies.

The crisis of the 1980s pushed STI policies to the bottom of the policy agenda in the developing world. As part of what has been called a 'counter-revolution in development theory and policy' (Toye, 1987), a radical neo-liberal programme in which 'development practically disappears as a specific question (remaining) only as the welfare achieved by the elimination of obstacles to market functioning' (Arocena & Sutz, 2005, 16) was introduced in the developing world. As this programme postulated the supremacy of the markets and assumed that even if market failures existed, imperfect markets were better than imperfect States, policy intervention was limited to the implementation of those mechanisms that did not interfere with market functioning.

Obviously this was reflected in STI policy and it was only after the liberal programme started to face problems in the late 1990s that old science and technology policies began to be renovated under the new label of the national innovation system approach. Beginning at the end of the 1980s, STI policies started to target more explicitly technological innovation. In a period in which foreign policy experts wielded huge influence, their internal policy formulation process introduced the 'innovation' theme at the core of policies, but with a distorted vision based on emerging conceptual models of OECD countries. The 'national innovation system' version that inspired policies was a narrow one that attempted to emulate what was perceived as the benchmark of the new economy—Silicon Valley and similar US experiences. Implicitly, policies were informed by the 'mode 2' of knowledge production (Gibbons et al., 1994), which advocated an entrepreneurial role for modern universities. The general constitution of STI policies was to manage instruments and mechanisms that could foster innovativeness in the economy, concentrating on providing infrastructure (external economies) and on stimulating technological entrepreneurship. According to Gibbons et al., the role of science in achieving national goals should be oriented towards 'the single question of how to hitch the scientific enterprise to industrial innovation and competitiveness'.

It is under such a framework that BRICS policies towards STI have evolved in the last 20 years. In the chapters of this book the reader will find that the BRICS pursued these policy lines, but in different ways. In particular, the BRICS countries connected in a different way explicit STI policy mechanisms of that type to other policies that are not geared directly to STI but have a significant impact on innovation outcomes.

India was one of the few developing countries to formulate an explicit policy for science and technology immediately after the end of the Second World War. The pursuit of technological self-reliance was given a central role in its development strategy after independence. This resulted in substantial public investment in scientific education and R&D infrastructure and involved the establishment of public enterprises for the production of inputs such as steel, oil and gas, petrochemicals, power, fertiliser and equipment and machine tools needed for the production of capital goods, as well as the creation of mission-oriented scientific and technological agencies and R&D institutions for the development of technological capabilities needed for the production of atomic energy, space equipment, clean coal, glass and ceramics, processed foods, pharmaceuticals, agro-chemicals. India accomplished self-sufficiency in food production and established a diversified industrial sector. This first phase also led to substantial achievements in areas such as atomic energy and space.

After 1980 the main thrust of India's STI policy continued to be strong emphasis on some strategic areas such as atomic energy, defence and space, and civilian R&D priorities continued to be neglected (Abrol, 2005). In 1983, however, a change in STI policy was proposed by the Technology Policy Statement (TPS), which set as main priorities both internal technological development and the absorption of foreign technology. After that at least eight major policy documents were issued by the Indian government with the aim of organising STI policy. One striking difference of the Indian policy is that it never adopted the emphasis on innovation and the national innovation system approach. Its legislation and policy mechanisms continued to target the scientific and technological infrastructure and technological development in the key strategic areas linked to defence but included a review of industrial property with a carefully designed change in patent legislation.

High-quality public research institutions are also a distinctive feature of India's NSI. In particular, those research institutions linked to defence have played a major role and have been one of the cornerstones of the STI policy. Worth pointing out is the role of the Defence Research and Development Organisation, which is credited by some authors for India's success in the area of software (Kumar, 2000). In India, even after liberalisation government spending on R&D continued to be crucial and more significant than private spending. But a few fields absorb the bulk of government support: the strategic areas of defence, space and nuclear energy[6] receive 64 per cent of central government expenditure in science and technology, while agricultural research comes next with approximately 10 per cent (Basant, 2000).

Another specific point regarding India is that the opening-up of its economy since the 1980s has been highly selective and a combination of active policies and strong regulation facilitated the emergence of large domestic entrepreneurial groups and technological learning. Some of these groups became multinational conglomerates, such as the Tata group, several pharmaceuticals firms (Cipla, Ranbaxy, Dr Reddys) and steel groups (Mittal). A well-known recent case of technological and production success is the US$ 2,000 automobile (the Nano) developed by the Tata Group, which was described by The Economist magazine (2007, p. 30) as an 'example of the smart but ascetic engineering that can produce an impressive car' for such a price. Tata expects to sell at least 300,000 of these vehicles in 2009–2010 in India alone (The Economist, 2009). A more liberal approach towards foreign investment was also introduced in India, even if there are several areas such as telecommunications and energy where foreign participation is still regulated.

In the case of Russia, the period immediately following the collapse of the Soviet Union brought with it a significant downgrading of previous accumulated capabilities. The first half of the 1990s was a period that Gokhberg (2003) described as one of 'market romanticism in science and technology policy, driven by vain hopes of reformers for quick and automatic transfer (of responsibilities) to the market economy' (p. 2). During this period the Russian scientific and technological system almost collapsed as a dramatic contraction of government funding (from 1991 to 1992 alone it fell from 1.85 per cent to 0.67 of GDP) meant a significant reduction of human resources and the liquidation of a large number of scientific organisations. According to the chapter on Russian STI policy in this book, the consequences of this crisis have not been overcome by the end of the 2000s.

STI policy started to change in the early 2000s. A first noticeable trend was a remarkable increase in government R&D funding, which in the 2003–2004 federal budget grew by 14.2 per cent, and in 2004–2005 by 51.1 per cent. Although initially using mostly traditional instruments—national programmes—STI policy started to be formulated in that period in a significantly more interventionist manner. First, the policy began to target areas and sectors: priority scientific and technological areas and critical technologies were chosen. More important big-scale innovation projects partly funded by the government were introduced and STI policy began to be closely connected to industrial policy.

Such change is associated with the rise of the new government in 1999, which at its inauguration stressed the need for State intervention in regulating economic forces in order to achieve strategic objectives, including the re-establishment of Russian geopolitical influences using domestic natural and technological resources (Putin, 1999).

In the new policy agenda, there is explicit mention of the need to pursue a strategy that focuses on 'progress in the high technologies and science-intensive commodities' (Putin, 1999). Among the main policy actions, the government singled out public procurement for advanced technologies and science-intensive production, support for the production of technology-intensive goods for export, support for processing industries geared to domestic demand and, finally, using novel instruments for stimulating the energy, oil and gas industries.

Besides a radical transformation of the industrial structure in the oil industry—with increasing control by the State—State corporations were set up in areas of State interests and priorities. The best example, perhaps, of such radical change was the creation of the Russian Corporation for Nanotechnology (Rosnanotech) in 2007 to address the challenges associated with the rapid development of nanoscale technologies. Rosnanotech is one of seven Russian State corporations, enjoys direct budgetary support and has special status since it is outside the control of regulatory bodies and its director is appointed by the Russian President only.

China is without doubt the most significant and complex case as regards recent STI policies among the BRICS. A major difference is that explicit technological policies have been accompanied by and have formed an important part of a sophisticated industrial policy since 1989, typified by huge State intervention geared towards industrialisation with emphasis on what are termed in China the 'pillar industries': the high-tech sectors, intensive in capital and technology. This intervention combined the selective attraction of MNCs (most of which were required to perform R&D activities inside China as part of the permission to produce there) and changes in the industrial structure in almost all sectors of activity which not only privileged locally controlled ventures but also retained State control of several important firms.

In the 1989 reform, science was given strong priority as the improvement of scientific and technological infrastructure was targeted and universities became major actors in the Chinese national innovation system. Through a series of policy programmes several universities were targeted to become world leading universities and, by 2010, China will probably produce more PhDs in science and technology than the United States. Universities were also prompted to strengthen research capabilities with the 973 Programme (Basic Research Programme), perhaps the most important component of the Chinese STI policy, launched in 1997 with the aim of strengthening the role of government in science and targeting areas such as energy, information technology, health and materials.

The upgrading of university capabilities was associated with programmes that addressed high-tech entrepreneurship, particularly the Torch Programme launched in 1988. Conceived basically as a follow-up to the 863 Programme (High Technology Development Plan), it aimed to diffuse the technologies emerging from the research carried out as part of the Plan (Baark, 2001). The success story was that new high-tech ventures were set up and were able to grow, as the programme was associated with other institutional changes that basically allowed universities and research institutes (including the Chinese Academy of Sciences) to keep control of these hi-tech firms. It provided the basis for the upsurge of a locally controlled high-tech sector that remains important in the Chinese national system of innovation.

High-tech zones have also been promoted and linked to these two programmes and universities were also given permission to set up and control firms in high-tech areas, which explains the creation of important firms that became leading actors in their sectors, such as Lenovo. The immediate result was that the share of the value added of high-tech goods in GDP jumped from 2.12 per cent in 1998 to 4.44 per cent in 2004.

One last factor worth mentioning is the change in direction of Chinese STI policy in 2006. Perceiving the limits to pursuing a technological strategy geared to exporting goods to western advanced economies, the new 2006 plan addressed two key issues: the environment and innovations addressing the needs of the domestic market. Perhaps prompted by concern about over-exposure to the global market, the policy aims to encourage firms and other actors in the innovation system to develop innovations more appropriate to the specificities of the large Chinese market. It contemplates the setting of priorities for indigenous innovation products in public procurement and some price advantages in public procurement for these products. More recently, in the middle of the crisis, China's economic stimulus package is providing approximately US$ 200 billion for eco-friendly projects (34 per cent of the total)[7].

Brazil and South Africa followed more or less the same pattern, as their development trajectories have been marked by the same type of integration in the world economy subjected to the abundance of natural resources within their borders. In both cases, but more markedly in the case of South Africa, mineral resources play a key role. In Brazil, although some institutional efforts were introduced in the 1950s with the establishment of the National Research Council, it was only in the late 1960s that an explicit policy for science and technology began to take off. Nevertheless, this policy concentrated on organising a postgraduate training and research system primarily within public universities. But these policies were much influenced by a broader import-substitution industrialisation policy which only in a small number of cases addressed internal technological capability building. The Brazilian production subsystems with high internal technological development are precisely those where technology policy has been the core of industrial policy: petroleum and gas, aeronautics, bio-fuels, most of the agro-industrial subsystems, some industrial inputs (raw materials) such as mineral ores, and paper and cellulose. Then, the decision to create State-owned enterprises in some of these sectors in fact reflected implicit technology policies insofar as these firms gradually built their own R&D labs.

There was a specific institutionalisation that proved crucial both for industrialisation and for technological development. Perhaps one of the main reasons for the successes of the Brazilian industrialisation process was the setting-up of the National Bank for Economic and Social Development (BNDES) in the 1950s. When expectations about a possible Marshall Plan for Latin America subsided, the domestic reaction was to create a financial institution to deal with problems of long-run investment. The BNDES, which is today twice as large as the World Bank, although not dealing specifically with technological development, has played an important role in the institutionalisation of science and technology in Brazil. It was there that in the 1960s the first programme directed towards scientific and technological development was created. Afterwards, a specific government agency for science and technology—Finep—was created, still in the 1960s. In the 1970s another crucial institutional development occurred with the setting-up in 1973 of the Brazilian Agricultural Research Corporation (EMBRAPA) with the aim of providing feasible solutions for sustainable development of Brazilian agriculture through knowledge and technology generation and transfer. EMBRAPA consists of a set of agricultural research and services units scattered across different parts of the country. Today it comprises 41 units: services (the units for technological information, technology transfer, instrumentation, etc.) product research units (for soy, fruits, etc.), units conducting research on basic themes (such as genetic resources and biotechnology) and research units specialised in the different Brazilian eco-regions (the cerrado, semi-arid regions, tropical forest, etc.). In 2007, EMBRAPA set up a research unit for satellite monitoring that concentrates on R&D on territorial management systems. In its labs researchers work on geographical information systems, electronic networks, processing of satellite images for remote sensors and data obtained at local level. The technologies and information produced by this unit have been crucial for the development and implementation of production strategies that are specific to different areas of Brazil and to different plots in each farm. Arguably the technological success of Brazilian agriculture is due to EMBRAPA.

After the crisis of the 1980s and 1990s, STI policies reverted to the Brazilian policy agenda which, similarly to what happened in other countries, concentrated on three main pillars: stimulating technological development and innovation in firms; upgrading the technological infrastructure; and incentives for setting up new technology-based firms (spin-offs from university research). For the implementation of this agenda the Brazilian Ministry of Science and Technology created 12 Sectoral Funds for Supporting Scientific and Technological Development, which essentially attempt to finance partnership projects between universities and firms, and projects aimed at restoring and expanding the scientific and technological infrastructure of research institutions and universities. Also, together with traditional mechanisms such as tax incentives for R&D, Brazil introduced an 'Innovation Law' inspired by French legislation in the early 2000s with the objective of stimulating the transfer of technology from the public R&D infrastructure to the private sector, but without any discernible positive results after more than five years.

In the case of South Africa, only with the elimination of the apartheid regime is it possible to speak of a national policy for science and technology. Before that period, programmes for training and research only existed for the white minority and one of the main policy challenges of the new democratic post-apartheid regime was to include all South Africans in its teaching and research system. After the end of the apartheid regime, science and technology policies were gradually and systematically changed using the NSI approach with the support of foreign donors and policy experts. The chapter on South Africa of this book points out that, as a consequence, the policy adopted afterwards did not adequately take into account the historical and contextual conditions of South Africa as a latecomer society and that is why it has not shown any perceivable results as far as innovation is concerned.

In one way or another both Brazil and South Africa set up a wide variety of policy programmes and funding mechanisms for innovation that focus primarily on scientific and technological institutions and joint R&D projects between universities and firms. Regarding the support for firms' innovations, mechanisms contemplate traditional, low-effectiveness tax incentives and loans for R&D[8]. However, in both cases it could be argued that extensive upgrading of the infrastructure has been achieved and that in some subsystems the results have been positive.

5. Concluding Remarks

At first sight it could be inferred that the BRICS countries have been implementing similar STI policies in the last 20 years. The analysis presented in this book suggests that even if they more or less followed similar policy lines that targeted innovation and infrastructure reform, the way in which these policy lines were implemented differed significantly. True, these countries increased their exposure to the global economy and went through major structural reforms. However, we cannot ignore their specific cultural and historical trajectories as well as the way and extent these countries understood structural reforms. The policy mechanisms adopted thus varied significantly. As a consequence, the impact on the production and technological structures of the BRICS has been extremely different. Part of these differences has to do with the specificities of the development process in each country, its historical evolution and the conditions that underpin the implementation of STI policy measures. In particular, it is argued that the geopolitical position of each country system plays an important role in the discussion.

This introduction makes the point that it is not possible to discuss the explicit STI policy without taking these factors into account. Take the case of India, where structural change benefited in the first place the domestic production capital and only later gradually allowed a partial penetration of foreign capital, and where there continues to be an important role for strategic defence-related innovations and technologies. These measures allowed the upsurge and consolidation of Indian private groups. Additionally, as part of its strategic development planning, important activities, such as telecommunications, were kept under government control.

An optimistic assessment of the Indian NSI would include a high-quality scientific subsystem that is rapidly expanding, a strong defence-related innovation system and a relatively weak industrial R&D system that is nevertheless growing rapidly in areas where local capital is strong: pharmaceuticals, chemicals and the auto industry. In important areas such as software there are human resources of high quality and well developed production capabilities.

China went through a profound transformation notable, among other things, for a significant increase in the quality and quantity of scientific and technological infrastructure, which, unlike India, was relatively underdeveloped up to the 1990s. Regarding industrial policy this country has linked access to its internal market to a series of obligations on foreign firms. At the same time the government has stimulated the upsurge of locally controlled firms. Some of these firms are novel ventures spinning off from university research but most were previously controlled by the government and were restructured in the 1990s under military supervision and gradually passed to private control. China's NSI has succeeded in mobilising the national education systems and in accumulating production capabilities that are growing at high rates. China also seems to have perceived technological opportunities in future areas such as the environment and is progressively redirecting policy towards innovation for the domestic economy.

In the case of Russia, the scientific and technological infrastructure has gradually recovered after the 1999 reforms. The importance of the industrial-military complex was restored and capabilities in oil and gas were given a prominent role. But the economy continues to be specialised in these activities and the results of STI policies in other areas are negligible. Russia's NSI has a solid position in higher education, with a powerful scientific system, particularly dedicated to space and defence activities.

Finally, Brazil and South Africa are still suffering from problems connected with their past and with excessive specialisation in commodities based on natural and mineral resources. The structural change that occurred in these two countries was more orthodox and the overall results are more modest. In the case of Brazil, even though the NSI has an increasingly qualified scientific infrastructure, particularly in important areas such as biology, agricultural sciences and space, its production system has presented mixed results with successes in aerospace, energy (including oil and bio-fuels), metallurgy and agro-business and weaknesses in several important innovation systems that were more innovative in the past, such as telecommunications. The South African NSI has to struggle with the legacy of the apartheid regime. It is showing increasing effort in high-quality education. Nevertheless, its R&D and innovation activities remain relatively weak, with some exceptions such as mining and wine-making.

In short, even if STI policies have been mostly dominated by a supply-side orientation in the last 20 years, the analysis of BRICS policies for STI show that in some cases, such as in China and India, it has been possible to subordinate them to a broader policy agenda. The recent crisis, however, brings some additional problems but also some opportunities for BRICS STI policies. Although there is an intrinsic difficulty in predicting the precise duration and intensity of the recession that has been afflicting more advanced economies since 2008, some trends that have become more apparent since the late 1990s have been reinforced. According to IMF figures, less developed countries have increased their share of the world's GDP from 36.9 per cent in 1998 to 45 per cent in 2008. The tendency towards increasing this share should be maintained as these countries, particularly those with large domestic markets, will be less affected by the crisis. The leadership position of the BRICS could even improve their bargaining position at international level and further contribute to reducing the inequality that persists between rich and poor countries.

Another particular point about the crisis and its consequences is essential for the issues treated in this book. The failure of a model that disregarded the importance of national policies orientating and regulating economic growth will certainly bring a more balanced notion of the role of the State. This and new ideas for long-term planning and for policies steering development will probably be one of the most significant outcomes of the crisis resulting from the transformations taking place at the end of the first decade of the millennium. Taken together with the more important role of large developing countries in the international economy and geopolitics, this renewed perception of the importance of policies should throw more light on the ways in which their potential can be mobilised.

The performance of the BRICS—their increasing share of the world product and trade, their impressive reserves and the size of their domestic markets— should reinforce interest in development issues and in how the inequality issue can be addressed. The huge task of evening out regional imbalances in countries of continental dimensions makes tackling regional and social development a core priority of the policy agenda. There are also enormous opportunities for the adoption of new policy models that foster sustainable and coordinated development at national, regional and local levels and are not geared solely towards integration into the global economy. For the organisations that design and implement policies, the choice and development of concepts, indicators and models that help to reduce the imbalances instead of reinforcing them and that associate economic and social development within a long-term perspective are extremely relevant.

References

Abrol, D. (2004). Dynamics of Innovation Systems amidst Neo-Liberal Globalisation: Lessons from India. Paper presented at the Globelics Seminar. Beijing, China.

Arocena, R. & Sutz, J. (2005). *Por um nuevo desarollo*, Madrid, 2005.

Arocena, R. & Sutz, J. (2003). 'Knowledge, Innovation and Learning: Systems and Policies in the North and in the South', in J. E. Cassiolato, H. M. M. Lastres & M. L. Maciel *Systems of Innovation and Development—Evidence from Brazil*. Cheltenham, UK: Edward Elgar.

Baark, E. (2001). 'Technology and entrepreneurship in China: commercialization reforms in the science and technology sector', *Policy Studies Review*, 112, Spring.

Basant, R. (2000). 'Corporate Response to Economic Reforms' in Nagesh Kumar (Ed.) Indian *Economy Under Reforms: An Assessment of Economic and Social Impact*, New Delhi: Bookwell.

Bielschowsky, R. (Ed.) (2000). *Cinqüenta anos de pensamento na CEPAL*, Editora Record. Rio de Janeiro.

Cassiolato, J. E. & Lastres, H. M. M. (1999). Globalização e Inovação Localizada: experiências de sistemas locais no Mercosul, Brasília: IBICT.

Cassiolato, J. E. & Lastres, H. M. M. (2008). 'Discussing innovation and development: converging points between the Latin American school and the Innovation Systems perspective', *Globelics Working Paper Series*, No 08-02.

Cassiolato, J. E., Lastres, H. M. M. & Maciel, M. L. (2003). *Systems of Innovation and Development—Evidence from Brazil*. Cheltenham, UK: Edward Elgar.

Cassiolato, J. E., Lastres, H. M. M., Mytelka, L. & Lundvall, B. A. (2005). *Systems of innovation and development: an introduction*, Mimeo, Economics Institute, Federal University of Rio de Janeiro.

Cassiolato, J. E., Guimarães, V., Peixoto F. & Lastres, H. M. M. (2005). 'Innovation Systems and Development: what can we learn from the Latin American experience?', paper presented at the 3rd Globelics Conference, Pretoria, South Africa.

Chesnais, F. & Sauviat, C. (2003). 'The financing of innovation-related investment in the contemporary global finance-dominated accumulation regime', in J. E. Cassiolato, H. M. M. Lastres & M. L. Maciel *Systems of Innovation and Development—Evidence from Brazil*. Cheltenham, UK: Edward Elgar.

Freeman, C. (1982). 'Technological infrastructure and international competitiveness', draft paper submitted to the OECD ad hoc group on science, technology and competitiveness, Paris: OCDE.

Freeman, C. (1987). Technology Policy and Economic Performance—Lessons from Japan, London: Frances Pinter.

Freeman, C. (2003) 'A hard landing for the "new economy"? Information technology and the United States national system of innovation' in J. E. Cassiolato, H. M. M. Lastres & M.L. Maciel *Systems of Innovation and Development—Evidence from Brazil. Cheltenham*, UK: Edward Elgar.

Freeman, C. & Soete, L. (1997). *The Economics of Industrial Innovation*, 2nd edition. Cambridge, Massachusetts: The MIT Press.

Freeman, C. & Perez, C. (1988). 'Structural crisis of adjustment, business cycles and investment behaviour', in G. DOSI et al. (Eds) *Technical Change and Economic Theory*, London: Pinter, 1988.

Furtado, C. (2002). *Capitalismo Global*. São Paulo: Paz e Terra.

Furtado, C. (1961). *Desenvolvimento e Subdesenvolvimento*. Editora Fundo de Cultura. Rio de Janeiro, 1961.

Furtado, C. (1958). 'Capital Formation and Economic Development' in A.N. Agarwala & S. P. Singh (Eds), *The Economics of Underdevelopment*, Oxford: Oxford University Press.

Gibbons, M. et al. (1994). The new production of knowledge—The dynamics of science and research in contemporary societies, London: Sage

Gokhberg, L. (2007). 'Russian System of Innovation', paper presented at the BRICS Project Workshop. Rio de Janeiro, Economics Institute, Federal University of Rio de Janeiro. 2007.

Gokhberg, L. (2003). 'A New Innovation System for a New Economy', paper presented at the First Globelics Conference 'Innovation Systems and Development Strategies for the Third Millennium', Rio de Janeiro, November 2–6.

Herrera, A. (1986). 'The new technology and the developing countries: problems and options', in R. Macleod (Ed.) *Technology and the human prospect: essays in honour of Christopher Freeman*. London: Frances Pinter.

Herrera, A. (1975). 'Los Determinantes Sociales de la Politica Cientifica en America Latina', in J. Sábato (Ed.) *El pensamento Latinoamericano en ciencia-tecnologia-desarrollo-dependencia*. Buenos Aires: Paidos.

Hirschman, A. (1958). *The strategy of economic development*. New Haven: Yale University Press.

IPEA (2008). 'Pnad-2007: Primeiras Análises: Pobreza e Mudança Social'. *Comunicados da Presidência*, n. 9, IPEA, Brasília.

Johnson, B. & Lundvall, B.-Å. (2003). 'Promoting Innovation Systems as a Response to the Globalising Learning Economy', in J. E. Cassiolato, H. M. M. Lastres & M. L. Maciel (Eds) *Systems of innovation and development*. Cheltenham, UK: Edward Elgar.

Kumar, N. (2000). 'New Technology Based Small Service Enterprises and Employment: The Case of Software and Related Services Industry in India', paper presented at the

National Seminar on Strategic Approach to Job Creation, ILO-SAAT and Ministry of Labour, Suraj Kund, Haryana.

Lastres, H. M. M. (1994). The advanced materials revolution and the Japanese system of innovation. London: MacMillan.

Lastres, H. M. M. & Cassiolato, J. E. (2005). 'Innovation systems and local productive arrangements: new strategies to promote the generation, acquisition and diffusion of knowledge', *Innovation: Management, Policy & Practice*, 7 (2), 172–187.

Lastres, H. M. M., Cassiolato, J. E. & Maciel, M. L. (2003). 'Systems of innovation for development in the knowledge era: an introduction', in J. E. Cassiolato, H. M. M. Lastres & M.L. Maciel *Systems of Innovation and Development—Evidence from Brazil*. Edward Elgar. Cheltenham, UK. Northampton, MA, USA. 2003.

List, F. (1841). Das Nationale System der Politischen Ökonomie, Basel: Kyklos.

Lundvall, B.-Å (2006). *National innovation system: analytical policy device and policy learning tool*. Mimeo. Department of Business Studies, Aalborg University, Aalborg, Denmark.

Lundvall, B.-Å. (1988). 'Innovation as an interactive process: From user-producer interaction to the National Innovation Systems', in G. Dosi et al. (Eds) *Technical change and economic theory*. London: Pinter Publishers.

Myrdal, G. (1968). Asian drama: An inquiry into the poverty of nations. London: Penguin Books.

Mytelka, L. K. (2000). 'Local systems of innovation in a globalized world economy'. Industry and Innovation, 7(1), 15–32.

Mytelka, L. K. & Farinelli, F. (2003). 'From local clusters to innovation systems', in J. E. Cassiolato, H. M. M. Lastres & M.L. Maciel (Eds) *Systems of innovation and development*. Cheltenham, UK: Edward Elgar.

Nelson, R. (1993). *National Innovation Systems. A Comparative Analysis*. New York: Oxford University Press.

OECD (1971). Science, growth and society—A new perspective (the Brooks Report), Paris: OECD.

Perez, C. (1988). 'New technologies and development', in C. Freeman & B.-A. Lundvall (Eds) *Small countries facing the technological revolution*. London: Pinter Publishers.

Perez, C. (1983). 'Structural change and the assimilation of new technologies in the economic and social system' *Futures*, 15(5), 357–375.

Presbisch, R. (1949). 'O desenvolvimento econômico da América Latina e alguns de seus problemas principais', Reprinted in R. Bielschowsky (2000) (Ed.) *Cinqüenta anos de pensamento na CEPAL*. Rio de Janeiro: Editora Record.

Presbisch, R. (1963). 'Por uma dinâmica do desenvolvimento latino-americano', in R. Bielschowsky (2000) (Ed.) *Cinqüenta anos de pensamento na CEPAL*, Rio de Janeiro: Editora Record.

Productivity Commission (2007). Public Support for Science and Innovation, Research Report, Productivity Commission, The Government of Australia, Canberra.

Putin, V. (1999). Russia at the turn of the Millenium, mimeo.

Ravallion, M. (2009). '*The Developing World's Bulging (but Vulnerable) "Middle Class"*' Development Research Group, World Bank, 2009, Washington, DC.

Reinert, E. & Reinert, S. (2003). 'Innovation systems of the past: modern nations—states in a historical perspective: the role of innovation and of systemic effects in economic thought', paper presented at the Rio De Janeiro Globelics Conference, Rio de Janeiro.

Rodríguez, G. & López, M. (2007). 'Introducción: sobre a diversidade da innovación.' in G. Rodríguez & M. López (Eds) *A diversidade da innovación: unha perspectiva sectorial*. Santiago de Compostela, Universidade de Santiago de Compostela.

Rodríguez, O. (2001). 'Prebisch: Actualidad de sus ideas básicas'. *Revista de la CEPAL* 75, pp 41–52.

Sagasti, F. (1978). Science and technology for development: main comparative report of the science and technology policy instruments project, Ottawa: IDRC.

Schumpeter, J. A. (1934). *The theory of economic development.* Cambridge: Harvard University Press.

Shukla, R. (2008). 'The Great Indian Middle Class,' *National Council of Applied Economic Research*, New Delhi.

Singer, H. W. (1950). 'The distribution of gains between investing and borrowing countries' *American Economic Review*, 15, 473–85.

Singer, H., Cooper, C., Desai, R. C., Freeman, C., Gish, O., Hall, S. & Oldham, G. (1970). 'The Sussex Manifesto: science and technology for developing countries during the Second Development Decade', *IDS Reprints* No 101, Brighton: Institute of Development Studies.

Sridharan, E. (2004). 'The Growth and Sectoral Composition of India's Middle Class: Its Impact on the Politics of Economic Liberalization,' *India Review* 3(4): 405–428.

Tavares, M. C. (1972). 'Auge e Declínio do Processo de Substituição de Importações no Brasil', in M. C. Tavares *Da Substituição de Importações ao Capitalismo Financeiro: Ensaios sobre Economia Brasileira.* Rio de Janeiro: Editora Zahar.

Tavares, M. C. (2001). 'O Subdesenvolvimento da Periferia Latino-Americana: o caso do Brasil no começo do Séc. XXI'. Seminário em Homenagem ao Centenário de Raúl Prebisch, UFRJ, Rio de Janeiro.

The Economist (2009a). *Inside the Tata Nano: no small achievement*, The Economist, 26 March 2009.

The Economist (2009b). *How green is your stimulus package?* The Economist web edition, 3 April 2009, available at http://www.economist.com

Toye, J. (1987). Dilemmas of Development—Reflections on the Counter Revolution in Development Theory and Policy. Oxford: Blackwell.

Chapter 2

ACHIEVEMENTS AND SHORTCOMINGS OF BRAZIL'S INNOVATION POLICIES

Priscila Koeller and José Eduardo Cassiolato

1. Introduction

Debates on innovation policy—its importance, scope, impacts, etc.—have taken place in the ambit of both developed and developing countries. The BRICS group of countries (Brazil, Russia, India, China and South Africa) stand out within this debate for their social and economic potential and also for the impact such development may have on other countries.

With a view to furthering this debate, this article presents the innovation policy adopted by the Brazilian Federal Government. The focus is on the period ranging from 1990 to 2006 even though some general remarks will be made about state intervention before this period that has influenced the Brazilian national system of innovation. The analysis will be tackled by means of an approach that is explicitly based on a combination of the neo-Schumpeterian and Latin American structuralist frameworks, conceiving innovation as the key element of the capitalist dynamics (Cassiolato & Lastres 2008).

Within this framework, the idea of a National System of Innovation[1] understands the innovative process as an integrated and systemic (and not linear) process. Although it focuses on the enterprise, institutions and organisations—and how they interact—are also important elements. Furthermore, context and history are crucial components and all policy elements affect the dynamics of the system. Thus, the analysis that follows covers not only innovation policy but science and technology and industrial policy and, more importantly, the overall economic policy of Brazil during the period.

The paper is structured in three sections. The first presents a brief history of the evolution of S&T, education and innovation policy in Brazil up to the 1990s. The second section discusses the institutionalisation of innovation policy in Brazil from 1990 onwards. A more detailed assessment of the main guiding principles and the programmes and mechanisms that were implemented is given for the period 1990–2006. Developments during 2007 and 2008 are also briefly discussed. The final section considers the outlook for innovation policy in Brazil and summarises its main achievements and shortcomings.

2. Brief History Up to the 1990s

2.1 Origins

The period when Brazil was ruled by the Portuguese crown—from 1500 to the early 1800s—featured some specific facts that significantly influence the country's scientific and technological capabilities. The Portuguese not only forbade the setting-up of any production activities that could be either performed in Portugal or subject to exchange with Portuguese commercial partners, but also impeded the establishment of any academic or research institution in its colonies. In Brazil, all training of local people in law, medicine or technical areas had until 1808 to be given in Portuguese institutions[2].

It was only when the Portuguese crown, fleeing French threats of invasion, moved to Brazil in 1808 that the Portuguese Regent signed a bill allowing the first Medical School to be organised in Salvador, Bahia, the first capital of the colony. Even after independence from Portugal was gained in 1822, institutionalisation of higher education and S&T in Brazil progressed very slowly. The predominantly commercial class that wielded power during the Monarchy Period (1822–1899) was not interested in such activities and rejected more than 20 bills proposing the creation of a Brazilian university. Only in the second half of the 19th century, with the setting-up of the Rio de Janeiro Polytechnic School (1874), was the first graduation school in engineering created; this was followed by technical centres in natural sciences, such as the Emílio Goeldi Museum, established in Pará in 1885, in agricultural research, with the setting-up of the Campinas Agronomics Institute in 1887, and in health and hygiene, with the establishment of the São Paulo Bacteriology Institute in 1893 and the Butantã Institute in 1899, also in São Paulo, and the Federal Seropathy Institute (later on the Oswaldo Cruz Institute) in 1908 in Rio de Janeiro, set up to produce serums and vaccines against the yellow fever that plagued Rio and endangered its position as Brazil's main port.

The need to set up the Oswaldo Cruz Institute and all the other research institutes during the late 1800s-early 1900s in the areas of health and agriculture was in fact basically economic. As Brazil's economy was firmly rooted in the production of two staple crops for export (coffee and sugar cane) there was a need to control agricultural pests and to improve planting and harvesting methods. The same is true for health and tropical diseases, as international vessels threatened not to moor in Rio until the yellow fever epidemic subsided. With an economy practically devoid of any manufacturing industry and heavily concentrated on the exploitation of a few agricultural products and on commerce and trade, there was hardly any need for scientific or technological knowledge.

During the 1920s, universities started to be created simply by a process of incorporation of isolated undergraduate professional schools existing in a given state, to be administratively managed by the state concerned and jointly funded by the union and the state. Six public state universities, typically agglomerations of isolated professional schools, were created during that decade.

Only in the 1930s was a university set up in Brazil as a complete project. The state of São Paulo, which in 1932 lost an internal war to secede from the union, decided to embrace modernisation and the establishment of the University of São Paulo was perceived as an important step in that direction. High-level teaching and research in fields such as physics, biology and chemistry was achieved with the "importation" of senior European researchers fleeing Nazi Germany and fascist Italy. The São Paulo project sparked similar efforts at the federal level.

2.2 From the 1950s to the Late 1970s

Like what happened in other less developed countries, the end of the second world war brought huge changes, including in the S&T area. As Brazil moved rapidly from being a typical supplier of a few agricultural goods, in this case coffee and sugar, to an economy based on manufacturing industry, several science and technology (S&T) initiatives were adopted. At the federal level, new institutions intended to organise the S&T system were created. Among such initiatives, it is worth highlighting the creation of the National Council for Scientific and Technological Development (CNPq—Conselho Nacional de Desenvolvimento Científico e Tecnológico) and of the Coordination Committee for the Further Training of Personnel with Higher Education (CAPES—Coordenação de Aperfeiçoamento de Pessoal de Nível Superior), both set up to organise and fund research and graduate studies.

Also worth noting is the creation by the Federal Government of some sectoral research and development (R&D) institutions in strategic fields. For the first time R&D institutions created were not restricted to the agricultural and biomedical areas. Examples of these institutions are the Aerospace Technical

Centre (CTA—Centro Técnico Aeroespacial), established in 1954, and the National Institute for Space Research (INPE—Instituto Nacional de Pesquisas Espaciais), created in 1961. Other institutional structures were adopted in several sectors, such as Petrobras (created as a stated-owned company in 1953) for petroleum, and local enterprises for mining and the iron and steel industry.

Import substituting industrialisation as it was planned in the 1950s—based on foreign investment and technology—significantly affected Brazil's prospects in S&T during this period. An understanding of how the NSI evolved should, then, be facilitated by briefly discussing some of the main features of the industrialisation process of the period.

Brazil embarked on a resolute path towards industrial transformation from the 1950s to the 1970s. Its performance was impressive[3]—Brazil had an average growth rate of value added in the manufacturing sector of 9.5 per cent per year between 1965 and 1980.

At the end of the 1970s, the Brazilian economy had acquired an almost complete industrial structure. The final phases of import substitution policies were carried out throughout the 1970s. Through the II PND (National Development Plan 1975–79),[4] whose objective was to complete the industrial structure and create export capacity for basic intermediate goods, the government coordinated a new phase of public and private investment in industries producing intermediate goods (such as petrochemicals, ferrous and non-ferrous metals, fertilizers, paper and pulp) and capital goods and public investment in infrastructure (energy, transport and telecommunications).

The industrial structure which evolved within a wide-ranging and constant strategy of protection, promotion and regulation had, by 1980, a high degree of intersectoral integration and product diversification. According to the 1980 Brazilian industrial census, chemical and mechanical engineering industries (including capital goods, consumer durables and the auto industry), which represented 47.5 per cent of total industrial production in 1970, were in 1980 responsible for 58.8 per cent of industrial output (Furtado 1990)[5].

The process of import substitution was responsible for the rapid changes in Brazil's production structure that were accompanied by social changes which were not negligible. The most important feature was, doubtless, the increase in social inequalities accompanied by high levels of absolute poverty. Another important macroeconomic feature worth mentioning is the accumulation of external debt, which in 1980 represented approximately 25 per cent of GDP and two and a half times the value of exports. The two features were to have a tremendous impact on Brazil's economy and society after the 1980s.

From the point of view of S&T development, it was only in the late 1960s that Brazil started again to include in its policy agenda the issue of scientific and technological development, as part of a series of policy measures that deeply transformed the Federal Government (such as the establishment of a Central Bank).

Brazil implemented a strategy that consisted primarily of really providing a good S&T infrastructure. The first serious attempt to mobilise financial resources for scientific and technological development in Brazil was made at the National Development Bank (BNDE) in 1964 when FUNTEC (the National Technical and Scientific Fund) was created. The basic aim of FUNTEC was to provide financial resources for upgrading the scientific and technological infrastructure. This was to be achieved primarily through the establishment of joint graduate and research programmes in (not exclusively, but almost entirely) public universities and research institutes[6].

The second important institutional change in S&T in Brazil was the setting-up of FINEP (Agency for Financing Studies and Projects) in 1969 as a separate agency of the Ministry of Planning. FINEP, which might be roughly described as a development bank for science and technology, started mainly by financing feasibility studies, but in 1971 its functions were greatly expanded. A new fund, the FNDCT (National Fund for Scientific and Technological Development), was created using federal budget resources with the aim of fostering scientific and technological capabilities[7].

Mention should be made of the transformation of the old National Research Council (CNPq) into an institution responsible for the coordination of all scientific and technological activities at federal level in 1973 and the subsequent two science and technology plans which were devised and implemented by the CNPq during the 1970s.

These can be broadly described as comprising, first, a statement of the main points of the strategy for S&T, as envisaged by the Federal Government and, secondly, a brief description of the projects and programmes of the institutions under the authority of the central government. As regards technological development the main political message was the need to increase the absorption of technology from abroad and the capacity for self-reliance, particularly of Brazilian enterprises. There is no explicit mechanism proposed in either plan setting out how these goals were to be achieved, apart from the budgets of state institutions and enterprises and FINEP's financing programmes.

Another crucial institutional innovation was the setting-up in 1973 of the Brazilian Agricultural Research Corporation (EMBRAPA), charged with providing feasible solutions for the sustainable development of Brazilian agribusiness through knowledge and technology generation and transfer.

In short, what can be said about this period is that, unlike the first attempt in the early 1950s, the abundance of budgetary resources (Brazil was growing at an average of 8.5 per cent per year in the late 1960s and early 1970s) that were channelled into the setting-up of good postgraduate courses and research in practically all scientific areas totally changed the landscape.

However, apart from the issue of technological infrastructure and despite all the planning effort, very limited results in fostering innovation and R&D activities by firms were achieved (Erber 1980, Cassiolato et al. 1981, Cassiolato 1982)[8]. True, some important policy mechanisms were set in motion in the early 1970s to promote such activities. In fact as early as in 1974, FINEP established the first programme to link firms with the S&T infrastructure and at about the same time it launched programmes such as ADTEN (Programme to Support Technological Development in National Industry)[9].

Low levels of internal R&D activities were accompanied by very weak linkages with government-owned industrial research institutes and universities, as documented by studies which analysed the technological behaviour of firms in the 1970s (Biato et al. 1973, Figueiredo 1972, Erber et al. 1974). The general impression was that:

> industrial entrepreneurs ... were ... "satisfied" with a low level of local technological activities and strong reliance on imported technology ... and ... such "satisfaction" can be understood in the light of the pattern of development followed in Brazil since the mid-fifties ... which reduced the importance of some of the reasons for a policy of more technological self-reliance (Erber 1980: 422).

Although many industrial firms were engaged in technical change and incremental technical change was present, general data on R&D expenditure suggest that firms were committing a very limited amount of resources to R&D. Also, the estimated number of firms which were engaged in explicit R&D was very low. In addition, one of the results of import substituting industrialisation was a very high level of technical heterogeneity in the industry. This heterogeneity was not only among different sectors, but most importantly inside the same industrial sector and sometimes even inside the same industrial plant[10]. Among other reasons such heterogeneity was associated with different levels of income in a very unequal society and the related different patterns of consumption.

Government behaviour in supporting technological development did not help very much. It is worth pointing out that the two most important mechanisms which supported the Brazilian industrialisation process never contemplated technological development[11]. The first was subsidies and tax exemptions granted by the CDI (the Industrial Development Council of the Ministry of Industry and Trade) to stimulate the setting-up of new import-substituting industries. The second was the long-term financing provided by the

BNDES (the National Bank for Economic and Social Development of the Planning Ministry) for new industrial investments. Investments in technology were never a prerequisite for the approval of projects submitted to both agencies. In the end FINEP's funds were the only source of R&D financing. These policies proved to be very limited: government expenditures on R&D infrastructure collapsed in the 1980s and long-term finance for R&D deteriorated.

State-owned public utilities found it necessary to create their own engineering and R&D departments in order to develop technologies specific to the country's environment and natural resources. These engineering departments fulfilled a vital role in designing and maintaining the new production facilities brought on stream by public-sector firms such as Petrobras in oil or Usiminas in the iron and steel industry. Within a short period of time, a large number of public R&D and engineering centres emerged, representing the core of the National System of Innovation of that period.

Foreign TNCs brought with them new product, process and organisational technologies that were often unknown in the domestic production environment. These firms did not come with the idea of developing a local technological infrastructure, but many of them found that they needed to do so in order to operate in a highly idiosyncratic production and institutional environment. Their technological efforts were generally aimed at "adapting" product designs and process and organisation technologies to local conditions.

Large, locally owned, conglomerates concentrated mostly in the raw material processing industries producing highly standardised "commodities" such as pulp and paper, iron and steel, vegetable oil, copper or petrochemicals. Unlike large industrial commodity producers in developed countries (pulp and paper in Sweden and Finland, copper in Canada or Australia, etc.), these conglomerates engaged in raw material processing industries did not undertake significant efforts for developing "in-house" engineering and R&D capabilities with the aim of increasing domestic value added and moving into more complex products and specialities. Quite on the contrary, they normally remained at the most elementary stages of the processing sequence of the locally available raw materials, making very little effort in moving toward a more sophisticated product mix.

In short, we may conclude that in this period some important institutional developments took place that would have significant positive impact in the long run. In the long run Brazilian industry was able to benefit from an ample, sophisticated and efficient infrastructure. From the point of view of technological development at firm level, policies did not show remarkable success but the roots for successes in the agro-industry (especially through the work of EMBRAPA), aerospace (Embraer, CTA, INPE, etc.), oil (where Brazil is the world leader in technology for deep water extraction), telecommunications (which was later lost) and energy (including biomass) were established.

Explicit S&T policy instruments linked to projects to develop local production capacity were set in place in these strategic sectors. In aerospace and oil these measures were put into practice in the early 1950s. In energy and telecommunications they gathered momentum in the 1970s. In all these sectors the State decided to control production, instead of letting the private sector take the lead.

2.3 The 1980s

The external debt crisis, which began to take shape at the beginning of the 1980s and deepened after the Mexican Moratorium of 1982, blocked Brazil's development and put an end to the impressive growth pattern that had been observed in previous decades. Under the external financing constraints, prevalent during the 1980s, the economy began to come apart as a result of the inevitable collapse of public finances and state companies. Brazil began to experience growing inflation and a forced compression of imports and had to accumulate a foreign exchange surplus to service the foreign debt under precarious conditions. The prolonged foreign exchange shortage, combined with wide-ranging and sophisticated mechanisms of indexation, pushed the economy toward an unprecedented regimen of super-inflation.

The debt crisis impacted the entire private sector as well as the large state enterprises holding dollar-denominated debts in the offshore euro market. The Federal Government absorbed most of the impact by assuming the dollar obligations of the private sector through various mechanisms, and ended up compromising its fiscal health and undermining its ability to continue fostering the development process. Fiscal weakness and a severe shortage of foreign exchange, coupled with the assumption of private debt by the Treasury as mentioned above, led Brazil to rampant inflation. From the point of view of the productive structure and its degree of competitiveness, potential problems that would affect the Brazilian economy—insufficient technological development, the low level of specialisation and the low degree of integration with the international economy—were already detected in the early 1980s (Cassiolato 1981, Serra 1982).

Obviously, this crisis period (and the consequent short-run stabilisation measures) had a significant impact on government S&T expenditures. The total expenditure of FUNTEC (the most important S&T fund) fell from US$ 1.2 billion (1970–1979) to US$ 754.32 million (1980–1989). The three main sources of funding for public science and technology institutions (the National Fund for Scientific and Technological Development of FINEP and the budgets for basic research of CNPq and CAPES) were allocated in 1985 only 40 per cent of the amount they received in 1979 (Bielchowsky 1985).

To counteract the budgetary crisis, in 1984 the Brazilian Government began the negotiation of a Loan Agreement with the World Bank (International Bank for Reconstruction and Development—IBRD). As a result a Science and Technology Reform Support Project (PADCT) was signed. The first PADCT aimed to increase and consolidate national technical and scientific competence in universities, research centres and enterprises but eventually only contributed to improve infrastructure with no impact on firms' technology strategies[12]. However, the World Bank loan was not sufficient to restore funding to the level of the 1970s.

Another important institutional development was the setting-up of a new Ministry of Science and Technology as part of the new democratic government of 1985. The Ministry placed innovation on the policy agenda for the first time, set up important programmes for human resources in the new areas of information technology, biotechnology and advanced materials and was able to restore funding to its 1970s levels. However, the deepening of the crisis in the late 1980s—when inflation reached three-digit levels— brought considerable institutional instability (the Ministry was downgraded to the level of a Special Secretariat with less political clout and resources) and the end of the decade witnessed another crisis for the S&T area in Brazil.

3. From 1990 to 2006: The Downgrading and Comeback of Innovation Policy

As pointed out in the introduction, it is essential for an analysis of innovation policy in Brazil to take into account the macroeconomic context of the period in question (1990–2006). This was a time when macroeconomic policy played a paramount, almost exclusive, role in the general economic and social policy of the Federal Government.

From this point of view, two distinct phases can be identified: the first, between 1990 and 1993, marked by intense monetary instability, and the second, from 1994 onwards, the year when the "Real Plan" (Plan for Monetary Stabilisation) was implemented. The period ranging from 1994 to 2006 unfolded against a background of restrictive macroeconomic policy, whose main aim continued to be preserving the monetary stability which followed implementation of the Real Plan (1994) and which used interest rates and exchange rates as the main adjustment variables.

In the first phase (1990–1998), there was no innovation policy and S&T policy was restricted to keep the scientific infrastructure alive. Industrial policy, which was essentially based on market liberalisation, deregulation and privatisation, induced significantly innovation strategies. Technological capacity building and innovation in general was primarily regarded as something to be left to market forces. In the second period (1999–2006), innovation policy came back to the government agenda as market forces had not brought any palpable result. During this period several policy mechanisms were introduced to correct "market failures".

3.1 The First Period: 1990–1998

The macroeconomic context of the period 1990–1998 was marked initially by intense monetary instability (1990 to 1993): inflation rates reached 2,477 per cent per year in 1993, according to the official extended consumer price index (IPCA), and growth rates fluctuated, with periods of recession (GDP growth was negative in 1990: –4.35 per cent and in 1992: –0.54 per cent) and recovery (GDP grew 1.02 per cent in 1991 and 4.92 per cent in 1993).

In 1994 a successful stabilisation plan was implemented (the Plan for Economic Stabilisation—Real Plan) and, at least up to 1998, macroeconomic policy was based on restrictive fiscal and monetary policies, using interest and exchange rates. The real interest rate was maintained at a high level during the whole period and the government adopted an exchange rate anchor, establishing a crawling peg system to operate the exchange rate flexibly. Policy-makers' strategy was to sustain the low level of economic activity and, simultaneously, to attract foreign capital in order to finance the balance of payments deficit.

This policy regime was based on the diagnosis that the Brazilian trade balance surplus was contributing to a deterioration of the fiscal balance, as inflows of foreign currency induced the government to increase the public debt (domestic bonds being sold by the Central Bank), worsening the fiscal imbalance and creating a "vicious circle". The idea was to enforce the integration of the Brazilian economy into the globalising economy in order to guarantee price competition between national and international (tradable) products, and to ensure that internal prices would be stable.

The implementation of such an exchange rate policy meant that imports increased more than exports, which generated current account deficits. The decline of the relationship between trade balance and gross domestic product (GDP) was managed by the combination of a fixed exchange rate and high real interest rate.

Arguably, such an economic policy ended up making the Brazilian economy increasingly vulnerable to a globalising financial economy. Without capital controls, financial liberalisation saw an increase in short-term capital inflows (mostly speculative) and generated increasing costs in rolling over the public debt. To deal with this problem, policy-makers increased taxes.

In summary, although Brazil did benefit from the abundant inflow of capital to stabilise inflation, the government opted for an onerous or "malignant" macroeconomic regime marked by five years of currency overvaluation and extremely high interest rates. The net results were very low levels of economic growth, a very high unemployment rate, burgeoning public debt, the hollowing-out of several productive activities, the persistence of retrograde corporate governance and widespread loss of national control over manufacturing and service enterprises.

In this context, the innovation policy of the 1990s was marked by a "laisser faire" approach[13]. Market liberalisation and encouragement of foreign investment were deemed to be sufficient. "Horizontal" policies directed towards the S&T infrastructure were designed to facilitate the operation of the market economy.

The central idea was that the process of trade liberalisation would induce enterprises to innovate, as part of their struggle to survive. Therefore, the State's role was essentially passive.

At the beginning of the 1990s, the Federal Government strategy towards production was in theory based on the idea of technological modernisation and capabilities building[14]. On one hand, there was the idea of a "competition shock" to be obtained by eliminating/reducing tariffs, eliminating subsidies and incentives, and strengthening competition. On the other hand, a "stimulus to competitiveness" package was devised.

Two programmes were created to support technology investments by private firms: the Brazilian Programme for Quality and Productivity (PBQP), which was basically a programme designed to increase awareness of these issues among industry managers, and the Programme to Support Technological Capacity of Industry (PACTI), which aimed to foster an increase in S&T expenditures by the government, the use of procurement as a way to encourage technological capabilities and the provision of tax incentives for R&D in firms. Eventually the only part of the programme that was implemented was the last one (tax incentives).

The PBQP seems not to have attained the expected outcomes, as the productivity gains accomplished by Brazilian economy in the period 1992–1994 cannot be directly ascribed to the programme. PACTI was a total failure as the goal for augmenting R&D expenditures from 0.5 per cent of GDP in 1989 to 1.3 per cent of GDP in 1994 was never fulfilled and tax incentives proved not to be enough to stimulate private R&D expenditures. R&D expenditures by private firms were in fact reduced in this period (Erber 1992, Erber & Cassiolato 1997).

In short, although this new government came to power with an agenda that included support for S&T, the continuing budgetary crisis meant that very little was done apart from exposing local firms to international competition. In fact, progressive and rapid liberalisation of the economy was set in motion with the aim of boosting the competitiveness of the productive sector and inducing the modernisation of local industry. Reforms—liberalisation (opening-up to foreign competition), deregulation of most markets and the privatisation of public-sector firms—did induce significant changes in the structure of the economy and affected microeconomic behaviour, but did not generate innovative capabilities.

The 1995–1998 period was basically a continuation of the previous regime, with inflation controlled. Innovation policy kept being shaped and implemented through horizontal measures. In 1995, the Federal Government issued the industry, technology and foreign trade policy, again oriented towards trade liberalisation and economic stabilisation. The main policy guidelines reflect the view of the Economics Ministries that totally opposed any type of industrial policy, as clearly expressed in 1996 by one of the main Central Bank officers:

> … a lesson was learned as to the effects of market inducements as opposed to heavy regulation or active industrial policies as the ultimate sources of entrepreneurial conducts leading to higher productivity growth. No question that the episode revealed the waste of time and resources involved in most instances of targeted industrial policies still in place in Brazil. Deregulation is surely on the rise and may reach other very sensitive areas, such as the labor market, in which the supply-side implications of deregulation may be very important (FRANCO 1996, p. 16).

It is no coincidence that changes in legislation on innovation policy in the period 1995–1998[15] followed such a vision as they even reduced tax incentives for R&D, the sole mechanism used in the previous period. The impact of this change in legislation on tax incentives was immediate, with a sharp fall in the (already small) number of firms which applied to make use of them: from 34 firms in 1997 to 20 in 1998. Although there is no comprehensive assessment of the use of tax incentives for R&D it can be suggested that, as only around 100 large firms took advantage of them, their effect was negligible: firms that used them would probably have invested the same amount in R&D without the programme (Doria Porto et al. 2000).

Admittedly, some other programmes were implemented during this period. The Ministry of Industry created the Brazilian Programme of Design (PBD) and FINEP, and set up the ALFA project for supporting innovation in micro- and small enterprises in the light of the US experience with the Small Business Innovation Research (SBIR) programme. Also, at FINEP, two specific lines for financing micro-, small and medium-sized enterprises (MPME) were set up

(AMPED and PATME), both implemented in partnership with SEBRAE—the Brazilian Service for Support of Micro- and Small Enterprises. In parallel, the government was negotiating the third phase of the above-mentioned World Bank loan (PADCT), which was never implemented as the necessary Brazilian counterpart did not materialise.

There were several consequences of such a policy regime for the National System of Innovation. First, liberalisation lowered the cost of imported capital goods and therefore encouraged their substitution for domestically produced machinery and equipment (Katz 1998). In Brazil, the coefficient of import penetration in machinery and electronic goods jumped from 29 per cent in 1993 to around 70 per cent in 1996. The same coefficient for some important inputs, such as chemical raw materials, fertilizers and resins, grew from 20 to 26 per cent in 1993 to around 33 to 42 per cent in 1996 (Cassiolato et al. 1998).

Second, under crisis and with the openness of the economy, MNC subsidiaries discontinued local engineering activities that they used to undertake in order to adapt or improve product and process technologies provided by their parent companies (Katz 1998, Cassiolato et al. 2001). As they could operate on the basis of imported parts and components, these firms reformulated their "adaptive engineering" strategies of the ISI period and discontinued domestic technological programmes that were justified in the more closed economy of the past.

Third, the general hypothesis that private agents should be playing a more important role in the financing and performance of technological activities at local level hardly came true.

Fourth, another hypothesis was that state-owned technological institutions and universities should obtain an increasing share of their funding from the private sector. The only perceived consequence was that these institutes started to change the mix of activities they conducted by reducing the number of research projects they undertook and by increasing the share of consultancy and technical assistance activities, which provided them with the resources they needed (Katz 1998).

Both in the case of the privatisation of state enterprises and in the expansion of domestically owned conglomerates in resource processing industries, the setting-up of new production capacity was based on the use of imported machinery and equipment and intermediate products. The final result was that production became less intensive in the use of local engineering and technical capabilities. Most of the few local innovative firms were acquired by subsidiaries of MNEs that, as part of their strategies, downgraded the technological activities carried out locally. The result was that Brazil specialised in sectors and areas of relatively low dynamism.

At the end of the 1990s, the general impression was that the Brazilian productive sector as a whole had become particularly fragile owing to: (i) weak competitive performance with outstanding trade fragility in all sectors of high added value and high technological content; (ii) widespread loss of national ownership in many sectors, weakness and reduced size of the remaining Brazilian business groups; and (iii) persistent financial vulnerability of Brazilian-owned businesses resulting from very high costs of capital and the lack of long-term financing mechanisms (Coutinho 2005).

3.2 The Second Period: 1999–2006

The second government term of President Cardoso (1999–2002) started with a huge crisis as the untenable foreign exchange position forced a devaluation of the real and a change in the foreign exchange regime in January 1999, from a fixed rate regime to a floating exchange rate that was supported by multilateral institutions, particularly the International Monetary Fund (IMF) and the World Bank. The adoption of the floating exchange rate aimed to prevent the persistent deficits in the balance of payments, which were to be counterbalanced by means of a positive trade balance. The IMF support for avoiding the deepening of Brazilian crisis had, as a counterpart, the requirement that the country should adopt strict fiscal and inflation goals through, again, high interest rates and the adoption of an inflation targeting regime.

Expectations regarding changes in economic policy subsided as the crisis unfolded. The only significant policy change was the adoption of a more aggressive foreign trade policy, which had positive impacts on the balance of payments as increasing surpluses in the balance of trade started to materialise.

It was basically against the same macroeconomic policy background that policies specifically directed towards innovation started to be designed in 1999; they followed more or less the same approach at least until 2006. The guidelines and objectives, however, followed a very similar framework to the one in place in the previous period (1995–1998), which advocated horizontal policies as the most appropriate approach for an innovation policy. The difference was that the Federal Government started to recognise the need for intervention to correct so-called "market failures", particularly to establish partnerships between scientific and technological institutions and firms.

The rationale was that the lack of interaction between scientific and technological institutions and firms was preventing the Brazilian scientific infrastructure from "producing" innovations. In addition, the characteristics of the innovative process, involving high risk, high costs and long maturation times justified, so the argument ran, action by the State. The policy was hallmarked by this view and was based on the creation of mechanisms and instruments aimed at encouraging interaction between the academic world and the production sector, as well as reducing both the costs and risks of inducing investments in innovative processes by the production sector. It has to be pointed out that this was nothing new in the Brazilian context as policies for fostering links between universities and businesses had been implemented since the mid-1970s (Cassiolato 1982).

Innovation policies remained restricted to the sphere of the Ministry of Science and Technology (MS&T). However, at the beginning of 1999, the Ministry of Development, Industry and Foreign Trade formulated a detailed plan for industrial, technological and foreign trade which explicitly recognised that one of the main problems of the Brazilian productive structure was a relatively low level of innovativeness. In this plan one of the main policy proposals was to step up the pace of technological innovation (Lemos 1999).

The Ministry of Development, Industry and Foreign Trade created in 2000 the Competitiveness Forums, which consisted of committees coordinated by its Department of Production Development whose main objective was to establish a dialogue between the productive sector, the government and Parliament. The forums aimed to promote debate and search for consensus.

Unfortunately, not much progress was achieved with the forums and the MS&T remained the sole body responsible for innovation policy. The Ministry was taken captive by the interests of the most vocal part of the Brazilian scientific community and shaped its strategy based on three main pillars: (1) incentives for technological development and innovation in firms; (2) incentives for the creation of new technological infrastructure; and (3) incentives for newly established technology firms (start-ups).

In order to enable such a policy to be implemented, the Ministry thought up an ingenious scheme to provide new funding. Funds for Scientific and Technological Development, the so-called sectoral funds, were set up (using new taxes) with the aim of rebuilding the capacity to grant incentives for financing R&D and innovation. Between 1999 and 2002, twelve sectoral funds were created, the first of them being the petroleum sectoral fund, as well as another two of a horizontal nature: the Yellow-Green Fund and the CT-Infra, which aimed respectively to finance projects involving university and enterprise partnerships for fostering innovation, and to restore and expand the scientific and technological infrastructure of universities and other research institutions.

The sectoral funds displayed two main novel features: the establishment of coordinating committees bringing together representatives of government, the production sector and academia and responsible for setting up guidelines, selecting and monitoring projects to be financed; and the rule that the research projects to be financed had to include both enterprises and scientific and technological institutions. The logic behind the creation of such a mechanism was, on the one hand, to allow for the participation of the private sector and academia in taking decisions about projects to be financed, and, on the other hand, to encourage the setting-up of partnerships in research projects, considering that innovation does not happen in isolation.

The restructuring of the MS&T's financing capacity allowed implementation of the policy's three pillars to begin. For the purpose of fostering partnership links between universities and enterprises, some schemes were also established for placing young researchers in enterprises. Such schemes were implemented by the National S&T Council, CNPq, through scholarships granted under the programme Human Resources for Strategic Activities—Innovation (RHAE—Inovação) and the Programmes for Incentives to Retain Human Resources (PROSET).

The originality of the sectoral funds, which rested on increasing otherwise scarce resources for S&T, was unfortunately outweighed by the very rudimentary notion of innovation adopted, i.e. joint R&D projects conducted by universities and firms. Implementation of the sectoral funds was based on the launch of calls for proposals with a view to the non-reimbursable[16] funding of "projects for research, development and innovation partnerships between scientific and technological institutions and enterprises". Eventually only R&D projects got under way.

To improve the technological infrastructure, the Ministry of Science and Technology launched, in December 2000, the programme Basic Industrial Technology and Technological Services for Innovation and Competitiveness (TIB Programme). This pursued the aim of adapting and expanding the technological services infrastructure in the areas of metrology, standardisation, technology management, support services for clean production, and support services for intellectual property and technological information.

The support for technology business enterprises was provided through the creation of the National Programme of Support for Business Incubators and Technology Parks (PNI) and the INOVAR programme for fostering seed and risk capital. These programmes were implemented by FINEP, the financing arm of the Ministry of S&T.

Several other programmes were created by the MS&T to support the technological development of micro-, small and medium-sized industrial enterprises. They consisted of actions directed towards technological extension, technological support for exports and technological services. The regional dimension was targeted by another programme, the Programme of Support for Innovation in Local Production and Innovation Arrangements, which was implemented in partnership between the Federal Government and state governments.

The third pillar of the innovation policy—encouragement of technological development and innovation in firms—was implemented via the revitalisation of tax incentives, the use of mechanisms for reducing interest rates on traditional lines of finance and the establishment of non-reimbursable financing mechanisms, i.e. grants. Although explicitly provided for in the policy, these new instruments were not implemented during the 1999–2002 government as no consensus was reached within government on how to put them into practice.

S&T policy, in its stricto sensu, was maintained with hardly any significant changes and concentrated in promoting S&T development via the concession of scholarships for students and researchers. There was however a significant increase in the government budget for the Ministry of S&T with the novel resources of the Sectoral Funds and three new initiatives, inspired by international agencies, were introduced.

The first was the launching of the Millennium Institutes programme. Similarly to what happened in other developing countries this program essentially aimed at consolidating high level research groups as it diverted some of the new budgetary resources to them. It did not represent any strategic change and rapidly lost its appeal, as it is only a way for members of the S&T community with a political clout to guarantee some resources. In 2008 a similar initiative was put into place, now with another name, National Institutes of Science and Technology.

The second was an attempt to restructure the research institutes associated to the Ministry of S&T. The idea was to introduce best managerial practices through the setting up of "Management Contracts" between them and the Ministry of S&T. The management contracts aimed at setting performance targets to the research institutes as a counterpart of guaranteed yearly budgets to them. The basic idea was to introduce a more professional management structure and to stimulate the institutes to get financial resources into the "market" through partnerships with the private sector. Such attempt was frustrated by two reasons: a strong internal resistance and the enormous difficulty in finding private partners.

The third initiative, the setting up of thematic research networks, was the most successful. The plan was to link different universities and research institutes working in the same theme in mobilizing research projects. As priority areas were chosen strategic areas such as biotechnology, with networks for genetic sequencing – the Genome project -, nanotechnology, etc. The success of this policy stimulated the setting up of other important networks, as for example the Genoma project, a thematic research network on environmental modelling of the Amazon region.

The new government of President Lula that held office in 2003–2006 launched the industry, technology and foreign trade policy (PITCE),[17] one of the main pillars of which was the encouragement and promotion of innovation in firms. In practice, the government maintained the same guidelines and objectives of the previous science, technology and innovation policy[18].

It is true, nevertheless, that the PITCE represented an advance in comparison to the national science, technology and innovation policy, as it took into account the need to identify strategic options, even though it limited such options to knowledge-intensive areas that were not even defined or specified in the policy documents[19]. However, for PITCE, unlike the national science, technology and innovation policy, there is no agency appointed to coordinate the policy[20].

In spite of the explicit acknowledgement of the need for an innovation policy and the need to select strategic areas, the new government implemented policies based on the same ideas and mechanisms created in the former period. In particular, sectoral funds remained the main sources of resources and the model for policy implementation.

Figure 2.1, which presents the evolution of sectoral funds as a percentage of GDP in the period from 1999 to 2006, indicates significant growth in the total amount of resources available for scientific, technological and innovation activities. As can be seen, funds collected and resources effectively spent were gradually growing. On the other hand, from 2001 on, a significant share of the funds were retained by the Economics Ministry as a contribution to newly created contingency funds. Such contingency funds were set up by the Economics Ministry to control budgetary expenditures and simply meant that portions of taxes collected and intended for the sectoral funds were retained by the monetary authorities as contingency reserves. In the period 2001 to 2005, the amount of the resources channelled to contingency funds was higher than the volume of resources effectively applied by the sectoral funds.

The creation of these funds is commendable at they substantially expanded the financing capacity of the Brazilian S&T system. However, it is a pity that the funds are mostly used in traditional instruments that attempt to foster university-industry links through joint R&D projects, which have been implemented in Brazil since the 1970s without much success. The mechanisms and instruments made available for promoting innovation do not promote systemic interaction of the actors, as they often remain geared to strengthening the research infrastructure of the country. As already emphasised, sectoral funds are implemented through public calls for proposals for research and development projects prepared by scientific and technological institutions (STIs) and, although the calls generally include requirements on partnerships with enterprises, the non-reimbursable resources are granted to the S&T institutions.

The main difference between the period 2003–2006 and the previous government was the creation of two new sectoral funds, adding to the 14 funds

Figure 2.1. Total Sectoral Funds as a Proportion of GDP—1999–2006

	Funds Collected	Budget Law*	Contingency Funds or Tender Restrictions	Amount Paid Out
1999	0.010	0.010	–	0.003
2000	0.021	0.025	–	0.011
2001	0.035	0.050	0.029	0.024
2002	0.062	0.057	0.023	0.021
2003	0.078	0.072	0.069	0.033
2004	0.073	0.073	0.042	0.031
2005	0.075	0.075	0.040	0.035
2006	0.080	0.074	0.029	0.042

Source: original data from IBGE (Brazilian Institute for Geography and Statistics) and Câmara dos Deputados do Brasil (Brazilian Congress).
Note:* The Budget Law includes approved appropriations and contingency funds or tender restrictions.

created in the period 1999–2002, and the establishment of the Coordinating Committee for the Sectoral Funds by the Ministry of Science and Technology. Perhaps the most important novelty was that some resources of the sectoral funds began to be used by the government to support policy actions that were not strictly sectoral as it earmarked 50 per cent of the resources to finance such actions. This measure was an attempt to remedy the prevailing lack of coherence between projects approved (and funded) by the Boards of the different sectoral funds and the strategic guidelines set by the Federal Government for the national science, technology and innovation policy and the industry, technology and foreign trade policy.

In addition to the sectoral funds, these two policies were linked to two basic legal instruments that were introduced: the Innovation Law, enacted in 2004, and the "Law of Good"[21], enacted in 2005, both aimed at promoting innovation by means of either tax incentives or non-reimbursable grants and interest rate subsidies. The mechanisms of grants and interest rate subsidies, which were created at the end of the Cardoso government and were not implemented, underwent some changes, and were eventually utilised.

In practice such changes meant the abandonment of the former requirement that firms would need to prepare R&D projects for approval by the Ministry of Science and Technology in order to qualify for the tax benefits. As the incentives became automatic and not subject to any type of assessment by the government, the number of firms which applied for incentives rose again in 2004 (20) and in 2005 (19) but the number of users remained insignificant.

Figure 2.2. Evolution of Federal Expenditures on Grants as a Percentage of GDP

	Amount Authorised	Amount Paid Out	Percentage Implementation
2005	0.00012	0.00012	99.3
2006*	0.009	0.002	20.3

Source: IBGE, Ipeadata and Senado Federal.
Note: The percentage implementation is the relationship between the amounts approved and those paid out (Liquidado).
* For 2006, preliminary results estimated on the basis of Contas Nacionais Trimestrais Referência 2000.

Figure 2.3. Evolution of Federal Expenditures on Interest Rate Subsidies as a Percentage of GDP

	Amount Authorised	Amount Paid Out	Percentage Implementation
2005	0.0019	0.0019	99.8
2006*	0.0028	0.0028	100.0

Source: IBGE, Ipeadata and Senado Federal.
Note: The percentage implementation is the relationship between the amounts approved and those paid out (Liquidado).
* For 2006, preliminary results estimated on the basis of Contas Nacionais Trimestrais Referência 2000.

The grants programme was effectively created in 2006[22] by FINEP, with the purpose of providing non-reimbursable financing for firms' innovation projects. Figure 2.2 suggests that, in spite of the increase in the amount authorised for grants since the programme was rolled out, the Federal Government either did not have the structure required for their full use or the public calls for proposals did not fit the Brazilian context as, in 2006, the percentage implementation was only about 20 per cent.

Another important new instrument was the interest rate subsidies provided by FINEP through the programmes Proinovação, aimed at medium-sized and large enterprises, and Juro Zero, aimed at small enterprises. The purpose of these programmes was to reduce the interest rates on loans granted to enterprises participating in joint innovation projects with scientific and technological institutions (STIs). The evolution of the budget and expenditures of the interest rate subsidy scheme is given in Figure 2.3, showing growing resources between 2005 and 2006.

Still aiming to finance innovation projects presented by enterprises, the National Bank of Social and Economic Development (BNDES), linked to the Ministry of Development, Industry and Foreign Trade, created two programmes in 2006: Innovative Capital, whose objective is the "development of capacity for undertaking systematic innovative activities", and Technological Innovation, designed to finance innovation projects of a technological nature.

Two further programmes for technological development are worth mentioning, which were both aimed at social development and were resumed in the period between 2003 and 2006: Habitare and Prosab. These social development programmes were created in the 1980s and were restructured in the 1990s. Habitare took on its current structure in 1994 and uses FINEP's financing modes—both reimbursable and non-reimbursable—to fund projects relating to housing technologies. Non-reimbursable financing is granted following calls for proposals. From 1994 to 2006, seven public calls were issued, three of them between 2003 and 2006. Prosab, which targets the development of sewage and water supply systems, was restructured in 1995, and launched a public call for proposals in 2006. Although social development is one of the guidelines of the national science, technology and innovation policy, these programmes are not coordinated either with the other programmes, directed at firms, or with the national industry, technology and foreign trade policy.

The analysis of both guidelines and implementation of the innovation policy, be it through the national industry, technology and foreign trade policy or through the national science, technology and innovation policy, reveals that in addition to problems of coordination and overlapping of objectives and actions, the support for research, technological development and innovation basically consisted in actions by the Ministry of Science and Technology and its agencies (FINEP and CNPq).

Continuity can in fact be observed between the innovation policy of the period 2003–2006, when all the Ministry's efforts were directed to improving/overhauling and implementing the instruments and the mechanisms conceived in the former period (1999–2002). The Innovation Law (which had already been drafted by the former government) and the "Law of Good" allowed for the availability of resources for interest rate subsidies and grants. Also the sectoral funds were reformulated slightly to bring them into line with the guidelines proposed by the government.

The guidelines and strategies of the innovation policy implemented in the period 1999–2006 were mainly aimed at creating an innovation-friendly environment by rebuilding the capacity for promoting/financing R&D and innovation and also by changing the legal framework, which was seen as hampering the innovation process in firms. These guidelines and strategies are explicitly anchored in the idea of correcting existing "market failures", being essentially a reformist liberal policy (Erber & Cassiolato 1997, p. 34).

The innovation policy devised and implemented since 1999 displays essentially a supply-side orientation and still follows the linear approach to innovation. Although labelling the projects to be supported with the words "research, development and innovation", policies supported basically R&D projects. The logic underlying both instruments and the implementation of innovation policy in the period 1994–2006 lacked a systemic view of the innovative process[23], failing to contemplate wider aspects of knowledge acquisition and learning that are essential parts of the innovation process (Cassiolato & Lastres 1999). Policy focused on scientific and technological institutions and on enterprises, considering, at best, the links and interaction between these two actors. Hence, other institutions that are vital to the innovation process continued to be ignored by this logic.

3.3 Current Innovation Policy

Discussion of the outlook for innovation policy in Brazil should include a brief explanation of some changes that have occurred recently and a few comments on other explicit policies besides macroeconomic policy, such as tax policy, education policy and commercial policy. The second Lula government (2007–2010) started with a wide debate on industrial policy which placed innovation policy as one of its central tenets. However, what is happening is in fact a continuation of the same policy as in previous years: a policy based on stimulating R&D in firms and encouraging partnerships between universities and enterprises, by means of tax incentives and financing of R&D projects. The policy makes use of the same instruments created in previous years: tax incentives, sectoral funds, grants and interest rate subsidies[24]. Out of these four instruments, the grants programme is worth noting: its implementation began, as a systematic programme, in 2006, and its volume of resources practically doubled between 2006 and 2007. Figure 2.4 illustrates the evolution of the budget availability for grants.

In 2007, awards of grants were based on two main strategies: resources allocated for research and development projects, and resources allocated for the retention of researchers within enterprises. The bulk of the resources were directed to R&D projects. It is worth noting the significant volume of resources in relation to the total budget of the Ministry of Science and Technology: in 2007 it represented nearly 8 per cent of the Ministry's total budget; in 2008 this percentage was reduced to 5 per cent of the budget. Even so, considering the total budget of the Federal Government, the available resources were quite limited: only 0.03 per cent in 2007 and 0.02 per cent in 2008. Nevertheless, the

Figure 2.4. Evolution of Budget for and Expenditures on Grants by the Federal Government—2007–2008

Grant	Year	Amount Authorised	Amount Paid Out	Percentage Implementation
Total (Brazilian reais (R$)—exchange rate: U$ 1 = R$ 2 2663 in November 2008, selling rate, monthly average)	2007	420 265 595	344 843 063	82.1
	2008	324 542 000	30 877 092	9.5
Percentage of MS&T's	2007	7.71	7.60	–
total budget	2008	5.45	9.31	–
Percentage of total budget	2007	0.03	0.03	–
of Federal Government	2008	0.02	0.01	–

Source: SigBrasil. Senado Federal. Own calculations.
Note: The percentage implementation is the relationship between amounts authorised and amounts paid out.
In 2008, data are updated to 12 April.

difficulties in spending all the available resources, a problem already identified in previous years—budget implementation was 82 per cent of allocated resources—reveal that the methods chosen for utilising these resources are still inadequate.

Analysis of the award of grants further highlights the problems in the design of the innovation policy. In 2007, the process of selecting enterprises which responded to public calls for proposals, and which could qualify for grants, identified five priority areas and initially provided 450 million Brazilian reais (around US$ 225 million) for up to three years' projects. Figure 2.5 provides information on the selection of projects proposed by enterprises for grant funding by area of operation. It can be seen that approved projects used about 70 per cent of the available resources.

Additional selection criteria were established, stipulating that 40 per cent of the resources should be earmarked for small enterprises, and another 30 per cent for enterprises located in the North, Northeast or Central-West regions of the country. Note that none of these percentages was attained by the end of the selection process: small enterprises selected received, during the grant period, about 31 per cent of the available resources. Enterprises located in the North, Northeast and Central-West regions were granted 16 per cent of the available resources.

Besides failing to use up all the budgeted resources, and also failing to fulfil the quotas in terms of small enterprises and regionalisation, the grants

Figure 2.5. Grants for Innovation 2007—Total by Area

Area of Operation		Percentage of the Total Grant Amount (%)	Percentage of the Available Resources	Number of Approved Projects	Percentage of the Total of Number of Approved Projects (%)
AREA 1	Information and communication technologies and nanotechnology	30.98	97.22	63	36.21
AREA 2	Biodiversity, biotechnology and health	8.13	25.51	28	16.09
AREA 3	Strategic programmes	33.73	105.83	34	19.54
AREA 4	Biofuels and energy	16.14	50.63	19	10.92
AREA 5	Social development	11.02	69.17	30	17.24
TOTAL	Grant 2007	100.00	69.73	174	100.00

Source: Own calculations using **FINEP** data (www.finep.gov.br).

programme is implemented in such a way that, although adopting priority areas, it uses a selection process similar to that adopted by the sectoral funds. That is, the enterprise must look for the finance and the project proposals are assessed and financed on an individual basis, while, again, the grants benefit a limited number of enterprises (only 174 projects were approved in 2007).

Summing up, innovation policy in 2007 was based on programmes that were conceived and created during previous government terms. The programmes that provide non-reimbursable finance are:

- Enterprises. The main instruments were: grants for projects, grants for retaining researchers within an enterprise, Próinovação (Pro innovation), Juro Zero (Zero interest), INOVAR (Venture Capital Programme), INOVAR Semente (Seed Money Programme);
- Scientific and technological institutions (STIs), with special reference to: PRO-INFRA, PAPPE, PNI;
- Partnerships between STIs and enterprises. The calls for proposals under the sectoral funds (former programmes such as PROGEX and PRUMO) continue to exist, although no further calls were issued in 2007.

However, the continuity in operation, during 2007, of innovation and industrial policies existing in previous years did not "silence" the debates on the inappropriateness of the policy and the need for coordination between the different agencies of the Federal Government. So it was that, in May 2008, the government launched the policy for productive development—Innovating and Investing for Growth, which showed major concern for coordinating the actions of the various ministries, particularly the Ministry of Science and Technology and the Ministry of Development, Industry and Foreign Trade.

In addition to the concerns about the governance of this new policy, strategic sectors were chosen and categorised as mobilising programmes in strategic areas—programmes for strengthening competitiveness, and programmes for consolidating and expanding leadership. These involve the following areas or economic activities:

- Mobilising programmes in strategic areas include: information and communication technology, nanotechnology, biotechnology, the defence industrial complex, the nuclear energy industrial complex and the health industrial complex.
- Programmes for strengthening competitiveness include: the automobile complex, the capital goods industry (on-demand and series production), the naval and coastal industry, the textile and clothing industry, the leather, footwear and artefacts complex, the personal care, perfume and cosmetics

sector, the wood and furniture sector, plastics, the biodiesel complex, agro-industry, civil construction and the services complex.
• Programmes for consolidating and enhancing leadership include: the bio-ethanol production complex, the oil, gas and petrochemicals industrial complex, the aeronautics complex and the production complexes for commodities such as mineral ores, iron and steel, cellulose and meats.

For each of these sectors, available policy instruments have been identified, as well as the indicators for monitoring their evolution.

Although it is somewhat premature to make an evaluation, we note the attention given to governance of the policy and to the distribution of responsibilities between the various agencies in charge of implementing it. However, two other points raise concerns: the first regarding the great number of areas and sectors included, with the possibility of including new ones, as expressed in the government's own statement of the policy; and the second regarding the instruments presented, which are the same as those created in previous years. In this latter case, what is at issue is not so much the use of existing instruments, but the way they are implemented, as several problems regarding implementation have already been identified.

4. Policy Outlook

The discussion of innovation policy must take place with reference to a background of restrictive macroeconomic policy and institutionalisation of innovation policy, which is to some extent still subordinated to this macroeconomic policy. As Coutinho (2005) emphasised, macroeconomic systems and policies, instead of being neutral, affect microeconomic decisions, having significant impacts on financing patterns, competitiveness and technical change[25]. Thus, the role of the State as designer of the innovation policy must be examined in the light of the macroeconomic policy adopted, which has a visible impact on microeconomic behaviour.

The brief characterisation of macroeconomic policy in the period 1990–2006 allows some fundamental aspects of innovation policy to be identified. After the implementation of the Plan for Economic Stabilisation (Real Plan) in 1994, a "stop-go" policy was set in place, under which the regime for inflation targeting controlled by high interest rates and the regime of floating exchange rates both allowed inflation rates to be reduced, but led to dismal performance in terms of GDP growth and employment, in spite of a largely friendly international context.

Investment rates after 1994 were close to 16 per cent of GDP, and never recovered to the historical levels of the 1970s and beginning of the 1980s,

Figure 2.6. Investment Rates and Exchange Rates—1995–2006

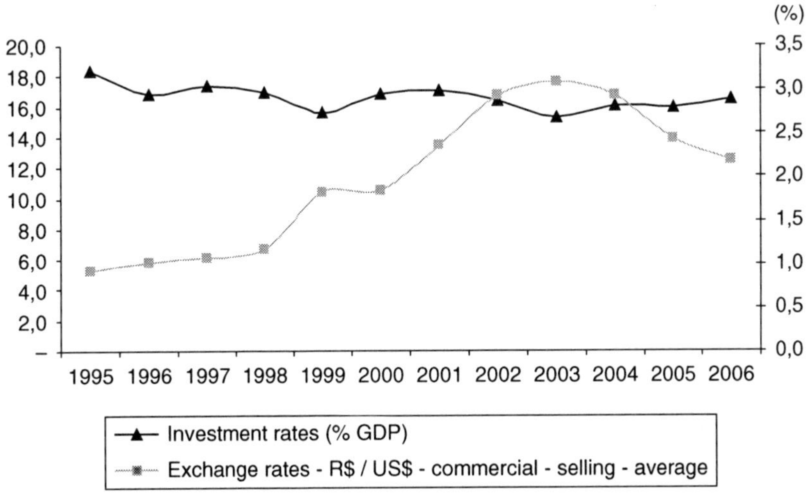

Source: IBGE and Banco Central.
Note: References for GDP values: for 1995–2005: Sistema de Contas Nacionais Referência 2000 (IBGE/SCN 2000 Anual). For 2006: preliminary results estimated from Contas Nacionais Trimestrais Referência 2000.

when they reached 24 per cent of GDP. Figure 2.6 and 2.7 illustrate the investment rates in relation to exchange rates and interest rates, revealing that investment rates reflected the exchange rate regime as well as the high interest rates adopted in the period in question.

Such a policy seems also to have affected expenditures on R&D and other innovative activities. As illustrated in Figure 2.8, expenditures on innovative activities in relation to gross fixed capital formation decreased between 2000 and 2005, in parallel with a reduction in the investment rate, which, in 2000, was 16.8 per cent of GDP and, in 2005, was 15.9 per cent of GDP.

The action of the State has been directly associated with the prevailing economic policy, that is, during periods when the Economics Ministry was unfavourable to the innovation policy, "disincentive" measures were adopted. In those periods when the Economics Ministry was favourable to the innovation policy, the State's role as a promoter of innovation increased but only by means of some innocuous policy measures such as tax incentives and the offer of new specific sources of finance aimed at innovation. Thus, throughout the period under analysis, the Brazilian government implemented a series of policy mechanisms aimed at stimulating businesses to enhance their R&D expenditures and expand the innovation rates of the country with no significant impact on the innovativeness of the economy.

Figure 2.7. Investment Rates and Interest Rates—1999–2006

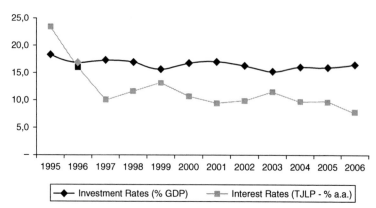

Source: IBGE and Banco Central.
Note: References for GDP values: for 1995–2005: Sistema de Contas Nacionais Referência 2000 (IBGE/SCN 2000 Anual). For 2006: preliminary results estimated from Contas Nacionais Trimestrais Referência 2000.

These different mechanisms were, altogether, based on the idea that sectors and enterprises to be assisted could not be chosen "ex-ante". Preference was given to "horizontal" policies, and stimuli that could benefit only a narrow group were rejected. Based on these same principles, the technology policy was not linked up with other government policies, particularly the trade policy, a practice that is usual in developed countries.

This policy can be summarised on the basis of its two principal mechanisms: tax incentives for innovation and encouragement of interaction between the academic world and the production sector. The implementation of these mechanisms, during the period in question (1990–2006), varied over time, with the tax incentives for R&D being implemented in the first period (1990–1998) and the mechanisms of public financing for innovation, as a stimulus to partnerships between universities and enterprises, being implemented in the second period (1999–2006).

Although tax incentives are widely used in most countries, a detailed analysis of the effectiveness of such incentives suggests that they are, at most, a secondary element and only subsidiary to support for innovation[26].

In Brazil, a quick look at the list of around 100 firms which used tax incentives throughout the 1990s suggests that this mechanism did not contribute significantly to the innovative potential of industry. These enterprises would probably spend resources on R&D, with or without tax incentives, since their competitive status relies significantly on such expenditures.

Figure 2.8. Brazil—Expenditures on Innovation Activities in Relation to Gross Fixed Capital Formation—2000, 2003 and 2005

Expenditures on Innovation Activities	2000	2003	2005
R&D expenditures/gross fixed capital formation	2.21	2.22	2.08
Expenditures on equipment and machinery/gross fixed capital formation	5.89	4.48	4.86
Total innovation expenditures/gross fixed capital formation	11.28	9.02	10.05

Source: Own calculations from IBGE's innovation surveys, 2000, 2003, 2005 and National Accounts, several years.
Note: Only manufacturing firms with more than 10 employees, which implemented either products or processes that were technologically new or substantially improved.

This trend is not restricted to the use of tax incentives for innovation but is common to all innovation policies. The industry survey of technological innovation indicates that only a small percentage of innovative manufacturing firms received any government support: 16.9 per cent for the years 1998–2000, 18.7 per cent for 2001–2003 and 19.2 per cent for 2003–2005 (PINTEC 2005, p. 20). According to the same source the data also show that, for the 2001–2003 survey, "large firms are the major beneficiaries of government programmes" (PINTEC 2005, p. 20) and, for the 2003–2005 survey, "firms with over 500 employees … are the ones that most benefited from government programmes" (PINTEC 2007, p. 55).

In spite of the growth in the percentage of firms that won government support, in 2005 only 5,800 firms managed to obtain such assistance. This is quite a small number compared with the nearly 150 thousand manufacturing enterprises and nearly 5 million enterprises existing in Brazil that year. Furthermore, the PINTEC survey also found that, as regards the government support, "… financing for the purchase of machinery and equipment stands out as the programme most used by innovative enterprises, and the Law on R&D [Law on Research and Development; refers to the Law on tax incentives for R&D] as the least used" (PINTEC 2007, p. 55).

At the end of the 1990s, some policy mechanisms that had been used in the 1970s with the aim of fostering relations between the production sector and the research infrastructure were rediscovered. Based on an outdated linear view of innovation (which suggests the existence of a "supply" of technology in the research institutions to be absorbed by a "demand" existing in the production sector), the programmes did not take account of the fact that enterprises, when interacting with the research infrastructure, must have a strong internal R&D capability. Such capability is a necessary condition for the establishment of cooperation and is encouraged and advanced by means of government programmes and actions much more complex than those that have been implemented in Brazil, as can be inferred from the preceding analysis.

Moreover, as already mentioned, attracting R&D by subsidiaries of multinational companies in order to increase local technological capabilities was at the core of the liberalisation policies of the 1990s. This strategy was in line with the whole industrialisation process conducted from the 1950s to the 1970s based on a massive inflow of foreign direct investment[27]. The aim in the second half of the 1990s was to renew foreign capital inflows, which declined in the 1980s as the domestic crisis deepened.

Such a policy was introduced at a time of increasing liquidity and availability of capital in the global financial market. It was not surprising that FDI inflows increased—from virtually nothing in the early years of the 1990s to an average of more than US$ 30 billion per year at the end of the decade[28]. Unlike the FDI of the 1970s which contributed to the establishment and enlargement of the Brazilian productive base, the FDI of the 1990s meant mostly a simple change of ownership. It concentrated heavily on the acquisition of local assets in privatised state-owned utilities, such as telecommunications and electrical energy, and other services such as those forming part of the banking system. Even the small amount of FDI in manufacturing consisted basically of acquisitions of local firms in sectors such as auto parts or IT. After privatisation subsided, FDI inflows were drastically reduced. At the beginning of the 2000s the relative flow of foreign investments declined, levelling off at approximately 2 per cent of total world FDI. This suggests that Brazil is becoming less attractive to productive FDI, particularly in subsystems with high technological intensity. This second period of FDI in Brazil did not result in structural modifications in the productive base and above all was not successful in stimulating technological and innovative efforts by foreign firms as expected in the 1990s.

Most importantly, the strategy aimed at boosting technological capabilities failed. Several empirical works confirm this pattern: Hiratuka (2008), for example, points out that as external investments were concentrated in the production structure of service provision to the detriment of manufacturing activities, domestic firms achieved higher rates of productivity growth in this period than MNC subsidiaries. Hiratuka's research concludes that foreign-owned subsidiaries of MNCs still keep using knowledge mostly developed by the R&D laboratories located in their headquarters and tend only to adapt the technologies to local conditions. This finding is in line with others.

Zucoloto and Junior (2005) compared the technological behaviour and strategies of local firms with those of MNC subsidiaries, controlling for the sector of activity and the level of control local firms and MNC subsidiaries have in the specific sector. They found a negative correlation between the relative technological effort (measured by the average R&D intensity in each sector in Brazil over the average R&D intensity in the sector in advanced countries) and the level of foreign participation in Brazilian manufacturing industry.

The authors demonstrated that, generally, the greater the foreign control over a particular sector, the lesser the relative technological effort developed by that sector. For example, in a sector such as pharmaceuticals where MNC subsidiaries control 75 per cent of net revenues the R&D intensity is just 8 per cent of the EU average. In contrast in sectors such as aircraft, wood products and paper and pulp where there is little influence of foreign capital (MNC subsidiaries control only zero, 9 per cent and 21 per cent), the relative technological effort is much higher, sometimes higher than the EU average (130 per cent, 116 per cent and 85 per cent respectively). Out of the 17 sectors studied, the authors note that if the relative technological effort is higher (lower) than the average of the manufacturing industry, then the foreign dominance in operating income is lower (higher) than that average.

It is worth noting also the lack of interlinkage between education policy and innovation policy. During the whole period analysed, there has been significant investment (particularly through the grant of scholarships), by both the Ministry of Education and the Ministry of Science and Technology, in MSc and PhD programmes with the explicit aim of increasing the number and calibre of lecturers. Brazil has in fact exceeded a score of 10 thousand PhD graduates per year. However, despite this commendable effort, there was no linking of this policy with innovation policy, apart from the recent programme aimed at fostering the use by productive firms of these human resources and slowing the brain drain. There is no integrated policy for learning and technical education linked to the innovation needs of the productive sector. It is no coincidence that in an overall environment characterised by a high level of unemployment, firms have difficulty in hiring people who fit their needs. There are several studies revealing that one of the main difficulties/barriers to innovation indicated by firms is the lack of qualified human resources, particularly at the level of basic and secondary education[29].

5. Concluding Remarks

In brief, the innovation policy adopted in Brazil since the late 1990s has been based on the idea of "market failures", being essentially a supply-side policy. As already pointed out "the problem raised by such thinking is not that of 'market failures' being irrelevant. On the contrary: the problem is that any empirical situation will hardly show significant similarity with such a 'standard'—for instance, in terms of the integrity of the market, the perfect nature of competition, the knowledge held by economic agents, the immutability of technologies and preferences, the 'rationality' of decision making, etc. (the list is indeed very long!" (Cimoli et al. 2007, p. 58).

The use of such an approach led to a mistaken diagnosis of the Brazilian situation that, added to the lack of planning, budgeting and coordination between policies and to the fact that the policies were "inspired" by those designed and implemented by developed countries, resulted in the shaping of policies, programmes and actions that were ineffective and insufficient. These programmes, at best, benefited a limited number of enterprises that probably would have invested in innovation activities without government support, given their need to retain a competitive position in the market. True, this is not specific to the Brazilian situation. The innovation policies adopted in many countries, as they are a spitting image of some of the policy proposals of more advanced countries, are still focused on traditional models, concentrating their support on the strong points of the system, instead of targeting measures at new elements (Lundvall 1998, Cassiolato 1999).

It is true that science, technology and innovation policy in Brazil has major achievements to its credit over the last forty years. One is the setting-up of a sophisticated infrastructure for science and technology represented by institutions, universities, research groups, etc. that work at the cutting edge of S&T. This is much more relevant if we consider that this happened also in areas of knowledge that are pertinent to the specificities of Brazil's biome such as tropical agriculture or biological processes. Such developments may prove crucial for the innovation of tomorrow. Brazil's economic success in production and exports in several areas of agribusiness can only be explained by the huge investment in S&T in agricultural areas by Embrapa and other state-level research institutes and agricultural technology diffusion programmes.

Other technological and innovation successes have occurred in areas/sectors where the explicit S&T&I policy played a minor role. Brazilian innovativeness in the oil industry (particularly offshore technologies), the aircraft industry (with Embraer being the third largest aircraft producer in the world), in commodities such as iron, steel and paper and pulp is much more related to implicit than explicit policies.

Finally, there has been in the last twenty years an increasing institutionalisation of science, technology and innovation policies at sub-national level. The 26 states of the federation have created agencies and policy organisations to deal with the issue and, although it is not the purpose of this paper to discuss these trends, their importance should be explicitly acknowledged. It is a pity that these positive outcomes are not accompanied by a systemic innovation policy at federal level. Hence, it can be concluded that Brazil's innovation policy lacks direction and guidance. For it to be effective, it should be, first, connected to a national strategy of development and should be structured on the basis of the idea that decisions by enterprises regarding technology and innovation depend significantly upon the existence of such a strategy. They should depend, also, on the establishment of government programmes developed in partnership with the productive sector which address the few variables that inhibit enterprises from raising their investments in collective learning and R&D.

Annex 1: Brazil—Legal Framework of Innovation Policy

Laws	Main Objective
1993—Lei 8.661	Created tax incentives to foster enhancement of the technological capacity of manufacturing and agricultural enterprises taking part in one of the programmes: Programa de Desenvolvimento Tecnológico Industrial (PDTI) and Programa de Desenvolvimento Tecnológico Agropecuário (PDTA).
1997—Lei 9.532	Reduced the tax incentives established by Lei 8.661/93, by approximately 50 per cent.
2000—Lei 10.168	Created a tax: Contribuição de Intervenção do Domínio Econômico (CIDE) to finance the programme Programa de Estímulo à Interação Universidade-Empresa para o Apoio à Inovação.
2001—Lei 10.332	Re-established the tax incentives created by Lei 8.661/93. Also instituted the grant for enterprises taking part in the PDTI or PDTA, and mechanisms for subsidising interest rates.
	During the period 1999–2002, 12 sectoral funds were created Provided support for the development of R&D projects in partnership between scientific and technological institutions and enterprises. The funds related to the following sectors: petroleum and natural gas, energy, water resources, transport, mineral resources, aerospace, telecommunications, information technology, health, aeronautics, biotechnology and agribusiness. There were also the Verde-Amarelo funds, and funds for infrastructure.
2004—Lei de Inovação— Lei 10.973	Aimed to promote interactions between scientific and technological institutions of the Federal Government and enterprises. This law also created new tax incentives for the innovative process within firms, establishing a grant for enterprises taking part in a project under the Fundo Nacional de Desenvolvimento Científico e Tecnológico (FNDCT).
2004 creation of two further sectoral funds	Related to the naval and coastal sector and to the Amazonian area; aimed to develop new technologies and stimulate the innovative process.

Annex 1: (*Continued*)

Laws	Main Objective
2005—Lei do Bem—Lei 11.196	Also related to tax incentives for technological innovation. This law replaced Law No 10.637 (2002) and its main instruments are: tax exemption, accelerated depreciation and the possibility of grants for researchers and graduates (masters and doctors). The difference between this new law and the former one is that the mechanisms for tax incentives became automatic; previously, it was necessary to participate in the Programa de Desenvolvimento Tecnológico Industrial (PDTI) or the Programa de Desenvolvimento Tecnológico Agropecuário (PDTA).

References

BACHA, E. (2003). Reflexões Pós-Cepalinas sobre a Inflação e a Crise Externa. In *Revista de Econômica Política*, vol. 23, n. 3, jul.-set.

Biato, F., Guimarães, E & Figueiredo, M. (1973). A transferência de tecnologia no Brasil. *IPEA/IPLAN Estudos para o Planejamento*, No 4.

Bielchowsky, R. (1985). *Situação do Apoio Financeiro do Governo Federal à Pesquisa Fundamental no Brasil*, Rio de Janeiro: FINEP.

Bielschowsky, R. & Mussi (2005). *O Pensamento Desenvolvimentista no Brasil: 1930–1964 e anotações sobre 1964–2005. Escritório da CEPAL no Brasil*. Brasília/DF, julho/2005.

brasil (2006). Ministério da Ciência e Tecnologia. Relatório de Gestão do Ministério da Ciência e Tecnologia – Janeiro de 2003 a Dezembro de 2006. Ministério da Ciência e Tecnologia. Brasília.

Brasil (1990). Ministério da Economia, Fazenda e Planejamento. Política industrial e de comércio exterior. Diretrizes gerais. – Brasília: Ministério da Economia, Fazenda e Planejamento, Secretaria Nacional de Economia.

Brasil (1998). Presidência da República. Nova Política Industrial – Desenvolvimento e Competitividade. Presidência da República, Brasília–1998.

Brasil (2003). Diretrizes de política industrial, tecnológica e de comércio exterior. Casa Civil da Presidência da República; Ministério do Desenvolvimento, Indústria e Comércio Exterior; Ministério da Fazenda; Ministério do Planejamento; Ministério da Ciência e Tecnologia; Instituto de Pesquisa Econômica Aplicada – IPEA; Banco Nacional de Desenvolvimento, Econômico e Social – BNDES; Financiadora de Estudos e Projetos – FINEP; Agência de Promoção das Exportações – APEX, Brasília, 26 nov 2003.

Bresser-Pereira, L C (2003). O Segundo Consenso de Washington e a Quase-Estagnação da Economia Brasileira. In *Revista de Econômica Política*, vol. 23, n. 3, jul.-set.

Cadastro de ações (2006). Secretaria de Orçamento Federal.

Cassiolato, J. & Lastres, H. (1999). Inovação, globalização e as novas políticas de desenvolvimento industrial e tecnológico. In *Globalização & Inovação Localizada Experiências de Sistemas Locais no Mercosul*. Ed. José Cassiolato & Helena Lastres. Brasília, IBICT/MCT.

Cassiolato, J. (1981). Notas sobre a evolução da idéia de planejamento e política científica e tecnológica na América Latina. Texto para Discussão Interna, No 02/81, CET/CNPq, Brasília.

Cassiolato, J. (1982). Evolução da política científica e tecnológica e o desenvolvimento econômico brasileiro na última década: algumas reflexões. In *V Seminario Metodologico sobre Politica y Planificacion Cientifica y Tecnologica*. Washington: Organisation of the American States.

Cassiolato, J. (1992). The user-producer connection in hi-tech: a case-study of banking automation in Brazil. In H. Schmitz & J. Cassiolato (eds) *Hi-Tech for Industrial Development*. London: Routledge.

Cassiolato, J. (1999). A Economia do Conhecimento e as Novas Políticas Industriais e Tecnológicas. In *Informação e Globalização na Era do Conhecimento*. Org. Helena Lastres & Sarita Albagli. Rio de Janeiro, Campus.

Cassiolato, J., Brunetti, J. & Paula, M. (1981). Desarollo y perspectivas de la politica de la ciencia y tecnologia en el Brasil. Paper presented at the conference "Estratégias alternativas para ciencia y tecnologia en América Latina en los anos 80", Cendes, Universidad Central de Venezuela, Caracas.

Cimoli, m., Dosi, g., R. Nelson, r. & Stiglitz, j. (2007). Instituições e Políticas Moldando o Desenvolvimento Industrial: uma nota introdutória. In *Revista Brasileira de Inovação*, Rio de Janeiro (RJ), 6 (1), pp. 55–85, janeiro/junho.

Coutinho, L. G. (2005). Regimes macroeconômicos e estratégias de negócio: uma política industrial alternativa para o Brasil no século XXI. In: Lastres, H. M., Cassiolato J. E. & Arroio A., (edit.) *Conhecimento, Sistemas de Inovação e Desenvolvimento*, Rio de Janeiro: Editora UFRJ/Contraponto.

Erber, F. & Cassiolato, J. (1997). Política industrial: teoria e prática no Brasil e na OCDE. In *Revista de Economia Política*, vol. 17, nº 2, abril/ junho, pp. 32–60.

Erber, F. et al. (1974). Reflexões sobre a demanda pelos serviços dos institutos de pesquisa. *FINEP Série de Pesquisas*, No 1.

Erber, F (1980). Desenvolvimento tecnológico e intervenção do estado: um confronto entre a experiência brasileira e a dos países capitalistas centrais. In *Revista de Administração Pública*, Vol. 14, No 4.

Erber, F. S. (2001). O padrão de Desenvolvimento Industrial e Tecnológico e o Futuro da Indústria Brasileira. In *Revista de Econômica Contemporânea*, vol. 5, edição especial.

Fanelli, J. M & Frenkel, R. (1996). Estabilidad y estructura: interacciones en el crecimiento económico. In *Estabilización Macroeconómica, Reforma Estructural e Comportamiento Industrial – estructura y funcionamiento del sector manufacturero latinoamericano en los años 90*. Ed. Jorge Katz. CEPAL/IDCR – Alianza Editorial, Chile.

Ferrari Filho, F. & Paula, L. F. (2003). The legacy of the Real Plan and an alternative agenda for the Brazilian economy. In *Investigación Económica*, Vol. LXII, n. 244, abril-junio, 2003, pp. 57–92.

Ferraz, J. (1989). A heterogeneidade tecnológica da indústria brasileira: perspectivas e implicações para política. In *Revista Brasileira de Economia*, vol. 43, No 3, pp. 373–392.

Ferraz, J. C., Kupfer, D. & Iootty, M. (2003). Made in Brazil: industrial competitiveness 10 years after economic liberalization. *Latin American Studies Series* No 4. IDE-JETRO.

Ferraz, J. C., Kupfer, D. & Iootty, M. (2003a). Economic liberalization and industrial competitiveness in Brazil. Paper presented at the conference "What do you know about innovation: a conference in honour of Keith Pavitt", Sussex, UK. Nov.

Figueiredo, N. (1972). A transferência de tecnologia no desenvolvimento industrial do Brasil. *IPEA Série Monográfica*, No 7.

Franco, G. (1996). The Real Plan. Remarks made at the seminar "Economics and Society in Brazil: new trends and perspectives", conference sponsored by the Department of Economics, the Department of Anthropology and the Center for Latin American Studies at the University of Chicago and Ministério das Relações Exteriores do Brasil, November 2 and 3, 1995 – Chicago. Brasília, Feb.

Franco, G. (1998). A Inserção Externa e o Desenvolvimento. In *Revista de Economia Política*, vol. 18, n. 3.

Freeman, C. (1987). *Technology Policy and Economic Performance: Lessons from Japan*, London, Frances Pinter.

Freeman, C. (1988). *Japan, a new system of innovation. In Technical change and economic theory*. Dosi, G., Freeman, C., Nelson, R. et al. (eds). London: Pinter, pp. 330–348.

Freeman, C. (1992). Formal scientific and technical institutions in the national system of innovation. In *National systems of innovation: towards a theory of innovation and interactive learning*. Lundvall, B-A. (ed.). London: Pinter, pp. 169–190.

Frenkel, R. (2003). Globalización y Crisis Financieras en América Latina. In *Revista de Economia Política*. Vol. 23, nº 3 (91), jul-set.

Furtado, J. (1990) *Produtividade na indústria brasileira: padrões setoriais e evolução – 1975/80*. MSc Dissertation, Campinas: Economics Institute, State University of Campinas.

Garcia, R. (2000). A reorganização do processo de planejamento do governo federal – o PPA 2000–2003. *Textos para Discussão*, n. 726. Brasília IPEA, May.

Guimarães, E. (1996). A Experiência Recente da Política Industrial no Brasil: Uma Avaliação. *Textos para Discussão*, n. 409. Brasília, IPEA, Apr.

Guimarães, E. (2006). Políticas de Inovação: Financiamento e Incentivos. *Textos para Discussão*, n. 1212. Brasília, IPEA, aug.

Hermann, J. (2004). O Trade Off do Crescimento no Brasil nos anos 1990–2000: análise crítica e alternativas de política monetária. In *Econômica*, Rio de Janeiro, v. 6, nº 2, Dez., pp. 261–289.

Hiratuka, C. (2007). Exportações das firmas domésticas e influência das firmas transnacionais. In: Negri, J. A. D. & Araújo, B. C. P. O. (Org.) *As empresas brasileiras e o comércio internacional*. Brasília: IPEA.

Katz, J. (1996). Interacciones entre lo micro y lo macro y su manifestación en el ámbito de la producción industrial. In *Estabilización Macroeconómica, Reforma Estructural e Comportamiento Industrial – estructura y funcionamiento del sector manufacturero latinoamericano en los años 90*. Ed. Jorge Katz. CEPAL/IDCR – Alianza Editorial, Chile.

Katz, J. (1996a). Régimen de Incentivos, Marco Regulatorio y Comportamiento Microeconómico. In *Estabilización Macroeconómica, Reforma Estructural e Comportamiento Industrial – estructura y funcionamiento del sector manufacturero latinoamericano en los años 90*. Ed. Jorge Katz. CEPAL/IDCR – Alianza Editorial, Chile.

Koeller, P. (2004). Interação Público/Privada – Um Estudo Sobre o Projeto de Lei de Inovação. Anais Seminário Abipti 2004, Belo Horizonte.

Kupfer, D. (2004) Política Industrial. In *Revista Econômica*. Depto de Pós-Graduação em Economia da UFF.v. 5, n. 2, pp. 91–108. Maio.

Lei Nº 10.973/04. Lei Nº 10.973 de 2 de Dezembro de 2004. Presidência da República, Casa Civil, Subchefia para Assuntos Jurídicos.

Lei Nº 11.080/04. Lei Nº 11.080 de 30 de Dezembro de 2004. Presidência da República, Casa Civil, Subchefia para Assuntos Jurídicos.

Lei Nº 11.196/05 (Lei do Bem), Lei Nº 11.196 de 21 de Novembro de 2005. Presidência da República, Casa Civil, Subchefia para Assuntos Jurídicos.

Lei Nº 11.306/06. Lei Nº 11.306 de 16 de Maio de 2006. (Lei Orçamentária Anual – LOA 2006). Presidência da República, Casa Civil, Subchefia para Assuntos Jurídicos. Vol. IV – Tomo I – Detalhamento das Ações – Órgãos do Poder Executivo (Exclusive Ministério da Educação).

Livro Branco: Ciência, Tecnologia e Inovação. Brasília: Ministério da Ciência e Tecnologia, 2002. Resultado da Conferência Nacional de Ciência, Tecnologia e Inovação.

Lopes, F. (2003). Notes on the Brazilian Crisis of 1997–99. In *Brazilian Journal of Political Economy*. Vol. 23, No 3 (91), July–Sept.

Lundvall, B-A (ed.) (1992). *National systems of innovation: towards a theory of innovation and interactive learning*. London: Pinter.

Modenesi, A. M. (2005). *Regimes Monetários: Teoria e a Experiência do Real*. Editora Manole. Barueri/SP.

OECD (1984). Industrial Structure Statistics – 1982. Paris: OECD.

Pastore, A. & Pinotti, M. (2000). Globalização, fluxos de capitais e regimes cambiais: reflexões sobre o Brasil. In: *Estudos Econômicos*, v. 30, n. 1, jan./mar.

Pintec (2003). *Pesquisa Industrial de Inovação Tecnológica 1998–2000*. Instituto Brasileiro de Geografia e Estatística – IBGE. Rio de Janeiro.

Pintec (2005). *Pesquisa Industrial de Inovação Tecnológica 2001–2003*. Instituto Brasileiro de Geografia e Estatística – IBGE. Rio de Janeiro.

Pintec (2007). *Pesquisa Industrial de Inovação Tecnológica 2003–2005*. Instituto Brasileiro de Geografia e Estatística – IBGE. Rio de Janeiro.

Plano Estratégico – Ministério da Ciência e Tecnologia, http://www.mct/gov.br/index.php/content/view/15854.html

Portaria Mefp nº 365 (1990). Portaria do Ministério da Economia, Fazenda e Planejamento (MEFP) nº 365 de 26.06.1990. Brasília: Ministério da Economia, Fazenda e Planejamento, Secretaria Nacional de Economia.

Prado, M.C.R.M. (2005). *A Real História do Real*. Editora Record, Rio de Janeiro.

Sagasti, F. (1978). *Ciência y tecnología para el desarrollo: Informe Comparativo Central del Proyecto sobre Instrumentos de Política Científica y Tecnológica (STPI)*. Bogotá, Centro Internacional de Investigaciones para el Desarrollo (CIID). 244 pp.

Schumpeter, J. A. (1943) *Capitalism, Socialism and Democracy*. London. G. Allen & Unwin, Chapters 7 and 8.

Serra, J. (1982). Ciclos e mudanças estruturais na economia brasileira do após-guerra. In *Revista de Economia Política*, Vol. 2, No 2, pp. 5–45.

Sicsú, J. (2003). Rumos e Definições da Política Econômica Brasileira: do Plano A de FHC para o Plano A+ de Lula. In *A Economia Política da Mudança – os desafios e os equívocos do início do governo Lula*. Org. J. A. de Paula. Editora Autêntica , Belo Horizonte.

Suzigan, W. (1988). Estado e industrialização no Brasil. In *Revista de Economia Política*, Vol. 8, No 4, pp. 5–15.

Suzigan, W. & Furtado, J. (2006). Política Industrial e Desenvolvimento. In *Revista de Economia Política*, vol. 26, n. 2, abr.-jun.

Tavares, M.C. & Lessa, C. (1984). *O Desenvolvimento Industrial da Década de 1970 – Impasse e Alternativas*. Mimeo, Economics Department, University of Campinas, Campinas.

Zucoloto, G.F.& Toneto, R. Jr. (2005). Esforço tecnológico da indústria de transformação brasileira: uma comparação com países selecionados. In *Revista de Economia contemporânea*. Rio de Janeiro, 9(2): 337–365, mai./ago. 2005.

Chapter 3

PROSPECTIVE AGENDA FOR SCIENCE AND TECHNOLOGY AND INNOVATION POLICIES IN RUSSIA

Leonid Gokhberg, Natalia Gorodnikova, Tatiana Kuznetsova, Alexander Sokolov and Stanislav Zaichenko

1. Introduction

The Russian Federation is one of the largest countries in the world, covering an area of 17.1 million km2 (1/3 of Eurasia), with the world's largest reserves of natural resources (45 per cent of the world's total natural gas, 13 per cent of oil, 23 per cent of coal, 22 per cent of forests, 37 per cent of lake water, etc.). However, Russia's climate and soil are mostly not favourable for agriculture and industrial activities, with only 13 per cent of the surface suitable for farming, while the population is concentrated in several regions leaving large areas almost unpopulated.

Russian history has also been rather turbulent. After the October Revolution in 1917, the centuries-old tsarist regime was brought to an end. The Union of Soviet Socialist Republics (USSR), comprising 15 such republics, lasted up to 1991. The Russian Soviet Federative Socialist Republic dominated the USSR for its entire 74-year history, the USSR often being referred to as 'Russia' and its people as 'Russians'. Russia was the largest republic of the USSR and contributed over half of its population. After the breakup of the USSR in 1991, social and economic reforms were launched. The Soviet ideology, economy and administration underwent a transition towards democratic principles and a free market system.

Russia as the successor of the USSR is also known for its contribution to the world's science and technology (S&T). The basic elements of the Soviet R&D system were put in place after 1917. The political objective of accelerating R&D

to serve military requirements and the industrialisation of the economy led to the strengthening of existing research institutes and the establishment of new bodies. From 1922 to 1940, employment in the science and scientific services sector grew from 35,000 to 362,000, and its share in total employment increased from 0.6 per cent to 1.1 per cent. There was intensive investment in R&D facilities and equipment to carry out research in the most important areas of science and technology. As a result, in the years up to the 1980s, an extremely large R&D base was developed, greater, in absolute terms, than that of most of the industrially developed countries (Gokhberg, 2003).

During and after the disintegration of the USSR, when wide-ranging reforms including privatisation and market liberalisation were being undertaken, the Russian economy went through a major crisis. This period was characterised by a deep contraction in output, with GDP declining by roughly 50 per cent between 1990 and the end of 1995 and industrial output falling by over 50 per cent. The collapse of the Soviet Union, and the transition to a market economy, radically affected the national R&D system inherited from the ex-USSR. This system developed in the Soviet era had three special characteristics: it was very large, centrally directed, and government-financed (Gokhberg, L., et al., 1997). These features were ill-suited to a market economy, so it was not surprising that the R&D sector suffered a crisis during the years of transition.

High oil prices and an initially weak currency, followed by increasing domestic demand, consumption and investment, helped the economy to grow for nine years, gradually increasing the quality of life. The period from 1999 to 2008 may therefore be considered as a time of stability and socio-economic recovery. However, this growth was not based on real labour productivity or innovation. Russian science and technology (S&T) and its 'national system of innovation' (NSI) are still mostly inefficient. There is a striking imbalance between resources devoted to research activities (carried out mostly in public institutions outside the higher education sector) and innovation performance. The sections below are devoted to the main challenges facing Russia's S&T and innovation policy and the institutional, legislative and regulatory reforms needed to address these challenges.

2. Russian S&T: Towards Competitiveness and Economic Growth

Following the drastic transformation of the 1990s, the R&D sector in Russia has faced a difficult situation, characterised by conflicting trends. On the one hand, many positive changes may be noted. Government R&D funding is now growing again (spending on civilian R&D grew by 43 per cent in 1998–2004 and by 54 per cent in 2004–2007, in real prices), with about 39

Figure 3.1. Innovation Activity in Industry (1992–2006), %

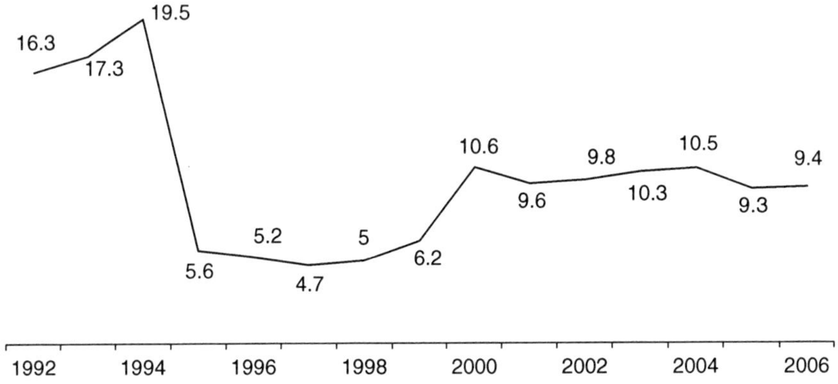

Source: Indicators of Innovation: 2008, 2008.

per cent devoted to basic research (Science and Technology Indicators, 2008). Financial support for R&D through contracts, programmes and calls for tender has also grown significantly. The number of researchers has stabilised (388.9 thousand, 48 per cent of R&D personnel in 2006). The salaries of R&D staff (about €450 on average) are almost the same as the average wage in the economy, and are gradually moving towards the average wage in manufacturing. The number of people employed by private research institutions is growing (17 per cent increase since 2000) as are the number of qualified top-level professionals. The number of government-owned research institutions has fallen by 9 per cent since 2000.

On the other hand, the systemic crisis in the R&D sector is evident. It stems from both the insufficient demand for and underdeveloped supply of R&D and innovation. As regards demand, private business does not show much interest in innovation. Since 2000, innovation activity in Russia has remained at a level of 9–10 per cent (Figure 3.1). The EU figures are significantly higher: ranging from 21 per cent (Hungary) to 73 per cent (Germany).

Demand for R&D in Russia comes mostly from the government, with the federal budget remaining the key source for R&D funding (in 1998–2007, it grew threefold in real prices). Investment in innovation is considered by private businesses to be more risky and less profitable than investment in mining and quarrying activities (especially natural gas and oil). Today, the most important feature of the Russia's geopolitics is energy production and distribution. The Russian Federation has the largest known natural gas reserves of any state on earth, along with the second largest coal reserves. It is the world's second largest oil producer and has the eighth largest oil reserves. It is also the world's biggest

Figure 3.2. Labour Productivity in Industry (2006), Thousand Roubles

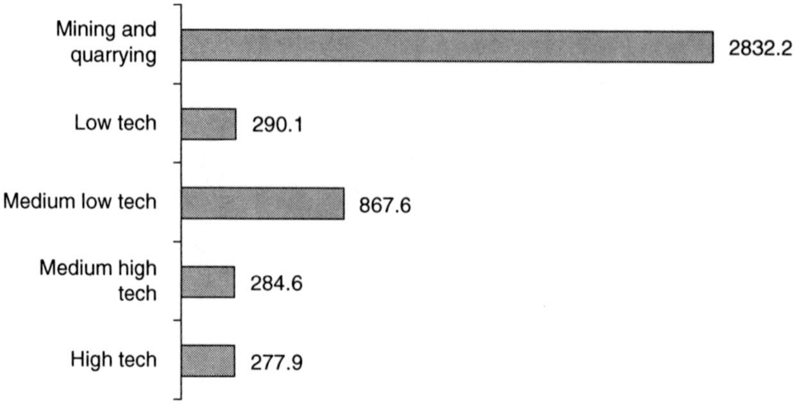

Source: Gokhberg, 2007.

natural gas producer with 22.3 per cent of global natural-gas production and the biggest exporter with 24.0 per cent of world exports (International Energy Agency, 2006). Crude oil makes up 34.4 per cent of Russia's goods exports, with just 1.2 per cent consisting of high-tech products (Gokhberg, 2007).

At the same time, labour productivity in the high-tech manufacturing sector in Russia is one of the world's lowest (Figure 3.2). Standing at an equivalent of about €8,200 in 2006, it was almost half that in Bulgaria (€15,200) and 15 times lower than in Ireland (€128,100). However, labour productivity in the Russian mining and quarrying sector is 10 times higher than in high-tech.

The supply of R&D and innovation is insufficient and is biased heavily towards R&D. Russia's annual technology exports amount to US$0.63 billion (by comparison, Hungary exports US$1.6 billion, Finland US$3.3 billion, and the United States US$ 75.4 billion). At the same time, the relatively high patenting activity in Russia (about 23 thousand patent applications a year, ranking sixth in the world) in combination with a low share of registered patent licenses compared with the number of annually registered patents (5–6 per cent) can be explained by the lack of competitiveness of Russian technologies (especially civilian applications). As regards publications, Russia now ranks 11th in the world in terms of leading scientific journals (or 2 per cent), down from 7th in 1995 and 3rd in 1980. To compare, China's share is 5.9 per cent or 5th in the world (Gokhberg, 2007).

Therefore the dual challenge for Russian S&T and innovation policies is to stimulate both sides of innovation — demand and supply. The Russian government is endeavouring to develop a system approach to this problem.

3. The Framework for S&T and Innovation Policies

The transition in Russia's S&T and innovation policies can be divided into four main stages. The first was a period of 'market romanticism' in the early 1990s, driven by vain hopes on the part of reformers for a quick and automatic transfer to a market economy. However, these high initial expectations were not met. Multiple mistakes in planning and implementing reforms resulted in a deep systemic crisis within the Russian NIS: a dramatic fall in funding, the shedding of human resources, and the disbanding of R&D organisations during the first wave of privatisation. The consequences of this crisis have still not been overcome.

In the next stage ('market formalism', in the mid-90s) the S&T sector fell into a deep stagnation. Change in this sector was lagging far behind the economic reforms. Government initiatives were reduced to urgent measures to slow down its definitive disintegration.

In the early 2000s, during the third period (the stage of 'market pragmatism') the first important strategic decisions were outlined for the future or began to be launched. But the strategy of delaying decisions on the Russian NIS resulted in serious risks and a narrow focus on the short and medium term at the expense of long-term programmes and projects.

The fourth stage, lasting from the mid-2000s to the present day, is characterised by a complex set of measures adopted by the government to bring about transition to an economy of knowledge. This approach has two main dimensions. The first is the creation of a structured NSI policy framework. The second is the implementation of policy mechanisms for efficient regulation in the main areas of activity: national priorities, performance-based budgeting, restructuring the government R&D sector, human resources and infrastructure development, etc.

The main official initiative at the current stage of the transition is the 'Concept for Long-Term Development until 2020' (CLTD)[1]. The Concept is based on three main elements: 1) a policy framework, 2) a 'roadmap' for reforms, and 3) target indicators.

The policy framework brings together the key policy directions. In particular, it establishes connections between NSI development policies and other areas such as education system development, environment protection strategies, health system development, regional development strategies, etc.

The 'roadmap' component of the CLTD sets out the structure of each policy direction as well as a basic plan of action. The goal of creating and developing the NSI is pursued by six initiatives, including the development of human resources for innovation, infrastructure support and the stimulation of demand for innovation, among others (Figure 3.3).

The 'target indicators' component is a statistical tool for tracking the main macro-effects in order to monitor the progress of reform. There are five key

Figure 3.3. Innovation Policy Structure in the CLTD

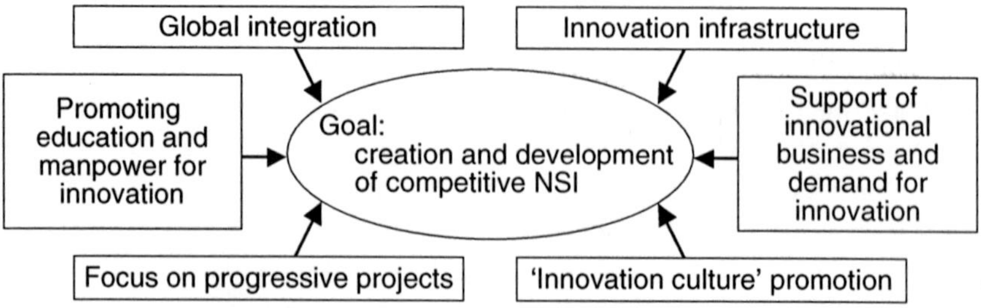

Figure 3.4. The Key CLTD Target Indicators for the NSI Development Goal

	2007	2020
GERD to GDP ratio, %	1.09	3.0
Labour productivity growth, %	6–7	9–10
Share of high-tech sectors in value added, %	10.5	17.2
Share of high-tech exports in world total, %	0.3	2.0
Share of innovative products in total sales, %	5.5	25–35

Source: Concept for Long-Term Development Until 2020.

indicators for the NSI development goal: GERD-to-GDP ratio, labour productivity, and three indicators for the high-tech industries (Figure 3.4).

The most significant growth is expected in the share of innovative products in total sales (5- to 7-fold increase) and in the GERD-to-GDP ratio (3-fold increase). However, four of the five indicators relate mostly to demand for innovation. The supply dimension is described only by the GERD indicator, which is not sufficiently informative.

Analysis shows that the innovation policies are aiming to establish a new network or rather 'chain' of actors involved in the innovation cycle (Figure 3.5). It can be regarded as a modified 'Triple Helix' chain (Etzkowitz and Leydesdorff, 2000) adapted to Russian circumstances. Public-private partnership (PPP) is emerging via state corporations, but interactions between business and academia are not being developed (dotted arrows).

The main instrument for enhancing demand for innovation is the development of public-private partnership. However, without efficient links between business, higher education institutions (HEIs) and R&D institutions, PPP will depend entirely on state corporations. This problem is not adequately addressed in the CLTD and may be a serious obstacle for further NSI

Figure 3.5. Actors and Interactions in the Russian Innovation Cycle

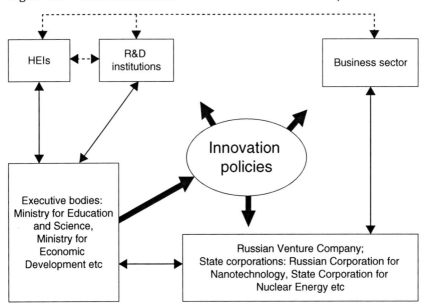

development. The integration of science and education also remains a problem. The section below is devoted to several main initiatives addressing the whole innovation policy system as well as its particular components.

4. Key Policy Actions

4.1 National Priority Setting

While the scope of scientific research is expanding from year to year, the highest research standards cannot be achieved without highly qualified specialists and sophisticated research equipment. In these circumstances, even the wealthiest nations cannot support simultaneous research in every field of science. In Russia, efforts to select S&T priorities were first launched at federal level in the mid-90s, and have since been continued on a regular basis. National S&T priorities are formulated in two lists: priority S&T areas and critical technologies.

The priority areas set the general trends for the country's S&T development. They are those S&T areas deemed capable of providing new technologies and facilities to contribute to the development of Russia's economy and society. These are specified in the List of Critical Technologies for the Russian Federation, which serves as a background for making decisions on concentrating public resources in the most important areas of science, technology and

Figure 3.6. Evolution of S&T Priorities in Russia

1996	2002	2006
1. Basic research	1. Information and telecommunication technologies and electronics	1. Information and telecommunication systems
2. Information technologies and electronics	2. New materials and chemical technologies	2. Nanosystems industry and materials
3. New materials and chemical technologies	3. Living systems technologies	3. Living systems
4. Living systems technologies	4. Ecology and rational utilisation of natural resources	4. Rational utilisation of natural resources
5. Ecology and rational utilisation of natural resources	5. Energy-saving technologies	5. Power engineering and energy saving
6. Fuel and power engineering	6. New transportation technologies	6. Transport, aviation and space systems
7. Transportation	7. Space and aviation technologies	7. Prospective armaments, military and special equipment
8. Manufacturing technologies	8. Manufacturing technologies	8. Security and counteracting terrorism
	9. Prospective armaments, military and special equipment	

innovation and on implementing the available S&T potential. The first priority list was established in the mid-90s. In 1996, the Government Commission on Scientific and Technological Policies approved a list of eight Priority Areas for Scientific and Technological Development. In 1999, this list was submitted to large-scale examination by more than 1000 leading Russian experts.

The expert analysis revealed an urgent need to reconsider the system of S&T priorities, concentrating on a small number of 'breakthrough' areas. In 2000–2001, new lists containing nine S&T priority areas and 52 critical technologies were developed. The aim was to optimise the number of priority areas so as to concentrate resources in the most important fields of innovation. In 2002 the Russian President approved the 'Basic Policies of the Russian Federation in the Sphere of Scientific and Technological Development for the Period Ending 2010 and Further Prospects'. This document has become an important element in Russia's social and economic development strategy, with its goals of innovation-based economic development, creating an effective national innovation system and making science and technology one of Russia's key priorities[2].

The S&T priorities and critical technologies approved in 2002 resulted in research areas that were too broad to become real targets for selecting technologies for priority government support and for private investment, so the Russian Ministry for Education and Science had these lists revised and corrected in 2003–2004.

This revision work was carried out during a period of sustained economic growth and great improvement in the state government system. International experience shows that long-term sustainable development is achievable only through high entrepreneurial and innovation activity in both the production and service sectors, the diversification of production and a greater share of sophisticated and hi-tech products. So concentrating resources in the areas where Russia's competitive advantages can be exploited helps to accelerate the introduction of innovation based on the latest research outcomes and technologies, which is now a key factor determining the competitiveness of a national economy. This is particularly important for Russia because of its present strong dependence on the international markets for fuel and mineral resources.

The following working definitions were used in reviewing the priorities:

- Priority areas for S&T development were deemed to be those with the potential to make a major contribution to ensuring the country's security, faster economic growth, and greater competitive capacity of Russian companies through development of the technological foundations of the national economy and R&D-intensive production facilities.

- Critical technologies were considered to be sets of technological solutions that offer the potential for further development of various technological areas, possess a broad range of innovative applications in various sectors of economy, and as a whole make the greatest contribution to resolving the main problems in implementing scientific and technological priorities.

During the final stage of the process, ministry officials and experts reduced and considerably modified the previous list of priority S&T areas. The new list included eight priorities (Figure 3.6). The first six correspond to current international technological development priorities. They have the greatest innovation development potential, and are defining new global markets. This is particularly true for information technologies, nanosystems and new materials, and living systems. The last two priorities on the revised list relate to national security.

The S&T priorities (as well as the set of critical technologies) are a powerful tool for innovation policies and especially resource distribution. All NSI development instruments and initiatives (including the policies discussed below) are based on the system of national priorities. Target-based budgeting and performance evaluation are the mechanisms most closely linked with them.

4.2 Budgetary Reforms

Most of the industrially developed countries are trying to find more efficient mechanisms and forms of government support for R&D. The complexity of the problem is explained by the obvious need for such support and by strictly limited resources. The solution found by the Russian government in the current situation looks quite realistic. It is based on more efficient budgetary resource allocation together with institutional reforms in R&D and innovation.

The federal budget for civil S&T is almost equally distributed between direct and competitive funding (Figure 3.7). The main part of the competitive funding stream (about 40 per cent of the total S&T budget) goes towards the federal goal-oriented programmes (one of which is discussed below) and scientific foundations. Almost half of the civil S&T budget is allocated to R&D institutions under the Russian Academy of Sciences (RAS) and under federal agencies. This second funding stream is not based on S&T priorities or the performance of R&D institutions. This is where new mechanisms for evaluation and institutional reform are to be implemented (see below).

The appropriate budgetary legislation was developed in Russia throughout the 1990s. The Budgetary Code adopted in 1998 put in place a framework for the 'normal' regulation of budgetary relationships. However, the restructuring of

Figure 3.7. Structure of the Budgetary Funding of Civil S&T (2008)

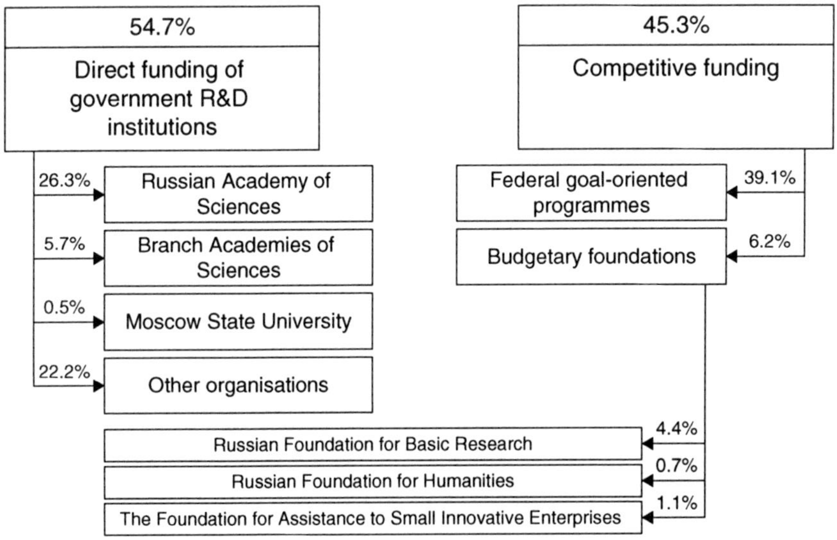

Source: Federal Law On the Federal Budget for 2008, 03.03.2008 (No 19-FZ).

the budgeting process did not start for another six years. In 2004, the 'Concept of Budgetary Process Restructuring' was approved. It was based on four key principles: 1) separation of existing and newly approved expenditure, 2) limiting approved expenditure to objectives clearly defined in advance, according to government policy priorities, 3) targeting and programming with the application of planning techniques, and 4) developing a system of real and objective (target) indicators to evaluate the performance of executive agencies, etc.

Now, Russia has entered a new stage of public fund management — mid-term performance-oriented budgeting. All of its principles were applied for the first time in the 2006 budget, when a prospective three-year financial plan was developed alongside the traditional one-year budgeting projections.

One of the most important elements in the development of the budgeting process was restructuring the budget classification and accounting. Under the 'Concept for Budgetary Process Restructuring', the new classification was brought into line with the main functions of government agencies and with international standards for accounting and public finance statistics. Under the new budgetary classification, R&D expenditure is divided into basic and applied research allocations, which in turn are split into sections. Basic research expenditure comes under the 'General Issues' section. Applied research expenditure mostly comes under other sections of the classification, to support R&D for education, economy, health, defence, etc.

The streamlining of the general budgeting process should encourage the development of a flexible and dynamic NSI as one of the top national priorities. It should be noted that there is potential for streamlining the budgeting process in the R&D sector at all stages—budget expenditure planning, shaping the budget and adjusting appropriations (allocation of funds to recipients), funding of R&D organisations (financial management techniques), the legal framework, etc.

As long as the state remains the largest R&D 'sponsor', the Russian government is planning to continue reforms in four areas:

- More concentration on the national priorities
- Further modernisation of the public S&T sector
- Optimisation of the funding structure
- New principles for budgetary funding

Concentration on the national priorities requires that direct government support for applied research and technologies should be reduced to a certain minimum, supporting only those most relevant to the national priorities. Foresight is considered to be the most useful tool for national priority setting. It is a highly discussed topic among both Russian scientists and officials. The first project for the practical implementation of foresight technology in Russia was launched in 2006–2008.

Further modernisation of the public S&T sector is related to the national reform of the government R&D sector, in particular the 'Concept for Budgetary Process Restructuring'. In 2005, the Concept was initially implemented in three key reform areas. First of all, it was decided to reduce the number of direct public funding recipients to concentrate on the most efficient organisations engaged in world-class R&D in both the basic and applied fields. The second step was to introduce new forms of R&D organisation to match market economy requirements. The legal and organisational structure of the R&D sector is gradually moving towards autonomous non-profit and private organisations and autonomous institutions. Finally, organisations that have completely lost their research profile, unable to retain personnel, material and technical resources, are supposed to be closed down. Organisations or divisions that have retained at least some of their research potential should be merged with more successful entities or privatised (provided that their research profile can be preserved—this would be an additional factor promoting corporate R&D).

Optimisation of the funding structure is an important measure especially when the total GERD is growing. A dramatic change in the structure of government expenditure is expected. Funding should be re-allocated in favour of target programmes and state R&D foundations (Figure 5). However, large-scale reallocation is impossible before reform of the R&D sector. A crucial principle of the forthcoming restructuring of R&D funding is the transition from subsidies towards credits in moving along the innovation 'chain' (basic research—applied research—development—implementation of innovations—consumption of innovation products).

New principles for budgetary funding can be defined as liberal funding and competition. The share of 'basic' funding in the R&D budget (funds allocated to particular organisations for specific purposes regardless of their performance) should be decreased. However, each government-owned R&D organisation that survives the restructuring of the government R&D sector should receive enough public money to meet its actual needs. The 'package funding' practice known in many countries is also being considered in Russia. It would provide a certain freedom in financial management and increase the operational flexibility of R&D institutions.

Streamlining the mechanisms of joint innovation programmes and project funding is an important element in the budgeting process. From the mid-90s the idea has been discussed of funding specific applied research outside the national priorities from the state budget through calls for tender, and only jointly with companies (up to 50 per cent of total project costs). However, the level of joint R&D funding and innovation projects remains low, not only because of the legal gaps and budget limitations but (most of all) because of the lack of mutual trust. Private investors are not ready to work without a specific long-term programme (which would also set out the government's obligations). Large-scale innovation projects can run for about 10–15 years, but specific programmes are drafted for much shorter periods and the budget in effect still covers just one year (ignoring the recently invented three-year budgetary planning tool). Many federal targeted programmes use one-year project planning as well. There have been negative experiences where the state refused to keep on funding R&D and innovation projects before they were completed. Short-term joint funding schemes are factors preventing the government, the R&D sector and business from joining forces. Investors and the state are acting separately, and their investment in innovation almost never matches each other.

Improvement in this area requires the creation and development of legal instruments regulating cooperative agreements in the R&D sector, grant support, and long-term government orders for R&D. In all developed countries, these are used to establish public-private partnerships and make efficient use of the R&D potential. Using such tools and mechanisms, and developing standards and frameworks for independent expert evaluation, would improve the quality of the entire system of R&D funding, promote a practical shift towards projects and programme funding, increase financial transparency and streamline procedures for making and spending profits, as well as sharing the risks of R&D and innovation activity.

In the context of the current debate, the federal budget can be said to have four main functions in the S&T sector: strategic, political, economic and management. The strategic budget function (with the aim of providing financial support for R&D reform) includes the evaluation of S&T prospects in Russia and the identification of the role of the government in developing R&D potential.

The political function (as a strategy and a set of measures to mobilise and allocate financial resources) is based on the creation of a hierarchical system of national objectives.

The economic function (as a financial plan to support sectors of the economy) is concerned with the development of the R&D sector, by increasing the effective demand for and commercialisation of R&D products.

The management function (procedures to establish objectives, structures, techniques and mechanisms for managing financial flows and for monitoring and evaluating results) includes the coordination, succession and transparency of the stages in the budgeting process and the realistic nature of obligations.

Despite all the changes, budgets have not yet become a real government policy tool, and do not fully carry out the functions crucial for developing Russia's R&D and innovation sector: the fourth function is implemented most widely (perhaps even too strictly), the third is implemented only partially, while there is still little evidence of the first and second. To improve this situation, the reforms should extend outside the budgetary sphere, taking the form of broad institutional changes.

4.3 Restructuring Government R&D Institutions

The predominance of government-owned budget-funded institutions in the S&T sector remains one of the most painful problems facing Russian science. Various types of commercial and non-profit organisations were allowed during the transition period of the Russian economy, but there was minimal change at the level of state R&D organisations. Over 73 per cent of all R&D organisations in Russia are public-owned and 37 per cent belong to the government sector (though many more R&D institutions, particularly those state-owned but serving industry, belong de facto to the state despite being formally placed in the business enterprise sector according to the Frascati Manual (OECD, 2005)). After federal executive agencies obtained the right to establish new institutions at the beginning of the 90s, their number even grew by 50 per cent (Science and Technology Indicators, 2008).

Russia has a huge system of state academies, a legacy of the former USSR. The most unusual feature of their legal status is its 'mixed' nature, which combines elements of a government institution, a public association and other forms (e.g. corporation and alliance). Another specific feature is the fact that academies act as holdings, 'owning' non-profit organisations. As government institutions, academies have control over a number of various other organisations and enterprises. The creation of an institution (academy) consisting of many other institutions (research institutes) causes property conflicts and is not in fact allowed by Russian civil law. However, under the Federal Law on Science and National Science and Technology Policy, state academies are an exception, organised exactly in this way. Finally, an important feature of state academies is that they operate as government institutions, even though by law they cannot have such authority as self-governing organisations. Academies receive and manage government funding provided by the state to support their research institutes. They can manage and control institutions and can create and close them.

This 'mix' of various organisational, legal and administrative forms has no precedent in other countries, and remains a big problem for the Russian government. The most worrying issue is the mismatch between performance and economic results in the R&D carried out by the academies and the amount of their public funding. There are other problems as well: inefficient monitoring of the use of federal property and public funds, along with insufficient transparency in the allocation and use of financial resources. At least 26 per cent of all public funds allocated to civil S&T go to the Russian Academy of the Sciences (Figure 3.7).

2005 saw the adoption of the 'Programme for modernisation of the structure, functions and funding mechanisms in the academic R&D sector', which envisages streamlining the network of academic organisations and introducing new forms for the organisation of R&D. The Programme also provides for increases in the salaries of staff while cutting their number. It was supposed to be implemented by 2008, but this did not happen. The resistance of the Academy's top management was strong enough to allow it to retain its operational and budgetary autonomy.

In the long run, more radical changes need to be considered. Since the system for the operation of the academies is too complicated, it has been proposed to divide them into two structures, separating organisation and property. There are some examples from other countries, where an 'academy' is a 'club' of prominent, well-known scientists without much administrative authority. On the other hand, academic institutes in future should retain government-sector status, and be controlled directly by executive government agencies.

Such proposals have been voiced repeatedly, but have always faced strong resistance from the academic community. Their top management's fears of the consequences of possible restructuring are well-grounded enough. There is no comparable situation in any other country where a legal entity exists and operates outside the general legal framework, or in conflict with it for so many years. The longer academies resist innovation, the more negative the consequences will be for Russian science should the academic system collapse.

The large number (and proportion) of government-owned R&D institutions makes Russia very different from other industrially developed countries. State R&D institutions funded by the government have to keep within budget limitations. They have almost none of the rights (or responsibilities) needed for adequate economic operation. While claiming large amounts of public money, they cannot guarantee that these resources will be used efficiently. In such a situation, the performance of the entire government S&T sector is affected.

A similar situation is found across the social sector of the Russian economy (education, culture, health care, etc.), showing the need to design and implement new, more flexible and independent organisational forms (Ozerova, 2004).

To meet this challenge, it was decided to create a new kind of government institution to operate in the social sector. The new flexible entity is known as an 'autonomous institution' (AI)[3]. The prospects for the transition of government-owned R&D organisations to the new form are outlined in 'R&D and Innovation Development Strategy in the Russian Federation until 2015'. At least 250 R&D institutions and HEIs should move to the new status over a fairly short period of time. Taking into account the period planned for this institutional transformation, this task looks quite complicated. It has been discussed now for more than two years but many questions and uncertainties still remain. The first autonomous institutions were due to appear by the end of 2008. By 2009, AIs should account for about 12 per cent of all government R&D institutions, and by 2010 this proportion should reach almost 22 per cent. Unlike existing budget-funded institutions, the new structures will not be funded by fixed budgetary grants, but rather will receive funding from various sources (including the government). This would increase their responsibility for the expected results. At the same time, they will remain government-owned entities. AIs will have a certain autonomy and independence in attracting (and spending) funds from non-government sources, including credits and investments. It will give them new development opportunities, not available to 'traditional' budget-funded institutions.

Another aspect of institutional reform (but still underdeveloped) is the integration of science and education (Gokhberg, L., et al., 2009). To this end, a new Federal Law on the Integration of Science and Education[4] was adopted at the end of 2007 to boost S&T and innovation at universities and to establish closer links between HEIs and research institutions. The new law legalises existing models for such integration and provides for efficient solutions, including a subset of necessary regulations. These regulations should help to eliminate the serious institutional barriers described above. Unfortunately, the discussion of the law dragged on for four years. The main problem was to achieve a compromise between the government, the university community and the Academy of Sciences. As a result, the final version of the law does not satisfy any of these sides. It just solves some evident problems with integration. But further amendments are required to make integration between science and education not only possible, but also efficient.

Another part of integration policy is support for the best 'innovative HEIs' or 'research universities'. The National Priority Project 'Education' contains specific policy measures to this end. An important component of this scheme, entitled 'Support Measures for Higher Education Institutions Implementing Innovative Education Programmes', is the distribution of competitive grants for developing university innovation (including human resource development, unique R&D and innovation projects, improvement of innovation infrastructure, acquisition of research equipment, etc.)[5]. There were 57 winners in the 2006–2007 competition. Each received funding in the range of 200 million to 1 billion roubles, depending on the scale of the project. The average annual R&D expenditure of the grant recipients was 123,300 roubles per member of R&D and teaching staff, but the difference between the minimum and maximum amounts (1,100 and 586,600 roubles, respectively) was very high. This meant that only some of the successful universities were really able to develop large-scale innovation projects. However, the scheme marked the first government experiment with earmarked support for research universities as centres of excellence. The main challenge for today is to continue this practice on a regular basis. If so, it could be a powerful driver similar to the university block grants in the UK or Japan.

As mentioned above, the two key targets for the current NSI transition in Russia are liberal mechanisms and competition. Within this framework, state support for R&D organisations (first of all state-funded bodies) should be oriented towards flexibility and selection of the best performers. The new mechanism meeting these requirements is discussed below.

4.4 Evaluation of the Performance of R&D Units

The efficient restructuring as well as the current operation of the state-funded R&D institutions also requires a set of comprehensive tools for performance evaluation. Such mechanisms are widespread in many countries and show positive effects. During the post-Soviet period, government funding of state R&D entities was not based on their performance. As a result, budgetary expenditure on R&D bore little relation to the output indicators (see the first section).

In 2008, a draft statement 'On the performance evaluation of R&D organisations' was prepared by the Ministry for Education and Science[6]. The main goals of this system are comprehensive planning and funding for R&D

Figure 3.8. Evaluation System Chart

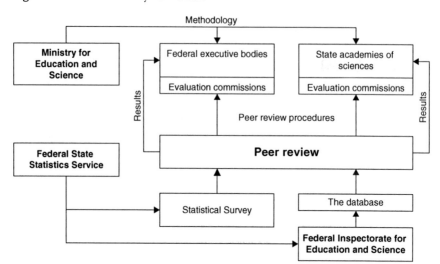

projects, optimisation of the network of R&D organisations, and benchmarking for non-public R&D organisations. The main tasks of the project are to organise regular surveys (every 3 years) and support the database containing statistical information on R&D institutions. Evaluation tasks are to be carried out by two official bodies: the Federal State Statistics Service (organisation of surveys) and the Federal Inspectorate for Education and Science (creation and development of the database). The second institution is subordinate to the Ministry for Education and Science, which is in charge of the whole initiative (Figure 3.8).

The evaluation commissions represent interest groups such as state executive bodies, business, academia, NGOs etc. They should be constituted in line with the principles of expert competence, authority and independence. Evaluation activities are to be based on independent peer review, transparency, involvement and minimal pressure on R&D organisations.

The key evaluation criteria are the same for different types of R&D organisations, but have different importance (weights) depending on the type of institution (as well as initial quantitative variables). Initial variables are combined into 7 key criteria. The criteria are put together in order to show the relationship between resources (inputs) and results (outputs). Output is measured by 1) R&D results (including publication activity, project results, etc.), 2) commercialisation and application of results (including patents, start-ups, participation to technology innovation projects etc.) and 3) scientific involvement (including international contacts, joint projects, etc.). Three further criteria relate to resources: 4) human capital (including quality and structure of personnel, salaries, etc.), 5) tangible and intangible resources (including equipment, facilities,

Figure 3.9. Main Categories of R&D Organisations by Performance and Recommendation Type

Category	Recommendation Type
'Poor performers'	Closure or reorganisation
'Candidates for reorganisation'	Reorganisation or renovation
'Stable institutions'	Stimulation of higher performance
'Leaders'	Special support

land, etc.) and 6) financial sustainability (income and expenditure structure, debts, etc.). The final criterion is 7) potential for further development (strategies, organisational structure, etc.).

A typical report by an evaluation commission consists of two parts: conclusions on performance against the key criteria and recommendations. Every R&D organisation should be assigned to one of four groups according to performance: from poor performers (all or almost all indicators below average) to leaders (all or almost all indicators above the national or even international averages). The recommendations therefore can vary from closure (for poor performers) to special support (for leaders) (Figure 3.9).

Unfortunately, this initiative faces the opposition by certain influential actors, and the final version may be considerably cut back compared to the initial one. However, this evaluation system will apply not only to the state-funded R&D institutions but also to other state NSI components, including innovation infrastructure institutions or PPP mechanisms (see below), and therefore should be extended rather than reduced.

4.5 Innovation Infrastructure

There are many different forms of innovation infrastructure in Russia. However, the most noteworthy are technoparks, science cities and special economic zones (SEZs). Technoparks are micro-level instruments for technology transfer, while science cities and SEZs are macro-level mechanisms for balancing the responsibilities of local and federal authorities in knowledge transfer support activities.

There are several dozen technoparks in Russia, although only some have official licenses. Technopark policies are full of hidden problems. First of all, multiple 'white spots' in the legislation dramatically weaken the technology commercialisation capability of universities and R&D institutions. For example, state universities or R&D institutions are not allowed to support other entities spun off from them. That means that a state university can create a start-up, but cannot provide any funding or facilities for it. That is why technoparks do not operate independently in Russia, as in other countries, but as a part of the 'host organisation' (university or R&D institution). In addition to the organisational inflexibility Russian technoparks lack performance monitoring and mechanisms for the diffusion of best practices. They also suffer from underdeveloped business consulting mechanisms.

In response to these negative factors, some new approaches to state policy for technoparks in Russia are appearing. A more streamlined development of technoparks has started with 'industry and manufacturing special economic zones' (see below). This makes it possible to reduce significantly the tax pressure and to attract investors. There are also other solutions such as business incubators and mechanisms to provide financial support for start-ups within technoparks; providing conversion and commercialisation mechanisms for defence 'dual-purpose' technologies, etc.

Currently, a number of legal mechanisms for technopark development and support are under construction. They mostly cover one of three aspects: 1) federal land provision for technoparks on a competitive basis (both for ownership and for long-term leasing), 2) direct investment in technopark infrastructure by federal executive bodies, and 3) creation of favourable conditions for technopark investment (including construction sites, transport, and housing infrastructure funding), sharing expenditure between federal and regional authorities.

An important instrument in the interaction between federal and local authorities takes the form of so-called 'science cities' or 'technopolises', or simply 'brain cities'. A typical science city is a large up-to-date research and industrial complex, including research institutions, universities, high-tech businesses and a residential area with a cultural and recreation infrastructure. The international concept of science cities aims to concentrate scientific potential in advanced and pioneering fields, providing a favourable environment for creative R&D activities. One of the features of a technopolis is beautiful surroundings and harmony with the natural environment and local traditions.

Russian science cities are the oldest such structures, secret communities created in the 1930s, 1950s, and 1970s in order to address major state defence objectives through R&D and new technologies. Almost all contemporary science cities were part of a larger system of closed cities in the USSR. About 70 cities, settlements and outlying districts were ranked as science cities, 29 of them being located within the Moscow region. About 40 per cent of national S&T potential is still concentrated in the science cities. They used to fall into two distinct categories. The first comprised communities with sensitive military, industrial or scientific facilities, such as arms plants or nuclear research sites. The second category consisted of border cities (and some entire border areas, such as the Kaliningrad Oblast), which were closed for security purposes. The locations of many of the closed cities were chosen for their geographical characteristics. They were often established in remote locations deep in the Urals and Siberia, out of range of possible enemy attack.

However, the most successful science cities today are located in the most populated regions. There are now 14 officially recognised sites with a specific status in Russia: Biysk, Dubna, Zhukovski, Koltsovo, Korolyov, Michurinsk, Petergof, Pushchino, Obninsk, Reutov, Troitsk, Fryazino, Chernogolovka, and Protvino. Nine are located in the Moscow region.

These cities are populated mainly by researchers and their families. The orientation towards scientific activity and specific tasks explains the lack of 'traditional' infrastructure elements such as agriculture. The Russian science cities were created mostly to contribute to military technologies. Consequently, after the dramatic decrease in state support in the 1990s, these cities faced extremely difficult economic and social problems.

Some Russian science cities still remain 'closed'. Others still have military connections, like Fryazino, which develops advanced radio and electronics devices, but most are now focusing on civilian activities with certain initial contribution by Western aid funding. Among the most famous are those operated by the Russian Academy of Sciences, for example Pushchino, a biological science centre, and Chernogolovka, a centre for physics and chemistry. Zelenograd (a city and an administrative district of Moscow, located forty kilometres from the city centre) is the Russian centre for research, education and production in microelectronics.

The main law defining the science city concept and special state support mechanisms was adopted in 1999. This was the Federal Law On the Status of a Science City in the Russian Federation[7]. According to the text, the science city is a municipal entity of the Russian Federation with a particular urban science and production complex. This complex consists of institutions carrying out research, development and innovation activities and training personnel in accordance with the national priorities in science and technology. Science city status is confirmed by the President of the Russian Federation for a period of 25 years. The President approves the priorities determined by the Government for the science city as well as the state programme for science development, which specifies the form of federal support for science cities in accordance with their specialisation. Science city funding, along with logistical and maintenance support, is provided from the federal budget, the budgets of the appropriate regional authorities of the Russian Federation, local budgets, and other funding sources in accordance with the constituting instrument.

Obninsk and Dubna were the first to obtain official science city status in the Russian Federation. The very first Russian science city, Obninsk (Kaluga Region), was opened in 2000[8]. It is famous for the world's first nuclear power station, built there in 1954. The Obninsk development programme provides autonomous mechanisms for city development without special state support.

In 2001, Dubna science city (Moscow Region) was 'reopened'[9]. The city of Dubna was founded in 1956. It is known for hosting the world-famous international Joint Institute for Nuclear Research which integrates research efforts from 18 countries. In the mid-80s, the city was transformed into a multidisciplinary research and industrial centre. R&D and production enterprises contribute over 40 per cent of tax revenues to the municipal budget.

The Dubna science city development programme aims to ensure the sustainable, autonomous social and economic development of the city, improvements in living standards, world leadership in R&D, including world-competitive high-tech products in accordance with national S&T priorities, as well as the training of highly qualified professionals.

From 1997, the issue of state support for science cities has been much discussed. Problems have included state responsibilities, efficient infrastructure creation and use, mechanisms for transition to autonomous grant-free development, etc. The creation of incentives and favourable conditions for transforming these regions into centres of high technology and advanced R&D is considered to be a major task for science city policies. The law on the status of science cities regards investment tax credit as the main support measure. For example, the plan was that the Obninsk administration should have the right to spend at least 50 per cent of tax revenues on innovation infrastructure development during the first five years. However, this mechanism was later rejected.

The reason for this rejection was the total absence of industrial activity in a number of cities (Dubna, Protvino, Pushchino, Troitsk, Chernogolovka). There was no industry, so no significant tax revenues to spend on innovation development. Finally, it was decided to use the internal resources of research organisations for R&D-intensive production.

Science city status presumes additional federal funding specifically for the implementation of innovation projects (on a competitive basis). The main problem today is the lack of mechanisms to transfer federal funding to specific scientific projects. In general, however, science cities are supposed to attract considerable investment as venture business centres and as hubs of science, education and technological excellence and integration[10].

There are also special mechanisms to promote the development of industry-oriented science cities and innovation-active regions. One is the 'special economic zone' (SEZ), which was introduced in Russia in 2005[11]. They are Russian Federation territories defined by the government where a special regime for entrepreneurial activity applies. SEZs are intended to promote high-technology industries.

Figure 3.10. Special Economic Zones in Russia

Type	Location	Description
Industry and manufacturing special economic zones	Elabuga Lipetsk	Automobile and oil industries Home appliances, building materials, chemical products
Technology and innovation special economic zones	Dubna Zelenograd Strelna Tomsk	Nuclear physics Microelectronics Electrolux, BSH Bosch und Siemens Hausgeräte GmbH Chemicals, pharmaceuticals, mechanical engineering
Tourism special economic zones	Krasnodar region, Stavropol region, Kaliningrad region, Altai region, Altai Republic, Irkutsk region, Republic of Buryatia	

There are three types of SEZs in the Russian Federation: industry and manufacturing special economic zones (special tax preferences, favourable investment regime), technology and innovation special economic zones (outside the customs zone, favourable for imports/exports), and tourism zones. Special economic areas can be created only on land owned by the government and/or municipalities. There are now thirteen SEZs in Russia (Figure 3.10).

However, official initiatives for innovation infrastructure development (as well as other mechanisms discussed above) do not guarantee growth in the demand for and/or supply of innovation. Particular NSI elements created directly to compensate for a lack of demand for (and investment in) innovation are the Russian Venture Company and several state corporations. They act as intermediaries, guarantors and sponsors in the PPPs (see Figure 3.5 above).

4.6 Public-Private Partnership Mechanisms

The Russian high-tech sector is still unable to absorb enough investment and to find demand for innovation. This problem has prompted state intervention in form of the Russian Venture Company and state corporations such as the Russian Corporation for Nanotechnology, the State Corporation for Nuclear Energy, etc.

The role of the Russian Venture Company is to promote venture investment and financial support for S&T throughout the country[12]. The Company invests in regional and sectoral investment funds (established under Russian legislation and regulated by the Federal Financial Market Service). A special management company manages each fund. The management companies compete for the right to sell fund investment shares to the Russian Venture Company. Funding can be provided only for projects related to the critical technologies (see above).

Once the venture fund has acquired all its funding, the fund management company can start investment activities (launch innovation companies in the areas of microelectronics, information and telecommunication technologies, biotechnologies, medical technologies, environment-friendly energy, and nanotechnologies). The management company team of each fund can finance from 10 to 15 innovation companies for several years. Thus, the result can be up to 15 venture funds and up to 150 innovation companies.

The capital resources for the Russian Venture Company are allocated from the Investment Fund of the Russian Federation. Initially, it was planned to allocate up to 5 billion roubles in 2006 and 10 billion in 2007 (total of 15 billion roubles). In 2008, however, the authorised capital stock amounted to 28.2 billion roubles (about €775 million at the currency exchange rate).

State corporations act as financial instruments to ensure the concentration and distribution of resources in line with state interests and priorities. For example, the Russian Corporation for Nanotechnology (Rosnanotech) was founded in 2007 by a special federal law[13] to address the growing challenge arising with the rapid development of new technologies on the nano-scale.

Rosnanotech, one of 7 Russian state corporations, enjoys initial lump-sum direct budgetary investment. Its 5-year budget is 130 billion roubles (about €3.7 billion). Due to its special status, the corporation is not government property and outside the control of regulating bodies. The Director-General is appointed directly by the Russian President. So far, 455 projects have been submitted to Rosnanotech (about 300 billion roubles in total), 17 have been approved and 2 have already started. Operational flexibility and stable support for projects should considerably boost their efficiency. However, such 'freedom' may also lead to unforeseen abuse.

The need to create such a corporation was expressed in 2007 by the Russian President in his annual message to the Federal Assembly of the Russian Federation. A new law sets out the legislative basis, organisational principles, and goals of the Russian Corporation for Nanotechnologies. Three key activities of Rosnanotech are assistance for state policies in the sphere of nanotechnology, the development of innovation infrastructure for nanotechnologies, and the launching of projects to create innovative nanotechnologies and nanoindustries.

In order to achieve its goals, Rosnanotech performs three main functions: R&D, nanotechnology education, and financial support for innovative projects. The first two functions are provided through financial support for R&D and nanotechnology education projects. The third function includes support for the entire innovation cycle, from project evaluation, financing and aid for commercialisation and production to supervision of projects after commercialisation.

One of the problems already being faced by Rosnanotech is the lack of human resources in this field. That is why education activities are closely tied with R&D. However the entire NSI requires the constant production and development of human resources. The last section below is devoted to the complex set of initiatives in this area.

4.7 Human Resources for S&T

A promising programme for developing human resources for R&D and innovation in HEIs and research institutions is to be implemented in the near future. The Federal Programme 'Science and Education Manpower for Innovative Russia' covers the period 2009–2013[14]. Its aim is to provide institutional support for the efficient development of human resources in S&T,

Figure 3.11. Task Chart for the Federal Target Programme 'Science and Education Manpower for Innovative Russia'

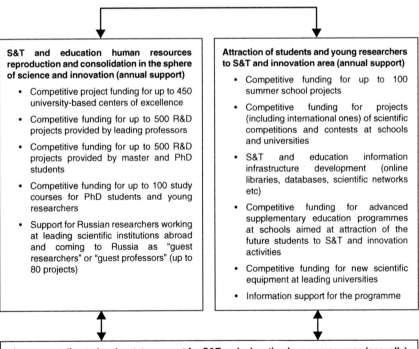

education and innovation. In order to achieve this goal, it is proposed to attract and involve young talent and highly skilled professionals in S&T and innovation projects and to consolidate excellent, competitive scholars in the best universities and R&D institutes. To this end, the Programme includes a number of actions and instruments: centres of excellence for science and education, a system of grants for young promising scientists and teachers, special schemes to attract young promising scientists and teachers from abroad, grants for innovation infrastructure development, etc.

The programme budget amounts to 90.5 billion roubles, or about €2.6 billion (88.9 per cent will come from the federal budget). The share of R&D funding is expected to be 73.6 per cent. The programme includes three main strands and 20 tasks (Figure 3.11).

The programme benchmarks call for a significant shift in S&T human capital:

- Annual support for up to 450 centres of excellence
- Decrease in average researcher age by 3–4 years by 2013
- Increase of 2–3 per cent in top-level researchers
- Increase of 4–6 per cent in top-level university teaching staff
- Increase of 1–1.5 per cent in Russia's share in the world scientific publications

One of the goals of the programme is to stimulate and develop non-government funding of supported projects. Therefore, projects attracting support from the business sector and NGOs should have an advantage.

5. Conclusions

This chapter has presented an overview of Russian S&T and innovation, emphasising the most recent trends and policies. Some years ago, the sector reached a turning point in the arduous transformation from a centrally controlled and administered structure to a flexible system operating in a free-market environment. Although the transition to a balanced demand and supply system is not complete, the demand for R&D has already shifted and the institutions meeting this demand are themselves undergoing transformation into more efficient and accountable forms.

However, initiatives for PPP development and stimulating demand for R&D will have only a temporary effect. In the long run, institutions such as Rosnanotech or RVC will not be able to replace the traditional market actors that ensure demand for R&D and innovation. At the same time, any institutional reform of the Russian R&D sector will not be complete without a deep transformation of the Russian Academy of Sciences (which has not yet happened).

Figure 3.12. The Forthcoming Model for Russian S&T and Innovation Policies

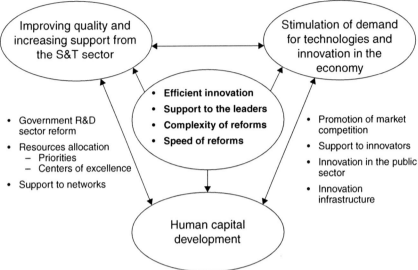

- Education sector reform
- Provision of an efficient contract, recovery if motivation for researchers/teachers
- Attraction and retention of young researchers

However, reforms of S&T cannot wait for full economic transition. Innovation activities themselves can contribute to the restructuring of enterprises and industrial change, as well as to the improvement of education, health care, and the environment. It is therefore crucial to speed up the reforms. There is a lot still to do to encourage this, especially in the fields of public policy and reorganisation of the R&D sector. S&T and innovation policies should be driven by top priority for complex and dynamic reforms aimed at efficient innovation and support for the best performers (Figure 3.12).

Future policy actions in this field will be coordinated within a complex framework including three key components: 1) development of the S&T sector (and supply of innovation), 2) increasing the demand for innovation, and 3) human capital development.

The future of the Russian NSI certainly depends on the reform of the entire economic system and the overall macroeconomic situation. It is evident that an economy based solely on oil and natural gas exports is unable to follow an innovation growth trajectory. Accordingly, enterprises can be encouraged to compete and play a central role in directing R&D and innovation only after broad structural shifts in the economy.

References

Etzkowitz, H.; Leydesdorff, L. (2000), The dynamics of innovation: from National Systems and 'Mode 2' to Triple Helix of university-industry-government relations. In *Research Policy*, Vol. 29, No 2, pp. 109–123.

Gokhberg, L. (2003), Science statistics. Moscow: TEIS. (In Russian).

Gokhberg, L. (2003a), Russia: A New Innovation System for the New Economy. Background material for a presentation at the First Globelics Conference 'Innovation Systems and Development Strategies for the Third Millennium', Rio de Janeiro, November 2–6, 2003.

Gokhberg, L. (Ed.) (2007), *Science, Technology and Innovation in Russia and OECD countries.* Moscow: State University—Higher School of Economics. (In Russian).

Gokhberg, L.; Kuznetsova, T.; Zaichenko, S. (2009), Towards a New Role of Universities in Russia: Prospects and Limitations. In *Science and Public Policy*, Special issue, March, 2009.

Gokhberg, L.; Peck, M. J.; Gacs, J. (Eds.) (1997), *Russian Applied Research and Development: Its Problems and Its Promise.* Laxenburg (Austria), IIASA.

Indicators Of Innovation: 2008 (2008), Data Book. Moscow: State University – Higher School of Economics. (In Russian).

International Energy Agency (2006), Key World Energy Statistics. Paris.

OECD (2005), The Measurement of Scientific and Technological Activities Frascati Manual 2002: Proposed Standard Practice for Surveys on Research and Experimental Development. Paris.

Ozerova, N. B. (2004), 'Restructuring the budget sector. Reasons, principles, directions. Financial monitoring of the budget sphere'. In *Financial Monitoring*, No 2, 2004. (In Russian).

Science And Technology Indicators (2008), Data Book. Moscow: State University—Higher School of Economics. (In Russian).

Sokolov, A. (2007) Method of Critical Technologies. In *Foresight*, No 4(4), pp. 64–74. (In Russian).

Chapter 4

SCIENCE, TECHNOLOGY AND INNOVATION POLICIES IN INDIA: ACHIEVEMENTS AND LIMITS

K. J. Joseph and Dinesh Abrol

1. Introduction

Policies that facilitate innovation in general and innovative performance in domestic industry in particular are an integral part of the development policies pursued by most countries. If the available evidence is any indication, India has been no exception. Both in terms of the institutional arrangements evolved over the years and of policy initiatives, India stands head and shoulders above developing country standards and in some respects is even on a par with some of the developed countries. Indian policymakers, particularly in the early years of independence, highlighted the crucial role of technology in addressing the development problems in the country and underscored the role of domestic generation of technology. The policies on technology imports in general, although initially liberal, were subsequently made restrictive for both embodied and disembodied imports to stimulate enterprises to take up and improve technology. Accordingly, almost all the policies formulated over the first forty years – including the policy statements exclusively for science and technology and others relating to industry, trade, investment and fiscal measures – were intended to influence either domestic generation or imports of technology or both. Apart from establishing its own agencies to promote innovation, the government encouraged the private sector, with the aid of various policy measures, to engage in in-house R&D activities. Also, with a view to promoting dissemination of technology, especially in agriculture, appropriate policy measures and other institutional action were taken from time to time.

In this context, technology policy – which has been defined, following Mowery (1994), as "policies that are intended to influence the decision of firms to develop, commercialise or adopt new technologies" – is linked closely to the overall development strategy and policy. Of course, as development strategy has changed, the strategy on development of S&T and promotion of innovation has also undergone substantial changes over the years. The strategy in place has been shaped by the changes brought about by the policy reforms to liberalise, privatise and globalise the economy and S&T. Broadly speaking, during the sixty years of independence India has witnessed at least two distinct phases of policies. The first (up to the 1980s) sought technological self-reliance under restrictive rules and the second (since 1980) took a more liberal approach to technology imports. The second phase has been deepened further in the mean time, especially after the 1990s. In general, the policymakers believe that the move away from a policy marked by the desire to achieve technological self-reliance, with a greater role for the public sector and a limited role for foreign capital, to a liberalised policy, with a greater role for the private sector and open access to foreign technology, was necessitated by two factors. First, the deteriorating technological performance under the earlier arrangement and, second, the changing external scenario following the end of the cold war and the emergence of a world dominated by the United States in S&T and economic terms.

This detailed account of the policy measures and institutional action focusing on industry during the two phases highlights the premises underlying the policy shift and argues that although the restrictive policy of the first phase was unable to achieve higher growth rates in productivity and output it did lay the S&T foundation for the sustained growth witnessed during the second phase. However, this paper also raises concerns about the inadequate investment being made at present in sustaining the current performance.

The remainder of this paper is organised as follows: The first section (2) gives a detailed analysis of the policy initiatives taken during the controlled phase to promote science and technology in the country, highlighting the achievements and limits. The second section (3) focuses on various initiatives during the globalisation phase and the last (4) puts the discussion into perspective by spotlighting certain concerns for the future.

2. Changing Stance of Technology Policy in India

2.1 Phase 1: Import Substitution for Technological Self-Reliance

As shown by the 1958 Science Policy Resolution (SPR), India is among the pioneering developing countries which recognised the role of science and technology in bringing about socio-economic change. To quote from the SPR, "the key to national prosperity, apart from the spirit of the people, lies, in the modern age, in the effective combination of three factors, technology, raw materials and capital, of which the first is perhaps the most important." Conceiving indigenous technological progress in a developing country like India as dependent on achieving scientific and technological self-reliance which, in turn, was an outcome of the combined effect of technology transfer from abroad and domestic R&D efforts, India was one of the first few latecomer countries in the post-colonial developing world to formulate an explicit Science Policy Resolution and evolve policy instruments to develop science and technology. This involved, inter alia, establishing public-sector enterprises for production of inputs like steel, oil and gas, petrochemicals, power, fertilisers and the equipment and machine tools needed for production of capital goods and setting up mission-oriented S&T agencies and R&D institutions to build up the technological capability needed for production of atomic energy, space technology, clean coal, glass and ceramics, processed foods, pharmaceuticals, agro-chemicals, etc. Emphasis was placed on importing technology to the extent possible in the public sector either by disembodied means (like licensing agreements) or by embodied means (like imports of capital goods). Policies were adjusted from time to time to regulate the technology flows, based on the attitude of companies in the western world to technology licensing. Since the private sector considered foreign direct investment fairly important for gaining access to foreign technology, both policy measures and institutional arrangements were devised with a view to keeping the nature and extent of FDI more or less in tune not only with the strategy upheld by the State but also with the behaviour of foreign firms. Various policy measures to help to build scientific and technological infrastructure and fiscal policies including incentives to promote R&D and various other policies, such as those relating to industry, trade and investment, were formulated to promote domestic generation of technology. Hence a proper understanding of S&T policy in India and its evolution over time presupposes an understanding of the changing stance on both domestic generation of technology and transfer of technology from abroad, which in turn has undergone drastic changes in response to changing economic conditions.

2.1.1 Promotion of R&D and Pursuit of Technological Self-Reliance

Immediately after independence, under Nehru, India embarked upon a journey with the declared objectives of growth, prosperity, economic development and equitable distribution of wealth (Nehru, 1947) by harnessing, amongst other things, the power of S&T. This era (1947–64) therefore saw impressive institution-building, with an affirming faith in the capability of S&T to catapult a primitive, predominantly agriculture-based, illiterate nation into an advanced country. Notwithstanding its emphasis on big science, the 1958 Science Policy Resolution underlined the need to pursue self-reliance in technology by stating that "in industrialising a country [a] heavy price has to be paid in importing science and technology... An early and large-scale development of science and technology in the country could therefore greatly reduce the drain on capital." Hence the SPR aimed to "foster, promote and sustain, by all appropriate means, the cultivation of science and scientific research in all its aspects – pure, applied and educational." The drive to promote industrial development with an emphasis on self-reliance was already evident in the 1956 Industrial Policy Resolution (IPR). As domestic private capital was in its infancy, and in tune with the declared objective of establishing a socialist pattern of society, the IPR reserved almost all the key industries (schedule B) and infrastructure for the public sector. Given the importance attached to development of the capital goods industries, as envisaged by the Mahalanobis model to achieve self-reliant development, a number of public-sector entities were set up to manufacture a wide variety of basic and capital goods. In the early years, however, most of the private-sector entities turned to foreign partners for both capital and technology and in licensing policy; preference was given to financial collaboration (Kidron, 1965).

To achieve technological self-reliance by promoting indigenous development, in addition to adopting a series of measures to restrict acquisition of foreign technology the government formulated a "comprehensive science and technology plan" for the first time in India, closely integrated with the country's fifth five-year plan. Also, there was a marked increase in investment in science and technology. By the end of the fifth five-year plan, a total of 13,800 million rupees had been invested against an outlay of 18,500 million rupees. This marked an almost four-fold increase in investment in science and technology compared with the 3,730 million rupees spent under the fourth (1969–75) five-year plan. What is more, the outlay for R&D during the last year of the plan (1978–79) was equivalent to 0.84 per cent of GDP against the target of 0.95 per cent (Parthasarathi, 2007).

The SPR noted that India's enormous resource – manpower – becomes an asset in the modern world only when trained and educated. This stand triggered substantial investment in science-based education along with R&D infrastructure. The number of engineering colleges and places increased strongly, from 38 colleges offering 2,940 places in 1947 to 138 and 25,000 respectively in 1970. The pace was maintained with further increases to 171 and 130,000 respectively in 1980. In the 1960s the Indian Institutes of Technology (IITs) modelled on the Massachusetts Institute of Technology were set up. The number of universities increased from 20 in 1947 to 150 in 1980. Enrolment in these universities increased from 0.15 million in 1947 to nearly five million by 1980, equivalent to an annual growth rate of 7.5 per cent sustained over 35 years. The proportion of the population over 25 years of age with third-level education rose from 0.5 per cent in 1951 to 2.5 per cent in 1981, by when the total number stood at 7 million compared with 1.5 million in 1950 (IAMR, various years). In this way, an environment conducive to domestic research had been created by 1980.

Alongside development of the human resources base for technological progress, a number of specialised laboratories and institutions providing a variety of services relating to science-based technologies were set up. Although the history of S&T institutions could be traced back to the pre-independence period[1], after independence a separate Ministry of Scientific Research and Cultural Affairs under the Prime Minister was set up – an indication of the high priority attached to development of science and technology in the country. Since then, elaborate scientific and technological infrastructure has been set up over the years under the CSIR, ICMR, ICAR and various government departments like the Department of Atomic Energy, the Department of Space, the Department of S&T, the Defence Research and Development Organisation and others. As Patel (1993) observed, "the maze of institutions for science and technology is an outstanding testimony to the wide spread of the scientific and technology infrastructure. India has no rival in the whole third world for the vastness of infrastructure and even many among the highly developed countries would not be able to rival India in the number and the spread of the institutions" (p. 34). Apart from their wider contribution in their specialist field, these institutions became the largest source of experienced scientists/technologists for in-house R&D activities in the country (Desai, 1980).

Governments in industrially developed and developing countries alike have been offering tax incentives and subsidies to support private R&D investment, as they are considered an effective means to address market failure in private firms' R&D investment decisions by eliminating the wedge between the private and social returns on R&D investment. Government subsidies have taken different forms in different countries. In South Korea, for example, Kim (1993) traced more than 94 per cent of industrially funded R&D in 1987 to low-interest R&D loans from State-controlled banks and other public funds. A number of European governments have used targeted subsidies to support R&D in selected areas, notably microelectronics. In Germany, R&D subsidy schemes included defraying part of the salaries of new R&D employees (Stoneman, 1991).

In India too the fiscal incentives offered by the State have played a key role. As early as 1974, the government started a scheme for recognising the in-house R&D units of industrial firms. Such units were given easier access to imported equipment, raw materials and various tax concessions. For example, expenditure incurred on scientific research was 100 per cent deductible from profit for the purpose of income tax calculations. The various fiscal incentives provided by the State continued in the 1980s and 1990s, notwithstanding major changes in the approach taken by government policy to technology development. The number of such registered units increased from 106 in 1973 to over 900 by the early 1980s. As regards tax incentives, however, a study (Mani, 2002) found that their effectiveness varied across different industries. Also, the importance of tax incentives for starting R&D and seeing it through varied positively with the R&D intensity of the firms. Firms with foreign collaboration were less motivated by tax incentives to start R&D.

The 1970 Patent Act has been considered the most innovative initiative by the State to foster indigenous development of technology. This comprehensive and extensive Act aimed at protecting the nascent domestic industry and has been a role model for many developing countries. The new Patent Act abolished product patents on food, chemicals and drugs. It also reduced the life of patents from fourteen to five years from the date of sealing of the patent or seven years from the date of filing, whichever was earlier. The Act included many other features to facilitate indigenous development of technology, such as the adoption of process instead of product patenting for chemicals, powerful compulsory licensing provisions, powers allowing State intervention in the pricing of patented products and so on.

2.1.2 Access to Foreign Technology

Although technological self-reliance and indigenous development have been considered the hallmarks of S&T policy in India during the first three decades and that, in turn, implied limited recourse to foreign capital and technology, the intensity with which these twin objectives were pursued varied significantly. The policy on foreign technology and capital was relatively liberal up to the mid-1960s, as is evident from the 1948 Industrial Policy Resolution and from the statement on foreign investment made by the Prime Minister in Parliament in April 1949. The overall approach remained liberal until the late sixties as foreign investment was considered to be a channel of technology transfer, but effective control was expected to lie with the local firms, keeping the national interest in mind.

However, the policy on foreign technology became more stringent from the mid-1960s on, in a difficult balance of payments situation. In 1966, on the recommendation of the Mudhaliar Committee on foreign collaboration, the procedure for approval of foreign investment proposals was streamlined. The Foreign Investment Board (FIB) was set up to deal with all cases involving foreign investment of less than 20 million rupees and within the 40 per cent equity limit. Any collaboration that exceeded this limit had to be referred to the cabinet committee on foreign investment. The government also made a list of industries where foreign collaboration was considered necessary and of those where technical collaboration could be permitted. It set a maximum ceiling for royalty payments (normally 5 per cent of sales) and their duration (normally 5 years). In general, foreign collaboration was severely restricted and FDI was allowed only in core industries where no alternative local technologies were available (Kumar, 1987). As a result, there has been a marked decline in reliance on foreign technology, as is shown by the fact that the number of foreign collaborations approved per annum during the early 1970s was less than half that approved in the early 1960s. More importantly, the number of cases involving foreign equity participation declined from 165 in 1961 to 27 in 1971.

Along with policy measures to regulate and monitor the inflow of disembodied technology with the aid of technology licensing, the inflow of embodied technology in the form of imports of capital goods was also subjected to monitoring and regulation by the State. Broadly, for the purpose of import regulation, capital goods were divided into two categories: the first comprised those with local availability and where imports were therefore banned, the second those under the open general licence (OGL) that could be freely imported by the actual users, although there were further restrictions if the total value of the import exceeded 0.1 million rupees. In 1976, a technical development fund was set up to allow industrial units to import US$0.5 million worth of technical know-how, consultancy services or capital goods for the purpose of modernising such units.

The 1970 Industrial Policy, drafted after the Monopolies and Restrictive Trade Practices (MRTP) Act, sought further to restrict the activities of foreign companies to certain industries involving complex technologies and high capital intensity. Later, the 1973 Foreign Exchange Regulation Act imposed a ceiling of 40 per cent on all foreign companies with the possible exception of export-oriented activities and industries involving a very high level of technology.

2.2 Phase 2: Liberal Policies for Science, Technology and Innovation

A number of committees appointed by the government in the seventies and early eighties, in response to the sub-potential performance of the economy, concluded that the excessive controls had been acting as a drag on growth. In the sphere of science and technology, it has been argued that, in terms of technological content, India's achievements under the restrictive policy were insignificant and costly. The advocates of this view actively promoted a policy of enhanced competition and deregulation. In undertaking these reforms, which were of far-reaching structural significance for the economy and innovation systems in the long run, the architects of the new economic policy (NEP) were largely guided by the neo-liberal assumption that the "government shackles" must be removed to enable firms to grow in terms of size of operations, improve their overall technological performance and develop their export competitiveness. By giving businesses not only total freedom to operate but also incentives for technological upgrading, policymakers attempted to unleash them to seize the opportunities opened up by the emerging growth routes of alliance-building with foreign companies to capture markets at home and abroad (Abrol, 2006). The policy shift observed in India, however, was a gradual process in two phases. The first was marked by internal liberalisation, whereas external liberalisation under globalisation was the hallmark of the policy reforms in the second.

2.2.1 Internal Liberalisation (1980–1990)

During the first phase, consisting of internal liberalisation and extending from the early eighties to 1991, the thrust was on internal competition. The policy initiatives during this period aimed at encouraging the corporate sector in India to acquire the means of industrial upgrading by importing technology and removing internal controls[2]. With external liberalisation policies still on hold, domestic firms were allowed to grow and increase their share of the Indian market. During this phase domestic firms had relatively stronger protection against imports. Domestic firms also got the government to protect the Indian market from the entry of new foreign firms. The government was persuaded to de-license the industrial sector sufficiently, relax the regulations regarding foreign collaboration and foreign exchange and dilute the controls over expansion of Indian big businesses to provide them with enhanced access to the home market. The government relaxed the restrictions on the scope, duration and payments for technology collaboration. The corporate sector was offered a wide range of fiscal and non-fiscal incentives to take an active part in strengthening its in-house technological capability. It was actively encouraged to consult the publicly funded R&D institutions for problem-solving, sponsorship of R&D and assistance with the take-up of imported technologies (Abrol, 2006).

The 1983 Technology Policy Statement (TPS) aimed to step up the pace of technological change by developing new policy instruments. The basic objective set in the Policy Statement was to develop indigenous technology and ensure efficient take-up and adaptation of imported technology appropriate to national priorities and resources. The policy highlighted the importance of building up human capital and of providing maximum gainful and satisfying employment to all strata of society, especially to women and the weaker sections of society, while harnessing their traditional skills and capabilities and making them commercially competitive. Given the context of increasing international competition and concern for the environment, the policy also underscored, among other things, the need to develop technologies which are internationally competitive, particularly those with export potential, and to reduce demand for energy, particularly from non-renewable sources, and ensure harmony with the environment.

Some of the initiatives under the 1983 TPS (1983) included the Programme aimed at Technological Self-Reliance (PASTER), now known as the Technology Development and Demonstration Programme (TDDP), which aims at technology adaptation by means of research, design and development work carried out by industry and overseen by experts from laboratories/universities, the Technology Absorption and Adaptation Scheme, the National Register on Foreign Collaboration, S&T for Weaker Sections, S&T for Rural Development and the Science & Technology Entrepreneurship Park (1984), along with financial institutions, State government bodies and academic institutions. Added incentives for in-house R&D and technology development were offered to industry, apart from setting up the Technology Development Fund (1987), by introducing a levy ("cess") on all technology import payments (Gupta and Dutta). Finally, a fully fledged Ministry of Science and Technology was set up in 1985, incorporating the earlier Department of Science and Technology (DST) and a new Department of Scientific and Industrial Research (DSIR) (Richardson, 2002). During this period the DSIR also launched the scheme for granting recognition to scientific and industrial research organisations (SIROs) in the private sector.

One major innovation in explicit policies for STI pursued during this period was the introduction of technology missions to promote civil development of technological applications and dissemination thereof in society. Significant positive outcomes were obtained from these missions in terms of technology development and dissemination in the fields of telecommunications, oilseeds and literacy. Successful establishment of the rural telephone exchanges developed by CDOT and improvements of almost 10 per cent in literacy are examples of what was achieved by technology missions. However, technology missions for societal development were no longer pursued consistently by the implementing agencies appointed by the government after 1991. India soon lost the momentum built up by these missions. The government failed to institutionalise this connection between S&T and development, particularly considering the need to consolidate the mission orientation emerging for societal development in the S&T agencies on the one hand and in the government line departments on the other. Therefore, after 1991 the policymakers in these agencies were also free to shift to projects that they believed to be far more consistent with the new goals of external liberalisation.

2.2.2 External Liberalisation (Since 1991)

In the second phase of reform, the thrust of the policy changes shifted towards external liberalisation, although it involved changes affecting many different aspects. First of all, the corporate sector, including foreign companies, was gradually freed from the controls imposed by the government to reserve and regulate access to the Indian markets. Second, Indian firms were permitted to enter into collaboration with foreign firms of their own choice. Third, both fiscal and non-fiscal incentives to the corporate sector for undertaking in-house R&D were enhanced to encourage enterprises to "innovate" faster in the form of development of new products and processes and take-up of imported technological know-how. Fourth, the IPR rules were changed to grant an absolute monopoly to the generators of intellectual property with the aim of encouraging corporations to invest in development of technology. Above all, the government offered the corporate sector a strategic role in the policymaking, planning and regulation processes with the aim of achieving closer coordination between the S&T institutions and Indian industry. In addition, new policy initiatives were launched to encourage Indian companies to invest abroad and facilitate access not only to their technology and human capital but also to their markets.

The technology import policy itself was allowed to turn into a vehicle for foreign firms to demand financial participation from the collaborating firms in India. The policy was implemented without any discipline over the entry of foreign capital. Considerable encouragement was given for Indian industry to enter into collaboration, seeking financial participation by foreign partners in the name of acquisition of new technologies. The Indian corporate sector was permitted to import foreign technologies not only under highly diluted restrictions but also without any technological coordination. Indiscriminate entry of foreign capital was facilitated by the changes made in the name of technology modernisation and improvement, yet no safeguards existed in the policy to make sure that broader, deeper technological know-how packages were imported.

During this period other new initiatives aimed at promoting scientific and technological innovation by means of public-private partnerships on pre-competitive R&D. They included, to give just a few examples, an Innovation Foundation to harness traditional knowledge, the New Millennium India Technology Leadership Initiative (2000) and the Technology Development Board (TDB) to provide financial assistance in the form of equity, soft loans or grants. This was followed by the setting-up of technology business incubators (TBIs) (2001) where grants-in-aid are provided by the government department, both on capital and recurring for a set period.

The shift observed in policy focus was built, however, on a vibrant innovation system which had evolved over the years, as evident, among other things, from the sound infrastructure base for science and technology – research laboratories, higher education institutions and highly skilled human resources. As stated in the 2006 Science Policy Statement, this was built up over the years on the strength of the commitment to promote the spread of science and the recognition of the role of technology as a key component in national development. In a context where the returns from science, technology and development were yet to reach large segments of society, the new Science Policy Statement put the emphasis on inclusive development, as can be seen from its focus on enhancing livelihood security, ending hunger and malnutrition, reducing regional imbalances and generating employment, by harnessing scientific and technological capability along with the traditional knowledge pool. Another important aspect of the new policy, in tune with earlier policies, is its renewed focus on human capital and emphasis on environmental protection while continuing with fiscal incentives and other measures to promote R&D and innovation.

3. Achievements and Limits

Assessment of technology policy is a relatively difficult task because both the policies and their outcomes are multidimensional and no single one-dimensional indicator could fully reflect the manifold dimensions involved. The issue is further complicated by the fact that, as times change, the policy focus in any economy undergoes major changes. This has also been the case in India, as evident from the discussion in the previous section. It is therefore almost impossible for any single indicator to measure the effectiveness of the policy supporting different objectives. This is not intended to play down the usefulness of conventional input indicators like R&D expenditure, R&D manpower and others and output indicators like patents, high-tech exports and others in addressing the issue at hand, but just to highlight their limits and underscore the usefulness of qualitative analysis with rich details and case studies. This section will begin with certain macro indicators of whether the policy has accomplished its aims. It will also make an attempt at exploring qualitatively the degree of success with certain other parameters considered important for building technological capability in a developing country like India.

3.1 Selected Macro Dimensions

3.1.1 Technology Imports and R&D

Looking back at the first phase, it is revealing to explore the extent to which self-reliance has been achieved and import dependence reduced in key areas, as these were the hallmarks of the policy during the first phase. Here India's well documented achievements in the spheres of atomic energy, space technology and, more importantly, self-sufficiency in food production along with establishment of a diversified industrial sector tends to suggest that India has much to its credit.

During the early years of development planning, with a relatively liberal policy on foreign technology, there was a substantial increase in the number of foreign collaborations. To be more specific, until 1955 the number of new foreign collaborations per annum was only in the order of 35. The pace accelerated during the second five-year plan with an almost three-fold increase to 104. The third plan and the period until the mid-sixties brought further increases in access to foreign technology, with an average of 356 agreements per annum. Thus there was an almost six-fold increase between 1948 and 1958 and 1954 and 1970. The FDI stock more than doubled to 560 million rupees between 1948 and 1964. Technology-related royalty payments jumped sixteen-fold between 1956–57 and 1967–68 (Richardson, 2002). Thus, as noted by Desai (1980), industrial capacity-building during the early years was based almost totally on imported technology.

Yet considering the first policy phase as a whole, India was able to achieve considerable progress towards its declared objective of reducing technological dependence and building technological self-reliance in terms of the capacity created for technology unpackaging in the system (Subrahmanian, 1984). There was also a drastic reduction in the cost of technology imported during the period of the restrictive policy. At the same time, domestic R&D effort increased at an unprecedented rate while the cost of technology imports increased at a much lower pace than national R&D. The annual average growth rate in R&D expenditure (8.34 per cent) remained higher than the corresponding increase in the direct cost of technology imports (7.7 per cent) throughout the seventies. On the whole, it has been demonstrated that the regulatory policy of the seventies did stimulate in-house R&D, especially industrial R&D.

The next question is how technology imports and local R&D have behaved under the liberal policy. It is evident that an unprecedented increase in the number of foreign collaborations was recorded during the post-liberalisation period. The number of collaborations during the five years beginning with 1980 was only 686, whereas it increased more than three-fold to 2,175 during 1996–2001 (Figure 4.1) and the available evidence indicates that the trend is continuing. This suggests that Indian firms' strategy, in the face of increasing international competition, is to depend increasingly on foreign firms to build their competitiveness and enhance their access to foreign markets.

Along with this increase in dependence on foreign technology, the kind of collaboration also changed. In the earlier period, when there was general disenchantment with foreign capital, the policy was to encourage technical

Figure 4.1. Trend in Foreign Collaborations Approved in India (Five-Year Average)

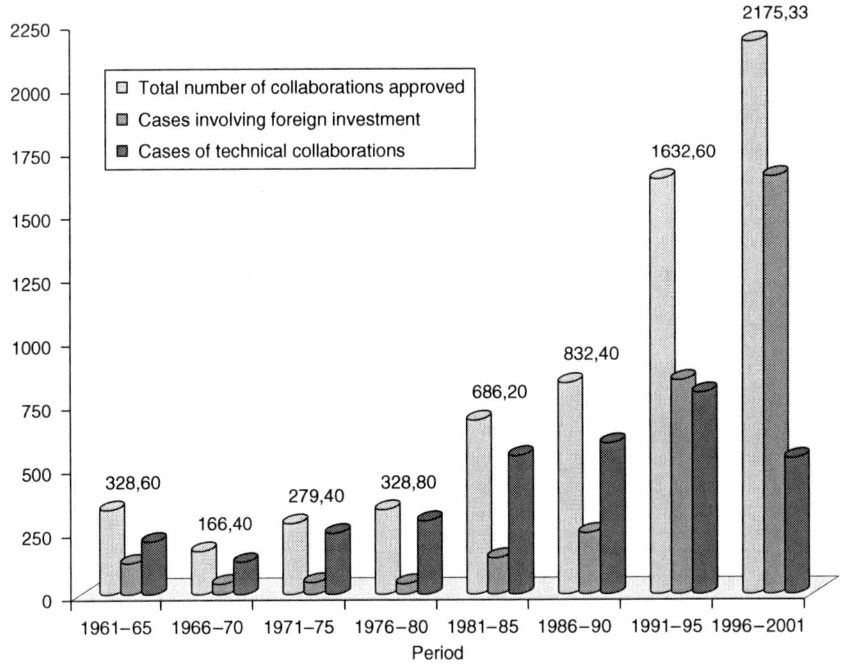

Source: Department of Scientific and Industrial Research, Foreign Collaborations, Ministry of Science and Technology, Government of India (different years).

collaboration. In 1960, for example, for every financial collaboration there were 1.4 technical collaborations and by 1977 this had increased to eight. But as the policy became more open to foreign technology and capital, the number of financial collaborations increased compared with technical collaboration and by 2001 there was only 0.1 technical collaboration for every financial collaboration (Figure 4.2). Here again there was an increasing incidence of cases involving majority equity participation. While there were only 4 per cent majority approvals in 1991, the share increased to almost 16 per cent by 1997. Mergers and acquisitions also grew at an unprecedented rate during the 1990s, rising from US$3.5 million to US$1 billion by 2001 (Basant, 2000; Beena, 2004; Kumar, 2000).

While the increase in the incidence of financial collaboration and in foreign equity participation has been in tune with the policy, and in a context of increasing competition between developing countries for FDI, in a country like India that is regionally more diverse than most continents, its contribution to national economic development would depend on the regional distribution of FDI. If the available evidence is any indication, foreign investment has been

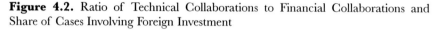

Figure 4.2. Ratio of Technical Collaborations to Financial Collaborations and Share of Cases Involving Foreign Investment

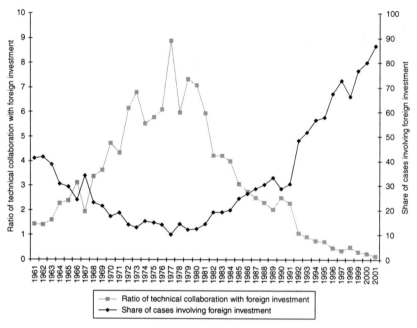

Source: Department of Scientific and Industrial Research, Foreign Collaborations, Ministry of Science and Technology, Government of India (different years).

becoming concentrated into a few regions and thus contributing to the widening of interregional disparities (Figure 4.3).

It has also been argued that indiscriminate entry of foreign capital was facilitated by the changes made in the name of technology modernisation and improvement, yet no safeguards existed in the technology import policy to ensure imports of broader, deeper technological know-how packages. Technology imports by big businesses were targeted particularly on acquisition of brand names. They were more interested in the brand names that came with these collaborations. National enterprises showed much interest in importing capital goods and transferring the advantage of assets like brand names (Abrol, 1995). There was also a lack of demand for any increase in the technology content in the collaboration from the corporate sector in most industries. This led purchasers of technology to persist with importing shallow technology packages. In this context, another point to note is that studies on the technology import behaviour of large corporate units under the liberalised policy have shown that, while the foreign collaboration led to enhanced profitability, it did not help to increase export intensity (Evenson and Joseph, 1997).

Figure 4.3. State-by-State FDI Approval (1991–1997, 1998–2002 and 1991–2002)

Serial No	State	Percentage Share 1991–2002	Rank	Percentage Share 1991–1997	Rank	Percentage Share 1998–2002	Rank
1	Andhra Pradesh	4.64	6	3.71	9	5.67	6
2	Bihar	0.32	18	0.08	18	0.60	14
3	Gujarat	6.50	5	4.42	7	8.80	4
4	Haryana	1.27	11	1.32	12	1.22	10
5	Himachal Pradesh	0.41	16	0.23	16	0.57	16
6	Karnataka	8.31	3	5.53	4	11.52	2
7	Kerala	0.54	14	0.36	14	0.72	11
8	Madhya Pradesh	3.37	7	4.44	6	2.26	7
9	Maharashtra	17.42	1	12.78	2	22.21	1
10	Orissa	2.90	9	4.96	5	0.61	13
11	Punjab	0.69	13	1.20	13	0.13	18
12	Rajasthan	1.06	12	1.46	11	0.60	15
13	Tamil Nadu	7.81	4	7.02	3	8.68	5
14	Uttar Pradesh	1.72	10	1.84	10	1.58	9
15	West Bengal	3.15	8	4.12	8	2.10	8
16	Delhi	12.48	2	14.25	1	10.54	3
17	Goa	0.34	17	0.24	15	0.45	17
18	Pondicherry	0.44	15	0.21	17	0.67	12
19	State not indicated	26.60		31.84		21.01	

Source: Naik (2007).

3.1.2 Research and Development

While there was increased emphasis on foreign technology and capital, the domestic technology-generating efforts showed no marked increase but took a back seat. This was true not only of a number of technology-intensive industries like electronics (Joseph, 1997) but also in many others and, hence, at national level. The R&D effort at national level showed a marked increase, especially in the first period. But the move to the second period triggered a steady decline in the R&D effort in terms of R&D expenditure at national level as a proportion of GDP (Figure 4.4). The target for R&D investment set by the latest Science and Technology Policy (STP 2003) by the end of the tenth plan, which the current policy is designed to implement, is 2 per cent of gross domestic product (GDP). After reaching a high of 0.91 per cent in 1987–88, there was a steady decline to 0.71 per cent by the mid-1990s. According to the statistics provided by the Department of Science and Technology, it slowly picked up again in 1998–99 to 0.81 per cent and stands at around 0.90 per cent today – still lower than the record 20 years ago.

It is evident that even today central R&D expenditure is concentrated heavily on a few departments like atomic energy, defence and space (Figure 4.5). Civilian

Figure 4.4. Expenditure on R&D in Relation to GDP in India

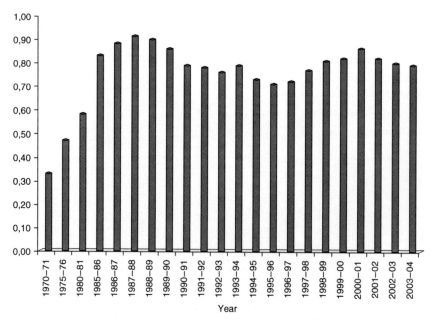

Source: Department of Science and Technology, Science & Technology Data Book 2002, NSTMIS.

Figure 4.5. Distribution of Central Government R&D Expenditure Across Different Agencies

Year	DAE	DRDO	DoS	CSIR	ICAR	ICMR	Total
	27	8			20	3	100
1969–70	30	21		27	20	2	100
1976–77	24	21	16	17	15	1	100
1980–81	19	20	13	18	17	2	100
1984–85	19	20	16	13	12	2	100
1988–89	14	27	20	10	9	2	100
1994–95	11	32	19	9	11	1	100
1998–99	12	32	21	10	12	1	100

Source: Department of Science and Technology, Government of India, R&D Statistics, different years.
DAE: Department of Atomic Energy.
DRDO: Defence Research and Development Organisation.
DoS: Department of Space.
CSIR: Council for Scientific and Industrial Research.
ICAR: Indian Council for Agricultural Research.
ICMR: Indian Council for Medical Research.

R&D priorities are still neglected. The annual budget on R&D relating to health, communicable disease control, nutrition and family welfare put together is only around 3,500 million rupees. Compare this figure with the spending of 25,000 million rupees on defence R&D and 8,000 million rupees on atomic energy R&D. R&D on meteorology, an area critical to agriculture, irrigation, flood control, drinking water and disaster prediction, is only about 1,300 million rupees. Put together, even today the outlays for botanical and zoological surveys (that are the basis for biodiversity assessment and protection in the country) are in the order of a mere 300 million rupees (Abrol, 2005).

Along with increasing concentration on certain departments, there has also been increasing regional concentration with R&D activity concentrated in selected, industrially advanced States (Chadha, 2006). Despite a number of policy initiatives including fiscal concessions from 1996–97 to 2006–07 to encourage investment in R&D by industry, judging from their impact any significant change in the growth of private-sector R&D activities has yet to occur. While there is empirical evidence that the private-sector share of industrial R&D increased from about 41 per cent in 1985 to 61 per cent in 2003–04 (Mani, 2008), private-sector R&D intensity (R&D expenditure as a per centage of sales turnover) in India is only about less than 0.1 per cent and has shown a declining

Figure 4.6. Percentage Changes in R&D Intensity Across Selected Countries

Country	Change (Phase 1)	Change (Phase 2)
Australia	−0.60 (1973–81)	0.55 (1981–2002)
Canada	0 (1973–81)	0.80 (1981–2002)
Japan	0.30 (1975–81)	0.71 (1981–2002)
Germany	0.40 (1973–81)	0.14 (1981–2002)
France	0.10 (1974–79)	0.47 (1979–2002)
UK	0.30 (1972–81)	−0.42 (1981–2002)
USA	0.20 (1974–81)	0.17 (1981–2002)
India	0.40 (1973–82)	0.01 (1982–1998)
Republic of Korea	0.20 (1974–81)	2.31 (1981–2002)
Brazil	0.50 (1974–82)	0.34 (1982–2002)
Philippines	−0.10 (1973–82)	0.02 (1982–1992)

Source: Department of Science and Technology, Government of India, R&D Statistics, different years.

trend since 1992–93 (Kumar and Aggarwal, 2005). Thus, as noted by Krishnan (2005), promotional efforts undertaken by the government to persuade the corporate sector to participate in development of indigenous technology have been far from effective. What is more, there is heavy concentration of R&D in selected industries. Seven industries (pharmaceuticals, transport, chemicals, electrical and electronics, defence, information technology and telecommunications) account for about 70 per cent of the total industrial R&D and the remainder is shared across 34 other industries. The pharmaceuticals industry is the single largest R&D spender, accounting for over a quarter of the R&D expenditure, followed by the automobile industry.

Figure 4.7. Ratio of Patents Sealed in India by Foreigners and Indians

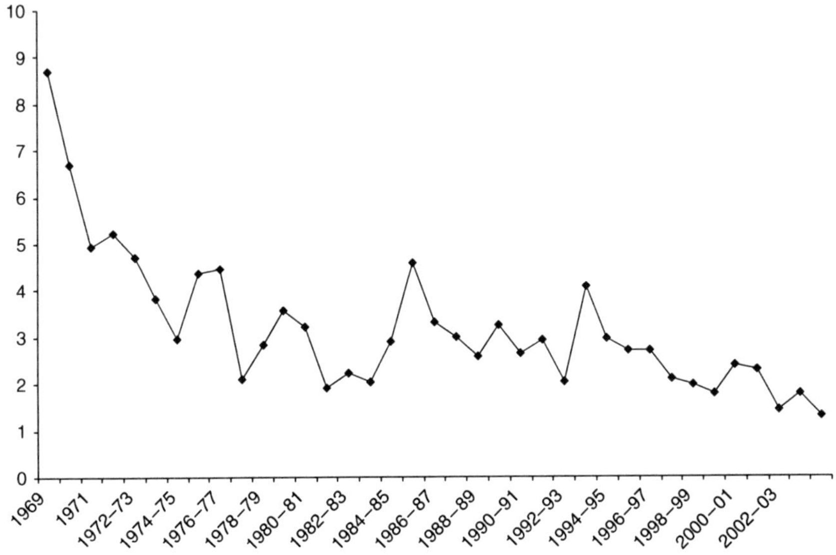

Source: Department of Science and Technology, Government of India, R&D Statistics, different years.

India's poor performance on the R&D front becomes highly revealing when compared with that of other countries. Figure 4.6 shows the percentage change in R&D intensity in India compared with selected countries broadly during the two periods under consideration. It indicates that during the seventies the country's overall R&D expenditure kept pace with the growth in the other countries. To be more specific, from 1973 to 1982 R&D intensity (R&D expenditure as a proportion of GNP) in India increased by 0.4 percentage points. Of the countries listed in the table – mostly developed and some developing – only Brazil recorded a better performance than India and only the Federal Republic of Germany kept pace with India. When it came to the second phase, the increase recorded in India was negligible (0.01 per cent) and most of the countries on the list recorded a much better performance than India.

As already mentioned, as early as in the 1970s India devised its own patent law to promote domestic innovative activity. In tune with globalisation and under the influence of the WTO, India moved towards a liberal copyright system. While it is true that the post-1970 period witnessed a decline or stagnation in the number of patent applications and the number of patents sealed in India, the process patenting mechanism led to a substantial increase in adaptive research, even by small and medium-sized enterprises, and proved especially effective for the development of industries like pharmaceuticals. More importantly, there has been an increasing incidence of patenting by Indians, as is evident from the drastic decline in the ratio of patents registered by foreigners compared with Indians (Figure 4.7). It has also been shown that there has been a dramatic increase in the number of US patents lodged by Indians since the 1990s and the observed increase has been at a higher rate than for China (Mani, 2008).

3.2 Technological Capacity-Building: Selected Micro-Level Experience

Experience with collaboration and in-house technological activity undertaken during liberalisation has been mixed. On the positive side, there is the experience of selected industries like pharmaceuticals and the automobile industry where substantial capacity was built. These two sectors benefited substantively from (a) the hold put on external liberalisation and (b) the government support given for in-house technological activity during this phase of internal liberalisation. There is also further evidence that all those domestic firms which did significantly better in terms of their technological performance were not under the control of big businesses.

In the case of pharmaceuticals, many of the technologically dynamic units were started on the initiative of technical entrepreneurs. They actively used the publicly funded R&D to obtain process know-how for the drugs reserved by the government for their benefit. They also consolidated their businesses with the help of protection and promotion made available by the government. The 1978 drug policy also played a role. Key markets were reserved for domestic firms with entry by foreign firms completely prohibited. In a way it would not be wrong to state that the emergence and consolidation of these firms is a result of the support that they received from the State during the internal liberalisation phase in the form of protection by the patent legislation, sectoral reservation, price regulation protection, supply of talent developed within the public sector and publicly funded R&D support (Abrol, 1994). Several Indian pharmaceutical companies have been able to build substantial process development capability. Because of this India has emerged as the world's most competitive supplier of a large number of life-saving generic drugs. Nearly a third of India's production of pharmaceuticals is exported. Nearly all the export effort is undertaken by domestic enterprises which have built up their own technological and industrial capability, brand names and overseas presence in several countries. India now has the highest number of US FDA-approved pharmaceutical plants (77) outside the USA. Indian companies are now moving up the value chain by innovating in new drug delivery systems and molecules. Besides their own investments and joint ventures, Indian companies are also acquiring companies abroad to gain access to marketing channels and boost their local presence (Aggarwal, 2007 among others).

Although experience in the automobile industry during the 1980s was not as impressive as in the pharmaceuticals industry, there was a considerable increase in internal competition as a result of broad banding and calibrated foreign collaboration in the passenger cars, commercial vehicles and two-wheeler segments and the introduction of products that, even today, are considered technologically "superior" within the market. In this sector, smaller firms' practice in respect of technology imports differed from the practice of big firms in that they used essentially technical collaboration to upgrade technologically (Abrol, 2006). Out of the total of 182 foreign collaborations approved for the automobile sector during the period 1982–91, as reported by Narayana and Joseph (1993), roughly 20 per cent were financial, 70 per cent purely technical and 10 per cent design and drawing agreements. The total number of collaborations was 32 for the vehicles sector and 150 for components. Entry of domestic firms in the automobile components sector was strengthened by the establishment of joint ventures (JVs) with Japanese original equipment manufacturers (OEMs) – referred to as the "Japanisation" phase (ACMA & SIAM, 2003). In the car segment the Government of India–Suzuki JV, Maruti Udyog Limited (MUL) was also set up. These initiatives laid the foundations for the better performance observed in the 1990s and thereafter. Tata Motors, for example, put a small pick-up truck based on indigenous know-how on the European market in the mid-1990s. Later it put on the market its Sumo and Safari sports utility vehicles. In the late 1990s it started producing its own small passenger car, Indica, followed by the middle-sized Indigo. Tata is among the very few new entrants into the passenger cars market in the world on the basis of indigenous know-how over the last few decades. Recently Tata Motors came up with the world's cheapest car designed in-house. It recently acquired Daewoo Trucks to complement its range of heavier commercial vehicles. Another firm, Mahindra & Mahindra, can report similar credentials (Singh, 2007).

In the electronics industry, although the growth record during the 1980s was impressive, there was an unprecedented shift in the product structure. The growth became concentrated in sectors with higher linkages to imports, whereas sectors with higher linkages to value added and employment lagged behind in output growth. The component sector remained marked by lack of investment coupled with the low scale of its operations and under-utilisation of capacity. By the end of the 1980s the share of the semiconductor industry in total electronics investment in India was around 10 per cent, as compared with figures of 30 to 35 per cent in the developed countries. There was a marked increase in the share of electronic consumer products at the expense of electronic intermediates and electronic capital goods (Joseph, 1987). However, such high growth could not be sustained and the growth decelerated in the 1990s and beyond (Joseph, 2007).

The situation in the capital goods industry, where the public sector was active, became desperate quite early during this period (Jacobbson & Alam, 1994). Despite the new investments, capacity was under-used as the orders were being placed with foreign suppliers. The first casualties were power equipment and machine building for the fertiliser industry. This had an adverse effect on the viability of units in the capital goods sector, including leading public sector units like Bharat Heavy Plates and Vessels (BHPV) and Bharat Heavy Electrical Equipment (BHEL). The co-existence of under-utilised capacity in the capital goods industry alongside utilisation of imported equipment was even affecting design, engineering and consultancy firms. For example, Project Planning and Development India Limited, the premier fertiliser consultancy firm with capacity to design two fertiliser factories per year, had work for only one factory in 1987, with nothing more in the pipeline (Abrol, 1995).

During the external liberalisation period a few other sectors, such as the performance in software and IT-enabled service exports, attracted worldwide attention. The recorded annual compound growth rate was over 50 per cent in the 1990s and has been 38 per cent since 1997–98, a record unprecedented in independent India. The value of output from India's software and services sector increased from less than US$0.83 billion in 1994–95 to US$36.3 billion in 2005–06 (NASSCOM, 2006). Software and services now account for over 20 per cent of merchandise exports, even higher than textiles and textile products, one of India's principal export commodities (Chandrasekhar et al., 2006). Needless to say, this remarkable export performance has attracted the attention of researchers and is well documented (Kumar, 2001; Arora et al., 2001; Joseph, 2002; Kumar and Joseph, 2005 to name just a few). However, the excessive export orientation has also been shown to have had an adverse effect on innovation activity in the industry (Parthasarathi and Joseph, 2002). Also the boom in the IT sector has been shown to have had an adverse effect on other sectors competing for skilled manpower because of the resource movement effect (Joseph and Harilal, 2001).

While a few sectors recorded remarkable performance, other important sectors like capital goods had a different experience. In the capital goods sector, the growth rate contracted from 15.24 per cent for 1985–91 to 5.27 per cent over 1991–97. Imports rose phenomenally faster during the period 1991–96 than over the period 1980–91. Since the mid-1990s, liberalisation measures like a reduction in tariff rates and liberal imports of second-hand machinery have had a serious adverse impact on the health of the machine-building industry. Imports rose even faster during 1991–96 than in the period 1980–91. While the related figure for imports was 21 per cent, exports' share remained at 6 per cent. There was a large inflow of foreign technologies into the capital goods sector during 1991–97. The share of non-electrical machinery in the value of output from registered manufacturing increased somewhat under the controlled liberalisation during the eighties but then decreased in the 1990s. In 1997–98 the share of non-electrical machinery (at 1993–94 prices) was 4.8 per cent – the same as in 1965–66 (Suresh, 2007).

As regards overall productivity and efficiency under economic liberalisation, Siddarthan (2004) reports that total factor productivity (TFP) growth in the 1990s was lower than in the 1980s. Similar results were reported by Balakrishnan et al. (2000). Siddarthan (2004) also concluded that: (a) the main gainers have been multinational enterprises (MNEs) and their affiliates which have better access to technology and other intangible assets; (b) in the case of domestic firms those which have adopted a strategy of relying on the non-equity route for technology imports as against royalty payments alone are reported to have done well; and (c) the other domestic firms that have no networking or non-equity strategic alliances have not done well. Furthermore, domestic firms did well under liberalisation only if their technology and productivity gap was small in relation to MNEs.

The accumulated evidence discussed above suggests that foreign technology licensors do not want domestic firms to become competitors by providing disembodied technology in high- and medium-tech sectors. Domestic firms are unable to catch up with their foreign competitors via the existing route[3]. Technological change is understood in the developing countries in terms of the combined effect of in-house R&D and technology imports, which implies looking into the practice of large private-sector firms for technology take-up and in-house R&D. Once again the evidence is not very encouraging. See Basant and Chandra (INTECH, 1999) for an analysis of the recent record of India's private sector on technological innovation in the form of case studies, which clearly confirms the continuing inadequacy of investment in the manufacturing and quality systems. Sectoral studies have confirmed the same passive tendency in respect of technology take-up in various sectors. In the case of the Indian basic chemicals industry this was confirmed by Narayanan (2004), who provided evidence not only that more than half of the firms in the basic chemicals industry are passive but also that higher vertical integration had a negative impact on technology investment. He also provided evidence that even in the post-liberalisation period the medium-sized firms in the Indian basic chemicals industry have been investing relatively (to their size) more on R&D than both larger and smaller firms.

3.3 *Influence on Publicly Funded S&T Institutions*

Publicly funded R&D institutions continue to account for the bulk of R&D expenditure in India, with industry funding only 28 per cent of national R&D. The decline in the proportion of national R&D expenditure was mainly due to the budgetary squeeze. Even the rate of growth of R&D expenditure in industry declined in the 1990s compared with the 1980s. In the 1990s R&D expenditure fell in 12 out of 28 broad industries and even where it rose the R&D to sales ratios stagnated or declined.

Policymakers tried to achieve a paradigm shift in the goals of civilian public-sector research to make the system market-friendly. This restructuring is vividly illustrated by the example of the Council of Scientific and Industrial Research (CSIR) – the largest civilian R&D agency in India. The goals set for 2001 were: to move towards self-financing by raising over 7 billion rupees from external sources, as against 1.35 billion rupees in 1994–95, of which at least 50 per cent was to be from industrial customers (up from 15 per cent in 1994–95); to develop at least ten exclusive and globally competitive technologies in niche areas; to hold a patent bank of 500 foreign patents (up from 50); to cover 10 per cent of operational expenditure from intellectual property licensing (up from < 1 per cent); and to derive annual earnings of US$40 million from overseas R&D work and services (up from < US$2 million).

Over two thirds of the CSIR's income continues to come from budgetary support. External cash flows continue to account for only about one fifth and this has remained more or less around the same level over the last decade and a half. The government (budgetary support plus contract revenue from government agencies as grants-in-aid) continues to be the main source of finance, accounting for over 80 per cent. The resources generated from industry continue to make up

Figure 4.8. The "Big Five" CSIR Laboratories Based on Patents Filed and Granted Abroad During the Period 1999–2002

CSIR Laboratories	Filed 1999–2000	Granted 1999–2000	Filed 2000–01	Granted 2000–01	Filed 2001–02	Granted 2001–02
CIMAP	68	1	38	7	31	25
IICT	32	6	72	4	92	17
NCL	18	12	63	16	43	16
CDRI	16	0	8	6	27	6
IICB	3	1	18	0	9	5
Total CSIR	199	35	452	56	580	86

Source: IPMD and CSIR.

Figure 4.9. Poor CSIR Performers for Patents Granted Abroad from 1999 to 2002

Laboratory	Granted 1999–2000	Granted 2000–2001	Granted 2001–2002
CBRI	0	0	0
CCMB	0	1	0
CEERI	0	0	1
CMRI	0	1	0
CSIO	0	0	0
CSMCRI	0	0	0
IMT	0	1	0
NAL	0	0	0
NBRI	0	0	1
NGRI	0	0	0
NIO	0	0	0
NML	0	0	0
RRL (BHU)	0	0	0
RRL (BHO)	0	0	0
RRL (JM)	0	0	0

Source: IPMD and CSIR.

about 25 per cent of the external resources (or about 6 per cent of the total receipts) and that too has shown little variation over the years. Foreign earnings turn out to be not more than 1.7 per cent.

Vision 2001 envisaged that the CSIR would hold a valuable portfolio of at least 1000 Indian patents and 500 foreign patents. It is well known that the propensity to patent also differs considerably between R&D organisations and inventors. However, the policymakers insisted on measuring the CSIR as a whole by patenting activity. The CSIR has successfully secured 591 Indian patents and 101 foreign ones (CSIR, 2001). The available evidence also tells that many of them are accounted for by a select set of five laboratories.

However, another equally important fact is that provisional figures from the CSIR indicate, by its own admission, that in the last five years only 4 per cent of the patents in force have been licensed. This achievement must be compared with the target of raising 10 per cent of the operational expenditure of the CSIR from intellectual property (Abrol, 2004).

This record of failure of the CSIR 2001 Vision and Strategy is yet another fact of the liberalisation period. The strategy contained a whole range of misapplied targets, to which the CSIR system could not be expected to respond favourably. The Vision and Strategy talked of globalising the CSIR system, making it a global platform for R&D. It said "patent or perish", when for several parts of the system this was a misapplied target. It put too much faith in market forces, but there was very little favourable response.

The primary function of the CSIR is to undertake R&D directed towards continuous improvement of indigenous technology and adaptation and development of imported technology. But during this period this primary function failed to receive the support of the CSIR. Out of the 984 technologies developed by 23 laboratories/institutes it has been found that 607, including 247 developed before 1996–97, have yet to be transferred (CAG, 2003). It was also found that these laboratories were unable to supply specific information on the actual expenditure on the development of technologies. Reasons for this non-transfer of 246 developed technologies showed that 77 were found unfit for transfer, while 87 required further improvement/development. In 82 cases, including 34 developed prior to 1999–2000, transfer negotiations were under way. The CSIR suffered losses of 99,310,000 rupees due to violation of its guidelines on technology transfer. Royalties/premiums totalling 134,580,000 rupees remained uncollected in 17 cases of technology transfer.

During this period the CSIR management also proceeded gradually to withdraw from the societal missions, where the strengths of the CSIR system were highly applicable. During the nineties the channels created during the eighties for all the efforts that the CSIR had initiated on a series of technology missions to reposition the agency with the objective of developing technologies for societal missions and rural industrialisation were dismantled. In 2000, the management even closed down the Societal and Technology Missions Division (STMD), a focal point set up to coordinate this work in the CSIR.

3.4 Opening-up of the National S&T System to MNEs

The national S&T policy was radically revised to open up the publicly funded research and development (R&D) structures to foreign companies by means of contract work. The current policy is to permit foreign companies freely to set up R&D facilities and venture capital funds in the country. All of these have a totally new set of strategic implications for the processes for integration of research and development (R&D) in industry[4]. Today foreign companies appear better placed than national companies in terms of access to S&T infrastructure. In fact, the country has been induced to open up the national laboratories to foreign companies for contract research in the fields of greatest interest to Indian companies.

The emerging trend towards deployment of the national scientific and technological capability by multinational enterprises or corporations (MNEs), which have been able to develop global intra-corporate networked innovation systems, is unlikely to lead to any major spillover by itself as the policies are not yet designed to harness such opportunities. More importantly, the interactions between academia at large and public laboratories in particular with industry that played an important role in the innovation process in developed countries have yet to take firm root in India. In this context, currently participation by India in R&D networking is likely to work in favour of foreign companies on account of their access to India's cheap but highly qualified S&T manpower that was built up over the years at substantial cost to a poor society.

3.5 Impact on Human Resource Development

For balanced development of the national innovation system, for a country like India it is critical that the support provided by the government to universities and technical institutions does not suffer due to financial constraints[5]. Most students enrolled in higher education are pursuing traditional programmes of studies, i.e. arts, humanities, social sciences and commerce, which in fact cost less than science, engineering or programmes directed towards the professions. There has been a tangible shift in demand and supply towards revenue-generating courses and short-duration education and crash courses. The budgets for libraries, laboratories and similar facilities remain severely affected.

Over the last decade, with the emphasis on deregulated privatisation of higher education, the problem of proliferation of sub-standard institutions has also been on the rise. There has been a mushrooming of "self-financing" engineering, management, medical and other professional institutions that operate on the principle that they have to finance themselves by generating revenue from student fees and service sales. Now there is pressure to extend the market mechanism to public-sector higher education (HE) in India as a means of increasing "efficiency". To reform the HE sector, the government is forcing these institutions to use funds and management expertise from private sources. HE institutions are encouraging their own faculties to make increased use of private funds to start new courses that are already of marketable value. There is a need for an urgent review of all these policy steps with a view to halting any further deterioration in the higher education sector.

The availability of manpower capable of taking up R&D has been declining and this must be linked to the increased demand for manpower from IT and related sectors in response to growing export demand (Joseph and Harilal, 2003).

Apart from viable financial support, the most critical input for R&D is manpower. While India has a strong pool of S&T personnel numbering over 6.3 million, the number of scientists actually engaged in R&D is only about 150,000. A clear drop in enrolment in basic sciences can be seen. The percentage of students taking up basic science courses declined from 30 per cent to 19.6 per cent in a matter of three decades. In post-graduate education and research in engineering and technology the situation is equally worrying. The average turnout of Master's degree-holders in engineering and technology is only around 5,000 per year against capacity of more than 15,000. The hype and lopsided emphasis on information technology and biotechnology have in turn contributed to the problem of achieving balanced development of human resources. The end-result of these policies is that even the drug and pharmaceutical firms which want to employ hundreds of PhDs are now facing extreme shortages of the manpower they need.

4. Conclusions

Against the backdrop of the leading role which India has given to development of science and technology as an instrument of socio-economic change, this paper has attempted to highlight various policy measures and institutional action taken over the years to achieve this goal. It looked at the changing focus of policies and strategies and their implications for innovation performance at both macro and micro levels. The paper identified two policy phases – the first phase advocating technological self-reliance with restrictions on technology imports and the second focusing initially on internal liberalisation and later extended to external liberalisation taking a very liberal approach to technology imports.

Drawing on the available evidence, this paper argues that the policy during the first phase successfully accomplished the objective of technological self-reliance and lower external dependence. While the achievements in terms of growth in output and productivity were far below the potential, the restrictive phase was effective in laying the foundations for future developments that enabled industry to withstand the competition from the global market in the globalisation phase. When it comes to the performance during the second phase the paper also paints a mixed picture and raises certain concerns. Along with better overall economic performance, some knowledge-intensive sectors like information technology have recorded remarkable performance. What is more, in some of these sectors, even though all the leading global firms are present, the domestic firms continue to hold the leading position. However, the national innovation effort, in terms of R&D expenditure as a proportion of GDP or R&D intensity at manufacturing level, has taken a back seat. R&D intensity, both at national level and for manufacturing as a whole, has not shown an upward trend but has either declined or stagnated, raising serious concerns about India's ability to sustain the current performance. The concern heightens when certain developments in human resource development and R&D outsourcing are considered, along with the growing neglect of national R&D infrastructure. Increased entry of the private sector into the field of education has brought with it a deterioration in the quality of manpower – an issue that needs urgent attention. While participation by Indian companies, especially the public-sector laboratories, in the global R&D networks has been growing, there have been hardly any policy initiatives to reap the spill over benefits from such participation. Without new initiatives to address these issues and challenges, India will be unlikely to be able to sustain its performance and make the development process more inclusive.

References

Abrol, D., 2006. "The challenge of transformation of Indian system(s) of innovation" in the International Conference on Innovation Systems for Competitiveness and Shared Prosperity in Developing Countries, GLOBELICS 2006 Trivandrum, Kerala, India, 4–7 October 2006.

Abrol, D., 2004. "Dynamics of innovation systems amidst neo-liberal globalisation: Lessons from India" in the 2nd Globelics Conference on Innovation Systems and Development: Emerging Opportunities and Challenges, Globelics & Tsighua University, Beijing, China, 30 September 2004.

Abrol, D., 2000. Science and Technology in *The Indian Economy 1999–2000: An Alternative Survey*, 81–87, New Delhi, November 2000.

Abrol, D., 1999. Readjusting S&T Policy in *The Indian Economy 1998–99: An Alternative Economic Survey*, 183–190, New Delhi, September 1999.

Abrol, D., 1994. Technology & WTO in *New Economic Policy (NEP) and Indian People* based on Proceedings of the National Seminar on NEP, Jan Vigyan Vedika, Indian Institute of Chemical Technology, Hyderabad, August 1994.

Abrol, D., 1994. Intellectual Property Rights in the Uruguay Round Negotiations: A Review of the Indian Debate in *Intellectual Property Rights* edited by K. R. G. Nair and Ashok Kumar, Allied Publishers, New Delhi, May 1994.

Acma & Siam, 2003. "Competitiveness of Indian automotive components industry, Delhi; A study commissioned by ACMA and SIAM" prepared by ICRA advisory services.

Aggarwal, A., 2004. Technology policies and acquisition of technological capabilities in the industrial sector: A comparative analysis of Indian and Korean experiences, Science, Technology and Society, 6(2).

Aggarwal, A., 2007. Pharmaceutical Industry, in Kumar, N. and Joseph, K. J. (Eds), *International Competitiveness & Knowledge-based industries in India*, Oxford University Press, New Delhi.

Arora, A., Arunachalam, V. S., Asundi, J., Ronald, F., 2001. The Indian software services industry, *Research Policy*, Vol. 30(3), 1267–1287.

Balakrishnan, P., Pushpangadan, K., Babu, M. S., 2000. Trade liberalisation and productivity growth in manufacturing: evidence from firm level panel data, *Economic and Political Weekly* 35 (10), 3679–3682.

Basant, R., 2000. Corporate response to Economic Reforms, *Economic and Political Weekly*, Vol. XXXV, No 10.

Basant, R., Chandra, P., 1999. Building technological capabilities in a liberalising developing economy: Firm strategies and public policy, INTECH, the UNU, 1999.

Beena, P. L., 2004. Towards understanding the merger wave in the Indian corporate sector: A comparative perspective, CDS Working Paper No 355.

Chadha, V., 2007. "An Assessment of the Regional R&D Effort in India: An Inter-State Analysis of some Selected Industrially Advanced States", seminar paper presented at Globelics India 2006, Trivandrum, available at: http://www.globelicsindia2006.org/Vikram%20Chadha.pdf, accessed on 13 May 2008.

Chandrasekhar, C. P., Jayati, G., Anamitra, R., 2007. The demographic dividend and young India's economic future, *Economic and Political Weekly*, Vol. 41, No 49, 5055–5064.

Comptroller and Auditor-General Of India, 2003. CAG, Report No 5 of 2003, Government of India, New Delhi.

Desai, Ashok, V., 1980. The origin and direction of industrial R&D in India, *Research Policy*, 9: 74–96.

Evenson, R. E., Joseph, K. J., 1999. Foreign technology licensing in Indian industry: an econometric analysis of the choice of pattern, terms of contract and the effect on licensees' performance, *Economic and Political Weekly*, Vol. 34, No 27, 3 July.

Gupta, A., Dutta, P. K., 2005. Indian innovation system: Perspective and challenges, *Technology Exports*, Vol. 4, April–June.

Institute of Applied Manpower Research (different years) "Manpower Profile India", New Delhi.

Jacobsson, S., Alam, G., 1994. Liberalisation and industrial development in the Third World: A study of Government policy and performance of the Indian and Korean engineering industries, Sage Publications, New Delhi.

Joseph, K. J., 1997. *Industry under Economic Liberalisation: The case of Indian electronics*, Sage publications, New Delhi, Thousand Oaks, London.

Joseph, K. J., 2002. "Growth of ICT and ICT for Development: Realities of the Myths of Indian Experience", discussion paper No 2002/78, Helsinki: UNU/WIDER.

Joseph, K. J., 2007. Electronics industry. In Kumar, N., Joseph, K. J., *International Competitiveness & Knowledge-based Industries in India*, Oxford University Press, New Delhi.

Joseph, K. J., Harilal, K. N., 2003. Structure and growth of India's IT exports: Implications of an export-oriented growth strategy, *Economic and Political Weekly*, Vol. 36 (34): 3263–70.

Kidron, M., 1965. *Foreign Investment in India*, Oxford University Press, London.

Kumar, N., 1987. Technology policy in India, An overview of its evolution and an assessment. In Brahmananda, P. R., Panchamukhi, V. R., (Eds), *The development process of the Indian economy*, Himalaya Publishing House, New Delhi.

Kumar, N., 2000. Multinational enterprises and M&As in India: Patterns and implications, *Economic and Political Weekly*, Vol. XXXV, No 32.

Kumar, N., 2001. Indian Software Industry Development: International and National Perspective, *Economic and Political Weekly*, 36(45):4278–4290.

Kumar, N., Joseph, K. J., 2005. Export of Software and Business Process Outsourcing from Developing Countries: Lessons from India, *Asia Pacific Trade and Investment Review* 1(1): 91–108.

Mani, S., 2002. Government, innovation and technology policy: An international comparative analysis, Edward Elgar Publications, Cheltenham.

Mani, S., 2008. "Performance of India's Innovation System", paper presented at the workshop on India's innovation system, IIM Ahmedabad, 3–4 January 2008.

Mowery, D. C., 1994. Science and technology policy in interdependent economies, Kluwer Academics, Boston.

Naik, S., 2006. "Regional determinants of FDI: A study of Indian states under liberalisation", Unpublished MPhil dissertation, CDS, Jawaharlal Nehru University, New Delhi.

Narayana, D., Joseph, K. J., 1993. Industry and trade liberalisation; Performance of motor vehicles and automotive industries, 1981–91. In *Economic and Political Weekly*, 28 (8 and 9): M13–20.

Narayanan, K., 2004. Technology acquisition and growth of firms: Indian automobile sector under changing policy regimes. In *Economic and Political Weekly*, 39(5): 460–471.

Nasscom, 2006. *The IT Software and Services Industry in India: Strategic Review 2006*. New Delhi: National Association of Software and Service Companies.

Suresh, P., 2007. Non-electrical machinery industry. In Kumar, N. and Joseph, K. J. (Eds), *International Competitiveness & Knowledge-based Industries in India*, Oxford University Press, New Delhi.

Parthasarthi, A., 1987. Acquisition and Development of Technology, *Economic and Political Weekly*, 28 November, M131–M138.

Parthasarthi, A., 2007. Technology at the core: Science and Technology with Indira Gandhi, Pearson Education, New Delhi.

Parthasarthi, A., Joseph, K. J., 2002. Limits to innovation with strong export orientation: The case of the Indian information communication technology sector, *Science, Technology and Society*, 7(1).

Patel, S., 1993. *Technological self-reliance in India*, Ashish Publications, New Delhi.

Richardson, P., 2002. *New science, technology and innovation development in India*, European Commission Directorate-General for Research, Brussels.

Siddharthan, 2004. Globalisation: Productivity, Efficiency and Growth, Special Number on Industry and Management, 1, 31, *Economic and Political Weekly*, Mumbai.

Singh, N., 2007. Automotive Industry. In Kumar, N. and Joseph, K. J. (Eds), *International Competitiveness & Knowledge-based industries in India*, Oxford University Press, New Delhi.

Subrahmanian, K. K., 1987. Towards technological self-reliance: An assessment of Indian strategy and achievement in industry. In Brahmananda, P. R., Panchamukhi, V. R. (Eds), *The development process of the Indian economy*, Himalaya Publishing House, New Delhi.

Subrahmanian, K. K., 1991. Technological Capability under Economic Liberalism: Experience of Indian Industry in the Eighties. *Economic and Political Weekly*, 31 August, M87–89.

Chapter 5

SCIENCE AND TECHNOLOGY AND INNOVATION POLICY IN CHINA

Xielin LIU and Jianbing LIU

1. Introduction

Science and technology (S&T) and innovation have been a strong force in Chinese economic growth. They are expected to play a more important role on the road to building a prosperous society according to the National Plan 2006–2020 for the Development of Science and Technology in the medium and long term.

S&T and innovation policy has been playing a key role in enabling China to catch up and move forward to become an innovative country. But in past decades, China had a different strategy for policy making and adopted a variety of policy tools. Some policies had a great impact on economic growth, some did not. As China has achieved double-digit economic growth for more than ten years, some would like to ascertain the role played by S&T and innovation policy in this long period of growth. The purpose of the paper is to analyse the origins and development of science, technology and innovation policy in China since 1978 and the challenges ahead.

Science policy is about how to promote science in a country. It was given the status of a special policy by Bernal in 1939 (Bernal, 1939). Later on, Vannevar Bush further clarified the role of science in the famous report Science: The endless frontier. According to Bush, the purpose of science policy is to contribute to national security, health and economic growth (Bush, 1945).

But these earlier views of science policy comprised a very strong element of the linear innovation model, which assumed that curiosity-driven scientific research would directly lead to innovation. Later on, the market-pull innovation approach was turned to, while governments in various countries started to spend more and more money on science. However, some authors also draw attention to the fact that political and commercial factors might restrain the freedom of science both in the direction it takes and in its size (Rip & van der Meulen, 1997; Jasanoff, 1997).

Technology policy is related to the development and acquisition of technology. It came to the fore when nuclear technology, space, computer technology, etc. were considered to be the most important factors for a country's security and economic growth. Those technologies were for a long time regarded as the strategic technologies.

Innovation policy is a relatively new policy area. In 1982, the OECD (1982) published a report entitled Innovation Policy. The goal of innovation policy, as it is described, is to promote the commercialisation of new knowledge (OECD, 1982, 1999, 2005). It regards innovation policy as the integration of science and technology policy and industrial policy (Rothwell, 1982).

In this chapter we show that, as a transition country, China has adopted a supply-side as well as a demand-side policy. China has opened to the world and so adopted policies that fit with WTO rules. But, at the same time, some conflicts are inevitable. Decentralisation also helps China to embark on a more innovative path as it stimulates different layers of government to innovate. However, this also widens the regional gap.

The chapter is structured as follows: section two describes the institutional context of policy making in China. Section three reviews S&T and innovation policy over the last thirty years. Section four discusses current policy in China and looks at the challenges ahead.

2. Institutional Context of S&T and Innovation Policy in China

Basically, for S&T and innovation policy to be effective in promoting economic development, there are three dimensions that need to be appropriately addressed:

- Supply vs demand side. The developing countries usually prefer to use supply-side policy to promote S&T development as well as economic development. In China as well as in Russia, government research institutes took a great deal of responsibility for R&D in the planned economy, so, by tradition, there are more policies on the supply side. Now China is going to make greater use of demand-side policy to promote innovation.
- Domestic vs global. In a global world, many policies that promote domestic companies have been under debate. The issue is whether a national innovation system is meaningful in a global world. If so, then indigenous policy making is appropriate. But then, how those domestic policies can fit with the WTO rules is a big question.

Figure 5.1. Chinese Innovation System in the Planned Economy

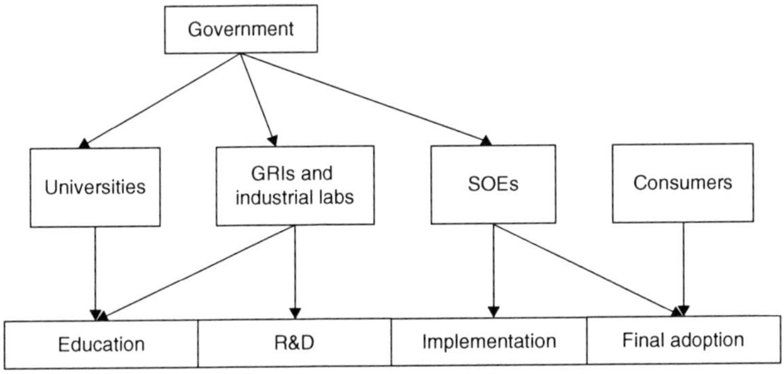

Source: Adapted from Xielin Liu & Steven White (2001), Comparing innovation systems: a framework and application to China's transitional context, *Research Policy* 30 (2001), p. 1094.

- Centralisation vs decentralisation. For a transition economy, the national plan is still the key for government to control and coordinate the economy. For example, the National Plan 2006–2020 for the Development of Science and Technology in the medium and long term in China introduced many new S&T and innovation policies. On the other hand, China has also opted for decentralisation to give local regions more freedom to innovate.

In this section, we will try to analyse the policy evolution in China from these three angles.

China is known as a transition country. It replicated many of the institutions of the former Soviet Union. So, in the BRICS context, China is more similar to Russia than the other three countries. In the era of the planned economy, the business sector was very weak in terms of innovation. Usually it did not perform any R&D. The government would tell firms when, where and how to introduce new technology. The main economic tools used by government were the five-year and annual economic and S&T plans. The main institutions were government research institutions. Even at government level, there was a carefully worked out division of labour. For example, the State Planning Committee (now the National Development and Reform Commission) was central in allocating production targets for enterprises and also had the powers and obligations to introduce new technologies into the economic system. The Ministry of Science and Technology would draw up five-year and annual plans in the area of science and technology (Figure 5.1).

But, overall, the whole system was less than efficient. Enterprises were output-based, with few if any incentives for efficiency and profit, and paid no attention to IPR. The research institutions and universities were funded by government and typically produced project reports with limited industrial use. The performance of innovation at that time was therefore poor, although reverse engineering made a great impact in some sectors. Many new industries started around the same year as Korea initiated her new growth path, such as the automobile industry, ICT industry and steel industry, but lagged decades behind Korea. "Import, lag behind, import again, lag behind once more" was the pattern in that period.

Since 1978, China has been going through a long transition period towards a market-based S&T system. Several major transformations relevant for S&T and innovation policy have taken place. First, the market has become the main force behind the innovation system. Second, the system centred on the state-owned company (SOE) has evolved into a triad company system (that is, SOEs, foreign related companies and private companies). Third, a general opening to the world, especially after WTO membership, has become a reality. Fourth, decentralisation has been introduced, allowing regional governments more autonomy to introduce innovation.

Before 1980, China had only a science and technology policy and no innovation policy. The traditional science and technology system was notable for the separation of science, technology and industrial development. It was copied from the Soviet Union and widely adopted in the planned economy. When China began to introduce the market economy and made economic growth the top priority, the previous S&T system faced a difficult situation. In 1985, the government started transforming the S&T system with the aim of breaking down the barrier between the S&T and economic systems. Innovation policy has emerged in China since that time.

After 1978 the so-called "market for technology" policy was widely used to press foreign companies to transfer technology to local companies. One of the results of this policy was that joint ventures became the main route for foreign companies to enter China. In recent years, there has been increasing criticism of this policy. Some researchers argue that joint ventures have led to little knowledge and technology spill-overs from foreign enterprises. Instead, Chinese companies have lost their original technology capability after being in joint ventures.

From the 1980s onwards, great efforts have been made to push firms to become the main players in the national innovation system. Under the National Plan 2006–2020 for the Development of Science and Technology in the medium and long term, China's current long-term S&T policy framework, the aim is to become "independent" and promote "indigenous" innovation. These two features have been put forward as the most important aspects of ST&I policy.

The Chinese economy is a mixed economy. Governments, both central and local, have strong influence on economic activity. To this day, the governments at different levels still control the land, large investment projects, infrastructure construction, market access for important industries such as automobiles, the financial markets. The same holds true in ST&I. By using the national R&D programme, policy and five-year plan or long-range plans and other policy tools, the government has a strong impact.

In China, many ministries have power over policy making related to S&T and innovation (ST&I). In terms of science policy, the main policy makers are the Ministry of S&T (MOST) and the Ministry of Education (MOE). As for technology policy, the Ministry of Commerce (MOC) and the National Development and Reform Commission (NDRC) can have a very large impact. Other ministries with responsibility for health, defence and security, energy, transportation, etc. also have a role in shaping ST&I policy.

The national programme is one of the very important policy tools in China, not just for reasons of funding. In China, the main contractors for the government programme are universities and government research institutes (GRIs). In addition, other regional and industrial funds quite often have their own regional projects.

3. S&T and Innovation Policy in China

3.1 Science Policy

In China, there is little scope for curiosity-driven research. S&T has generally been viewed as a practical economic activity (Hu, 2005). Most Chinese cannot distinguish between sciences and technology. Although the share of the R&D budget and human resources for basic research is increasing gradually, it is still quite low compared to developed countries. Even now, the proportion of basic research has been kept to a relatively low level of 5–6 per cent of total R&D expenditure. In addition, most of the government funds for basic research are targeted at limited areas such as biology and nanotechnology with a strong practical purpose (Hu, 2005).

Before the 1980s, the major actors in basic research were the government research institutes (GRIs). From the 1980s onwards, universities became more and more important. There are two important organisations supporting science research in China: the National Science Foundation and the Department of Basic Research within the MOST. Most regions have their own regional science foundation system, but their functions are more practical and geared to local economic and social needs.

3.1.1 Actors in Scientific Research

Before 1980, the GRIs were the main players in the S&T system. From the 1950s to the 1980s, China established different layers of GRIs with various missions. At national level, the most important GRI was the Chinese Academy

Figure 5.2. Structure of China's R&D Expenditure in 2005 (Unit: %)

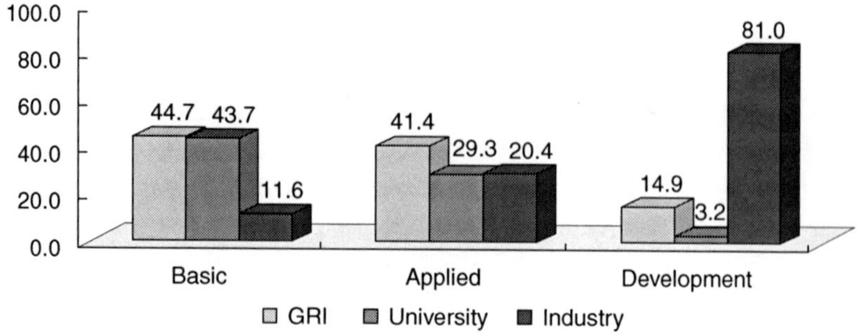

Source: MOST. Chinese science and technology statistics, 2006. http://www.sts.org.cn/

of Sciences (CAS), focusing mainly on basic research. There were also hundreds of industrial research institutes under a wide range of industrial ministries, mainly focusing on applied science and experimental development. Regional GRIs would carry out research and development work according to the needs determined at regional level (Commission of S&T, 1986).

At that time, enterprises were no more than manufacturing plants. Most of them did not perform any R&D. Only some large state-owned enterprises had their own R&D labs, but their work mainly focused on experimental issues (Liu & White, 2002).

Most of the universities were not involved in research either, except a few research universities such as Tsinghua University and Peking University. Many were specialised universities (such as the university of light industry, of metallurgy, of printing, etc.) focusing on industry-specific technology.

Following the dramatic reform of the S&T system, most GRIs have been transformed into enterprises. Universities have been given a much more important role in science. In 2003, the share of universities in the big three foundations, that is, the National Science Foundation of China, the National Basic Research Programme ("973" Programme) and the National Laboratories for Basic Research, was respectively about 67 per cent, 47 per cent and 56.79 per cent. In 2005, the share of basic research performed by GRIs, universities and industry was 44.7 per cent, 43.7 per cent and 11.6 per cent respectively (Figure 5.2). This confirms that universities are nowadays a very important actor in terms of basic research.

3.1.2 National Programmes

The National Science Foundation of China (NSFC) plays a unique role in the Chinese science system. For a long time, there was no special fund for basic

Figure 5.3. Budget of the NSFC (Unit: Billion RMB)

	1996	1997	2005	2006
Total	0.65	0.78	2.26	2.68
For general projects	–	–	1.74	2.03
Projects for young scientists	–	–	0.45	0.56
Region-based projects	–	–	0.07	0.09

Source: www.nsfc.gov.cn

science. After 1978, a fund similar to the US National Science Foundation was set up. It was established in 1986, firstly under the MOST and subsequently becoming an independent body in 2000. This system works mainly based on peer review rather than on government plan. The Foundation gives curiosity-based research a place in the whole R&D set-up in China.

The NSFC is mainly funded by government budget. From 2001 to 2005, about ten billion RMB was spent on basic research. The channels of support were greatly diversified, from teams to talented scientists, from general to key projects. In 2006, the overall budget for the NSFC was 2.68 billion RMB (Figure 5.3).

As the Foundation mainly operates on a peer review basis, it is widely regarded as the backbone of the Chinese science system.

The National Basic Research Programme ("973" Programme). "973" is a national mission-oriented science programme for big science and transnational cooperation, launched in 1997 with the aim of strengthening the role of government in science. The target areas are the so-called strategic areas, such as energy, information, health and materials. From 1998 to 2005, more than 5 billion RMB was allocated to this Programme. More than 143 key projects are being supported. In 2005, the main fields sponsored by the 973 Programme were: population and health care (17.4 per cent), IT (12.1 per cent), materials (14.3 per cent), agriculture (17 per cent), energy (10.5 per cent), resources and the environment (17.4 per cent) interdisciplinary study (14.7 per cent) and others (2.8 per cent) (MOST, 2007).

The Knowledge Innovation Programme was launched in 1998, mainly to allow the CAS to survive in the context of rising university research. With this meta-project, the CAS has been reorganising itself to upgrade its core competence in the face of the universities. The budget is about one billion RMB a year. The main goal is to make the CAS the leading international basic research centre. In reality, this project helps the CAS greatly in facilitating the work of and attracting key scientists, making the CAS the largest basic science centre in China and in the world.

Talent People Policy. China has a large pool of human resources spread around the world. How to use this pool is a critical problem for Chinese science policy. In order to attract talented scientists back to China, special grants for returnees have been prepared by the government. The result is positive. More and more have returned (Figure 5.4). For example, from 2001 to 2005 under the Knowledge Innovation Programme, the CAS attracted 422 scientists with special money for their research and labs via the One Hundred Talents Programme.

Figure 5.4. Overseas Chinese Students and Returnees

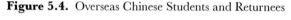

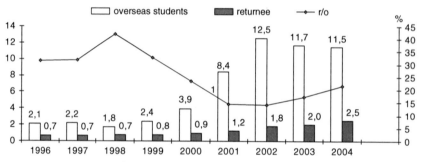

Unit for number of overseas students and returnees: 10 000
Sources: MOST, 2006a, China Science and Technology Development Report, 2006. China S&T Literature Press. Beijing.

Performance. Publications and citations are one way of measuring a nation's scientific output. Since the 1990s, the number of papers published by Chinese researchers both in English and in Chinese has been rapidly increasing. In terms of the SCI, China is already the fifth country in the world (Figure 5.5).

There are several reasons for this rapid growth:

First, since 1978, the government has been promoting science and technology in various ways. The size of Chinese R&D is increasing in terms of both grants and human resources. Universities are expanding. China now employs the largest number of human resources in R&D in the world with more than 35 million people in the S&T system.

Second, many universities and research institutions have introduced new incentives to promote publishing. Researchers can win prizes and awards for publishing in highly ranked journals. Now even PhD students are required to

Figure 5.5. Percentage of World Share of Scientific Publications

	China	France	Germany	Japan	Korea	UK	US	EU-15
1995	2.05	6.09	7.62	8.65	0.79	8.88	33.54	34.36
1998	2.90	6.48	8.82	9.42	1.41	9.08	31.63	36.85
2001	4.30	6.33	8.68	9.52	2.01	8.90	31.01	36.55
2004	6.52	5.84	8.14	8.84	2.70	8.33	30.48	35.18

Source: Adapted from P. Zhou and L. Leydesdorff, The emergence of China as a leading nation in science, Research Policy 35, No 1 (Feb 2006).

Figure 5.6. International Joint Papers by Chinese Researchers

	1996	1999	2002	2003
Number of total papers	15 218	23 174	33 867	59 543
Number of joint papers	4 489	7 413	10 840	17 751
With US	1 364	2 104	3 267	5 791
EU	1 320	2 068	2 881	4 568
UK	430	646	895	1 561
Germany	429	615	949	1 381
France	213	294	441	827
Canada	294	402	566	1 109
Australia	180	353	593	974
Japan	530	945	1 461	2 222
Singapore	75	204	359	726
Korea	108	177	342	646

Source: Evidence Ltd, Patterns of International Collaboration: China's growing research collaboration (Leeds: Evidence Ltd, Dec 2006).

publish at least one article in a journal listed in Thomson's Science Citation Index, the main citation database.

Third, the open door policy is also contributing to progress in science. The most important means is international collaboration. From Figure 5.6, it can be seen that Chinese researchers published four times more joint papers in 2003 than in 1996. Among the countries concerned, the US is the largest partner country engaged in joint research with China.

Although the overall quality of publications is not high, it has been increasing, as measured through citations, especially in some emerging fields such as nanotechnology.

Science policy in China has been implemented through a supply-side as well as a demand-side approach. But as a developing country, the national strategy has downplayed the demand side. Sometimes, scientists are not happy with that. Neither are they glad to see that the government cannot give as much support as developed countries do, since the funding for basic research in China remains about 5–6 per cent of national R&D funding.

3.2 Technology Policy

3.2.1 Technology Import

For a long time, from the establishment of the People's Republic of China in 1949 until the 1970s, the main aim of technology policy was to cover shortages of technology and enhance China's military strength. In the 1950s, the Soviet Union was the main source of foreign technology; 156 key projects with that country were the most famous. They became the incubators for later industrialisation in various industries. But after the break-up of the alliance with the Soviet Union, China began to emphasise independent technology development, although imported technology still played a very important role. The success of the nuclear bomb and artificial insulin projects was the result of the technology policy in this period. China nevertheless imported technologies on a grand scale from the Soviet Union, Germany, Japan and other countries. Those technologies laid the foundations for many Chinese industries, including chemicals, automobiles, steel, textiles (Wang, 2000). But the absorption capacity of Chinese firms is rather poor. So "Import, lag behind, import again, lag behind once more" seems to be the pattern of technology importing. Many new industries started in China at around the same time as Korea, such as the automobile industry, the ICT industry and the steel industry, but now, decades later, China lags behind Korea.

3.2.2 Market for Technology

Foreign direct investment came to China in the 1980s. In the first stage, the government hesitated as to how to deal with FDI. China was in great need of foreign technology and capital. But for a long time, under traditional ideology, foreign investment was not regarded as a good thing for Chinese society. So "market for technology" became a practical technology policy, although the government never formally used the term.

First, government used the big Chinese market to press foreign companies to transfer technology to local companies and to protect local companies from international competition. In IT and the automobile industry, the specific policy tool was to require multinationals to license technology to Chinese companies as a precondition for their investment. For example, "Industrial policy for the automobile industry (1994)" stated that "the preconditions for a joint venture are that the companies have to set up institutes for technology development and the products introduced have to be at the level of the 1990s in developed countries (Article 31)". Second, multinationals were required to sell most of their products internationally. The purpose of that requirement was to protect domestic companies. As only local companies could sell their products to customers in China, the result of these policies was to make joint ventures the main route for foreign companies to invest in China.

This policy has been very effective for international technology transfer. Here the large market provides effective leverage for technology transfer. A very interesting case concerns power plant equipment. For the construction of the Three Gorges Dam, in June 1996 the government explicitly required bids for the project to include foreign companies. For the left bank of the Three Gorges Dam, the winner of the first 12 out of 14 equipment contracts could be foreign companies, but Chinese companies had to be involved in the bidding and the building. A Chinese company had to be the main player in the last two equipment contracts. At the same time, foreign companies had to co-design and co-manufacture the equipment jointly with Chinese partners. If foreign companies did not agree to these terms, they would lose their chance to bid. This kind of special arrangement helped Chinese companies a lot. Through this way of learning, Harbin Electricity Power Station Equipment has now become the largest player in this business (Yu, 2007).

The "market for technology" policy was stopped by China's entry into the WTO. After that, the foreign wholly owned firm became the main channel for multinationals to invest in China.

The issue of the spill-over of FDI through the establishment of joint ventures is very controversial in China. For example, in the automobile industry, the first mover was Volkswagen in the 1980s. Later on, Citroën, General Motors, Mazda, Nissan, Honda, Ford, Hyundai, Toyota and Suzuki all became key players in the Chinese market. Most of them engaged in joint ventures. In 2004, in the passenger car industry, about 2 million passenger cars were produced in China, but only one tenth of them by local brand manufacturers. These are quasi-private companies: Chery and Jeely. The rest are joint ventures with large TNCs throughout the world. The passenger car industry is therefore dominated by TNCs. Some observers have argued that there is little spill-over from them to domestic firms. On the contrary, domestic companies have in their view been losing their innovation capability after entering into joint ventures with foreign companies (Lu & Feng, 2005). Firstly, as the foreign partner in the joint venture cannot have an equity share of more than 50 per cent to control the new company, it would normally not open up much to the domestic partner in terms of technology transfer. Secondly, TNCs would care more about the contract than the market, so they would lack incentives to innovate in China. Those multinationals have usually used Chinese partners as their production base and no real technology has been transferred to the Chinese partner. The result is that local companies have made little progress in product innovation (Lu & Feng, 2005). Thirdly, the TNCs see importing core parts from their parent structure as a more cost-effective route to profit than Chinese production. Lastly, at the same time, market protection has sometimes given the local companies less incentive to innovate as they can enjoy high profits with no innovation.

3.2.3 Encouraging Multinationals to set up R&D Centres in China

With the new trend towards globalisation of R&D driven by multinationals seeking to localise their products and R&D, and to take advantage of the cheap R&D human resources available in China, the Chinese government, with the intention of getting the latest technology from foreign R&D facilities, adopted some special policies to attract multinationals to set up R&D centres in China. Up to now, there are no precise data about the number of R&D centres established by multinationals in China. According to von Zedtwitz (2006), there were 199 foreign R&D facilities in China at the beginning of 2004 (Figure 5.7). The number has increased rapidly since then and possibly amounts to 250–300 at present. Most of these R&D centres are located in large cities, such as Beijing and Shanghai.

Figure 5.7. Number of New Establishments of Foreign R&D Labs in China, 1987–2003

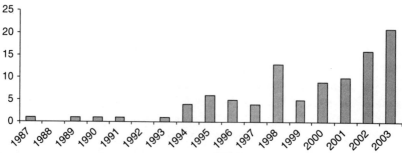

Source: Von Zedtwitz (2006).

Figure 5.8. Select List of Research Cooperation Projects Between Domestic Research Institutes and Multinationals in the Biomedical Industry

Foreign Company	Chinese Partner	Details
GlaxoSmithKline	Shanghai Institutes of Materia Medica (SIMM)	Chemical compound database
Roche	Chinese National Human Genome Centre	Diabetes and schizophrenia
Novartis	Shanghai Institutes of Materia Medica (SIMM)	Herbal compounds, Chinese traditional medicine
AstraZeneca	Shanghai JiaoTong University	Gene linked to schizophrenia
DSM	Joint lab with Fudan University in Shanghai. JV with Chinese vitamin makers	Nutritional products activities
Novo Nordisk	Collaboration with Tsinghua University in Beijing	Diabetes

Source: Liu & Lundin (2006a), Table 23.

But the spill-over cannot easily be seen. More time is needed to observe the positive results. A recent study by the Office for Technology Transactions operating under the Commission for Science and Technology of Beijing shows that the spill-over effect is very low. According to the study, from 2001 to 2006, about 94 per cent of the technology sold by 52 multinationals having R&D centres in Beijing is bought by their headquarters and other subsidiaries or joint ventures of multinationals located in China. This means that the R&D system of multinationals in China is mainly a closed one, with little linkage with Chinese actors in the national and local innovation system (OTTB, 2007).

However, this result should be taken with caution. There may be other important ways in which spill-over takes place that have not been discerned. Liu & Lundin (2006) have observed a great deal of cooperation between FDI companies and Chinese universities and GRIs, and have suggested some benefits of such cooperation (Figure 5.8). They think that it will not only provide local universities and research institutes with additional funding and more advanced equipment, but, more importantly, it will also generate positive demonstration effects and spill-over to the universities and allow them to become better informed about the international research frontier.

3.2.4 The 863 Programme and Breakthrough Programme

Besides the technology importing and "market for technology" policies, the most important technology policy is Chinese high-tech policy. The main policy tool for high-tech industry is the National High-Tech R&D Programme (863 Programme), which is the largest national programme in China. It was launched in 1986 with the aim of tracking and catching up with the development of high technology in developed countries. The 863 Programme is divided into two parts: defence technology and civil technology. From 2001 to 2005, about 15 billion RMB was spent on civil technology (Figure 5.9).

From Figure 5.10, it seems that this high-tech programme has performed well in terms of the output of patents and papers.

Figure 5.9. National S&T Plans Unit: Billion RMB

	2004	2001–2005
973 Basic Research	0.9	4.0
863 National High-Tech R&D Programme (from 1986)	3.77	15.0
Key Technologies R&D Programme (from 1983)	1.61	6.85
SME Innovation Fund	0.83	3.8
Torch Programme (1988, for high technology)	0.08	0.05
Spark Programme (1988, for rural SMEs)	0.05	0.12

Source: MOST, 2006b, Annual report on the state programmes of science and technology development, 2005.

Figure 5.10. Some Indicators of Achievement of the 863 Programme

	1999	2000	2002	2003	2004	2005
Patents granted	108	286	245	1249	2173	3106
Patented inventions	67	180	141	745	1422	2252
Number of papers published in Chinese	6828	12329	9533	26832	29467	34462
Number of papers published in English	1629	3005	2056	6699	7590	9830
Number of new products or production processes	357	868	1105		3455	9328
Items of technology transferred	107	779	264		2009	3359

Sources: MOST, 2006c, Chinese science and technology statistics, 2006. http://www.sts.org.cn

Figure 5.11. The Share of High-Tech Industry in GDP and Manufacturing Industry

	1998	2001	2002	2003	2004	2005
Share of high-tech industry value added in GDP (%)	2.12	2.82	3.13	3.71	3.97	4.44
Share of high-tech industry value added in all manufacturing value added (%)	8.1	9.5	9.9	10.5	10.9	–
Share of high-tech industry value added in STIPs (%)	59.4	70.1	71.7	84.7	87.2	86.6

Sources: MOST, 2006c, Chinese science and technology statistics, 2006. http://www.sts.org.cn

High-tech zones are a second additional instrument for promoting high-tech industry in China. They are a mixed result of policy, institutional reform and government action.

Zhongguancun was the first high-tech zone to be created and there are now 53 national high-tech zones in China. Their purpose is to establish efficiently functioning infrastructure to serve as a platform for innovation activities and interactions among universities, research institutes and firms. More specifically, high-tech zones have the following functions: to provide preferential treatment for high-tech firms in the form of a broad range of tax incentives; to create a new governance model, described by the watchword "small government, but big service"; to reduce transaction costs and to establish a cluster structure in order to promote active interactions and close cooperation among the firms.

In the past two decades, these high-tech zones have expanded rapidly in terms of their size and scope of activities and have therefore played an important role in promoting the development of the high-tech industry in China. In 2004 there were 53 National Science &Technology Industrial Parks (STIPs). In 2004, the total value added of all high-tech zones was 634 billion RMB, about 3.97 per cent of GDP; high-tech companies in STIP accounted about 86.6 per cent of high-tech industry value added. Most of them are spin-offs from universities and GRIs, new private firms and FDI firms (MOST, 2006).

3.2.5 Special Industrial Policy

To foster strategic industries and Chinese local companies, some policies have been implemented, including subsidies to R&D labs in big companies. Under this policy, about 512 large companies were selected to enjoy special support. Among them, more than two hundred companies were chosen as leading innovative companies to be given direct support under the National Programme 2006–2020 for the Development of Science and Technology in the medium and long term implemented in 2007.

In 2000, a special policy was adopted for the integrated circuit and software industry in China, because integrated circuits and software are assumed to be the key sectors of the information industry and deserve a special policy to promote them. The main policy tool is tax abatement for businesses. The result of this policy is very interesting. While most foreign companies criticise the policy for giving too strong support to local companies as against foreign companies, many local companies also criticise the policy on the ground that they derive less benefit from it than foreign companies.

3.2.6 Actors in Technology Policy

For a long time, the main players in technology development were the GRIs. From 1949 to the 1980s, the main task of many industrial GRIs was the assimilation of imported technology. In order to replace the imported technology and to save foreign currency, incremental innovations based on imported technology were implemented according to the principles of a planned economy. Enterprises were only the users of the technology developed

Figure 5.12. Expenditure on In-House R&D and Technology Importing and Assimilation (Unit: Billion RMB)

	Expenditure on R&D	Expenditure on Technology Importing	Expenditure on Technology Assimilation	Ratio
1991	5.9	9.0	0.4	1:1.54:0.06
1993	9.5	15.9	0.6	1:1.67:0.06
1995	14.2	36.1	1.3	1:2.55:0.09
1998	19.7	21.5	1.5	1:1.09:0.07
1999	25.0	20.8	1.8	1:0.83:0.07
2000	35.4	24.5	1.8	1:0.69:0.05
2001	44.2	28.6	2.0	1:0.65:0.04
2002	56.0	37.3	2.6	1:0.66:0.04
2003	72.1	40.5	2.7	1:0.56:0.04
2004	95.4	36.8	5.4	1:0.39:0.06

Source: MOST, China Science and Technology Statistical Yearbook, 1991–2003, Beijing.

Figure 5.13. Ratio of R&D/Sales in Large and Medium-Sized Companies (%)

Year	1991	1995	2000	2001	2002	2003	2004	2005
R&D/ sales	0.49	0.46	0.71	0.76	0.83	0.75	0.71	0.76

Source: MOST, China Science and Technology Statistical Yearbook, 1991–2003, Beijing.

by GRIs and a few universities. Enterprises typically operated as plants or production units with few if any R&D activities and little capability for technology development. Imported technology was the main source enabling companies to maintain and upgrade production capability.

Since the 1980s, state-owned enterprises (SOEs) have been given more autonomy to invest and innovate based on their own strategic decisions. Also, entrepreneurs have been allowed to set up millions of SMEs. This wave of privatisation and competition provided enterprises with the motivation to invest in product development and innovation on top of exploiting cost advantages or diversification. As shown in Figure 5.12, although enterprises still spent a lot of money on imported technology, large and medium-sized companies quickly increased their R&D inputs and entered a stage in which they were more "making" than "buying". But generally, their level of R&D is still very low compared to other companies in developed countries (Figure 5.13). This is why, in China, companies have introduced more incremental innovations and few radical innovations.

3.3 Innovation Policy

In China, the innovation policy was born to break down the barrier between R&D outputs and their commercial application. The planned economy gave GRIs and universities the freedom to do their research without caring much about its application. The traditional system is closer to the linear model of innovation. The market-oriented policy pressed the S&T system to operate around economic needs. A variety of innovation policies have since then been brought forward.

3.3.1 Spin-off Policy

In order to speed up the process from research to commercial products, in the 1980s the government encouraged GRIs and universities to set up their own spin-offs and scientists to leave their research position to engage in commercial activities.

Figure 5.14. Spin-Offs From Universities

	Number of Spin-Offs	Revenue (Billion RMB)	Profit (Billion RMB)
1999	2137	26.7	2.2
2000	2097	36.8	3.5
2001	1993	44.8	3.1
2002	2216	53.9	2.5
2003	2447	66.8	2.8
2004	2355	80.7	4.1

Sources: Statistics on university-based industry in 2004 in China, Centre for S&T for Development, Ministry of Education, 2005.

Although the size of the spin-off business in China was small compared to that of Chinese industry (Figure 5.14), it was valuable for the high-tech industry in China. Spin-off companies gave many scientists in universities or GRIs good opportunities to access market knowledge.

The result of the spin-offs policy is that it gave birth to many dynamic domestic high-tech companies, such as Lenovo, spun off from the Chinese Academy of Sciences, or Beida Founder, from Peking University. Most biotech companies are also the result of spin-offs.

But the policy gradually faced many challenges. For example, spin-off companies are not well regulated for producing further innovation. In addition, the conflict between profit-seeking and the public goal of universities put the universities and GPIs in a more risky position. To cope with this awkward situation, a new policy was implemented that separates the business from the university, leaving universities only as shareholders. At the same time, from the end of the last century, as the government has continuously stepped up its support for research and education, the universities stopped thinking of setting up and developing spin-off companies as their primary function. The same applies to the GRIs.

3.3.2 Industry-Science Linkages Policy

As there was a functional division of labour in knowledge creation and diffusion for many years in China, a strong barrier existed between knowledge creation in GRIs and universities and the use of knowledge in enterprises. But since the introduction of market mechanisms in China and the stronger

Figure 5.15. Share of Universities' Research Funding from Industry

		1999	2000	2001	2002	2003	2004
Total S&T funds (in billion)		10.3	16.7	20.0	24.8	30.8	39.2
From firms		5.4	5.5	7.2	9.0	11.3	14.9
	Share (%)	52.2	33.3	36.2	36.2	36.7	38.0
From government		4.9	9.7	11.0	13.7	16.5	21.1
	Share (%)	47.8	58.4	54.9	55.4	53.6	53.8

Source: MOE, 2006, Statistics on Science and Technology in Higher Education, 2000–2005, Department of S&T, Ministry of Education.

Figure 5.16. R&D Outsourcing to Universities and R&D Institutes – From Large and Medium-Sized Industrial Enterprises

	2000	2001	2002	2003	2004
Total R&D expenditure (billion RMB)	35.4	44.2	56.0	72.1	95.4
Funds for universities (billion RMB)	5.5	7.2	9.0	11.2	24.9
Share of total businesses' R&D (%)	15.5	16.2	16.1	15.5	26.1
Funds for R&D institutes (billion RMB)	3.8	2.5	3.6	4.7	5.0
Share of total businesses' R&D (%)	10.7	5.6	6.4	6.5	5.2
Total outsourcing to domestic univ. and R&D inst. (%)	26.2	21.8	22.5	22.0	31.3

Source: MOST, 2006c, China Science and Technology Statistical Yearbook, 2005. Beijing: Chinese Statistical Press.

Figure 5.17. Papers Co-authored by Industry and Universities, 2000–2003

First/Second Author	2000		2001		2002		2003	
	Papers	Share	Papers	Share	Papers	Share	Papers	Share
Total	51079	100	53246	100	87688	100	100310	100
Industry/university	4499	8.81	1123	2.11	1381	1.57	1567	1.56
University/industry	867	1.7	5301	9.96	6448	7.35	7421	7.39

Source: Chinese Institute of Information, China Science Paper and Citation Analysis, 2005.

pressures from competition, industry-academic linkages have improved greatly in the last 20 years.

Firstly, universities and GRIs were allowed to set up their own spin-offs so that they could commercialise their technology directly. In this way, universities and GRIs would be more integrated in China's process of economic growth. Secondly, spin-off companies served also as a way for GRIs and universities to compensate for the operating budget cuts that the government had been making since the 1980s.

At the same time, universities and GRIs began to do more contract research for industry. This benefits industry, as most companies, especially SMEs, have limited R&D capabilities and outsourcing of research to universities is thus a strategic component of their development. As a result of this, from 2000 to 2004 the share of universities' budgets coming from industry increased; it was about 38 per cent of their total research funds in 2004 (Figure 5.15). In 2004, about 26 per cent of industry's total R&D expenditure went to the universities (Figure 5.16).

Joint publishing of scientific papers between university and industry is an alternative indicator of industry-academic linkage. For IPR and other reasons, industry is reluctant to publish papers. But from Figure 5.17, it is clear that universities are increasingly willing to have industry engineers as their co-authors for joint publishing.

3.3.3 Indigenous Innovation

The National Programme 2006–2020 for the Development of Science and Technology in the medium and long term is China's current long-term innovation policy framework. The most interesting element of the new plan is the declared intention to strengthen "independent" or "indigenous" innovation. The essence of the policy is to strengthen the innovation capability in domestic companies. The main routes to indigenous innovation are: original innovation based on basic research, integrative innovation and second innovation

There are three different factors behind this decision to push for indigenous innovation.

First, China's economic growth has been strongly dependent on foreign technology and FDI. Since 2000, foreign-invested enterprises have accounted for more than 85 per cent of all high-tech exports (NBS, 2006). But it is commonly believed that the "market for technology" policy has not resulted in the immediate and automatic knowledge and technology spill-overs from FDI that policymakers had hoped for.

Second, a culture of imitation and copying is common not only in product development and design, but also in the field of scientific research. Hence, innovations based on domestic knowledge and intellectual property rights are strongly needed in China.

Third, the Chinese economy's high growth rate path of the last twenty years will not be sustainable without a dramatic change over the next twenty years. The government has adopted a new nationwide strategy called "Scientific development". In future, China will use more energy-efficient and environment-friendly technologies, new management skills and new organisational practices to ensure sustainable growth.

There are three main policies selected to implement the indigenous innovation strategy. Firstly, the government plans to increase R&D by 2020 to 2.5 per cent of GDP (from the current level of 1.3 per cent in 2005). Since GDP growth is projected to increase at a similar pace, boosting R&D expenditure as a share of GDP requires a faster increase in absolute terms. Already today, China has the third largest expenditure on R&D in terms of purchasing power parity, trailing only the US and Japan (Serger & Breidne, 2006). Secondly, fiscal policy to activate innovation capability at the company level is assumed to be the most important tool. The new tax policy will make company R&D expenditure 150 per cent tax deductible, thus effectively constituting a net subsidy, as well as allowing accelerated depreciation for R&D equipment worth up to 300 000 RMB. Thirdly, public procurement of technology will be widely used. This policy is the result of learning from the United States' and Korea's best practices.

The aim of current public procurement practice is to cut costs rather than promote indigenous innovation. Under the new policy, government agencies have to prioritise innovative Chinese companies by procuring their goods or services even if these are not as good or as cheap as those of other companies (both Chinese and foreign). The main points of the new public procurement policy are:

- Giving priority to indigenous innovative products in public procurement. China will establish a system of procurement of innovative products on the current finance base, including a certification of what is an innovative product, and will give priority to innovative products in the procurement list;
- In the purchasing process, domestic products have priority over foreign products. Only those products that are not available in China can be purchased from abroad. More than 30 per cent of technology and equipment purchasing should go to domestic equipment if using public money. As for key national projects using government money, domestic equipment purchase should be not less than 60 per cent of total value. For purchasing products of foreign companies, those companies that are willing to transfer technology to local companies and let them assimilate it will be given priority listing over other candidates;

- Establishing a system of procurement of innovation. This means that the government should purchase the first vintage of innovation products created by domestic enterprises or research institutions if the innovative products have proven to have big potential markets. This gives government the scope to purchase R&D projects for commercial purposes;
- Giving indigenous innovative products some price advantage when it comes to procurement. In price-based bidding, even if the price of indigenous innovative products is higher than that of other products, their price can be reduced in the real bidding. If the price of the indigenous products is not higher than other products, they will be selected — assuming that the quality is appropriate and comparable to the foreign products.

In its innovation policy, the Chinese government is trying to balance the supply side with the demand side. Recent policy such as public procurement of technology is a strong demand-side policy. But overall, demand-side policy is weak compared to supply-side policy. In China, the government controls large amounts of resources and so prefers to use supply-side rather than demand-side policies.

3.4 Regional Aspects of S&T and Innovation Policy

China, as a big country, has different regions with different cultures, geography and resources. This kind of diversity is also very important for innovation. Historically, the north-eastern part used to be China's core industrial base, with heavy industries and important technologies imported from the Soviet Union.

In the western region, there were some isolated industrial bases following the construction of the third-line defence in the 1960s and 1970s, that is, the mass transfer of the defence industry from the coastal region to the western region. This made Xian, Guichou and other western cities centres of heavy industry. Currently, Chongqing, Xian and Chendu are three examples of innovative cities in the western region.

The coastal area used to be the most recently developed region. For example, in the planned economy era the government invested very little in the Fujian, Zhejiang and Guangdong provinces, so there are few big SOEs in those regions. But those regions had been the commercial centres since the Ming dynasty. Once opened to the world, they adapted to the market economy much faster than other regions. Private SMEs with great entrepreneurship flourished and Guangdong, Zhejiang, Jiansu and Fujian become the main regions of the new Chinese economy.

Figure 5.18. Regional Gap in R&D Inputs

	Eastern	Central	Western
Share of national GDP (2003)	58.9%	24.6%	16.5%
Share of national R&D	71%	17%	13%

Source: China Science and Technology Statistical Yearbook, 2005. Beijing: Chinese Statistical Press.

Figure 5.19. R&D Expenditure and R&D/GDP by Region, 2003

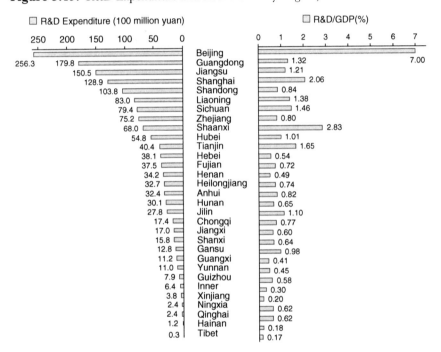

Source: Science and Technology Indicators, 2004.

But the diversity of innovation across China is also due to the decentralisation of decision-making over both resource allocation and operational issues since the 1980s.

One result but also a serious challenge to China's R&D activities after decentralisation is the large regional S&T disparity. The gap among the eastern, central and western regions in terms of R&D can be seen in Figure 5.18. Encouraged by an unbalanced growth approach and uneven FDI inflows, the eastern region, with Beijing, Shanghai, Guangdong and Jiangsu, became the

Figure 5.20. Scoreboard of Regional Innovation Capability, 2005

Regions	Final Score		Knowledge Creation		Knowledge Acquisition		Company Innovation		Infrastructure		Performance	
		Rank		Rank		Rank		Rank		Rank		Rank
Shanghai	56.97	1	46.96	2	59.51	1	61.19	1	50.07	2	65.9	1
Beijing	56.11	2	80.94	1	40.41	5	42.52	7	59.71	1	61.77	3
Guangdong	50.22	3	29.13	5	44.05	4	58.17	3	48.83	3	62.44	2
Jiangsu	48.41	4	25.47	6	57.41	2	59.7	2	45.9	4	47.9	6
Zhejiang	45.29	5	23.21	7	50.5	3	54.36	4	44.21	5	47.95	5
Shangdong	37.96	6	19.92	13	35.98	6	51.64	5	37.09	6	36.99	7
Tianjing	37.43	7	30.56	4	32.19	7	36.19	11	29.17	9	58.37	4
Liaoning	32.05	8	22.5	8	30.68	8	46.02	6	31.97	8	22.89	17
Fujiang	30.74	9	20.19	12	28.35	11	39.09	9	26.79	14	34.94	8
Chaoqing	28.63	10	17.66	16	29.45	9	39.7	8	25.11	18	26.8	12
Xiannxi	27.27	11	21.75	9	24.13	15	33.21	16	28.13	10	25.25	14

Source: X. Liu et al., Chinese Report on Regional Innovation Capability, Chinese Science Press, 2006.

hub for R&D activity in China. Those provinces have a much higher level of R&D expenditure and R&D intensity than other regions.

Aware of the divergence among regions and the risk of the gap widening, the central government launched the "go west" strategy in 2000, aiming to energise the less developed regions through a combination of fiscal, regional, FDI and S&T policies. But even with that, R&D expenditures and R&D intensities in the central and western regions have still not been increasing. In addition to R&D expenditure, there are large regional disparities on a broad range of criteria, e.g. human resources, high-tech industries and openness of the regional economies in general (Figure 5.19).

The performance of regional innovation capability can be seen in a report on regional innovation capability in China (Liu, 2006). Based on indicators of knowledge creation, diffusion, company innovation, infrastructure and performance, Shanghai, Beijing, Guangdong, Jiangsu, Zhejiang and Shangdong are the top six most innovative regions in China. They are all located in the eastern and coastal region (Figure 5.20). According to the report, Beijing is a science superpower in China, but the innovation capability of enterprises lags behind in relative terms. Shanghai is the number one in China on every aspect of innovation. Guangdong is similar to Shanghai. Jiangsu, Zhejiang and Shangdong score well in company-based innovation and knowledge acquisition, but lag behind in knowledge creation. Liaoning scores well in other aspects, except on performance, meaning that the region has a strong base for innovation, but lacks capacity to turn this base into strong performance (Figure 5.20). Liaoning is a region with significant national investment, especially in heavy industries, but is still influenced by the traditions and cultures of the planned economy. The same is true for the whole north-east region. Chaoqing is the only western region in the top ten. Its company system performs well in innovation and knowledge acquisition, but suffers from a relatively poor infrastructure.

4. Discussion of Policy Implications in China

S&T and innovation policy has played a very important role in helping China to become a real global power. The making and implementation of those policies has become a strategic issue in China. Traditional S&T policy has gradually been replaced by a market-based policy in line with WTO rules.

In science policy, new means of support and evaluate systems have been introduced. The number of SCI papers has been steadily increasing in recent years. Following the open policy and globalisation of science, the Chinese science system has been gradually integrated into the global science system.

In technology and innovation policy, technology importing and FDI still loom large in China. But as more and more international IPR conflicts arise and most industries are found to lack core technology, indigenous innovation has been raised to the status of a national strategy.

The following three dimensions of S&T and innovation policy-making still matter a great deal in China.

Supply vs demand. In China, supply-side policy via government programmes has been a common means of promoting S&T as well as economic development. Overall, demand-side policy is weak compared to supply-side policy. In China, the government controls large amounts of resources and so prefers to use supply-side rather than demand-side policy.

But there is a large gap between what the academic sector produces and what industry needs. The indicator is that there are more SCI papers from academics in China than patents taken out by industry. In many areas, such as in nanotechnology, papers outnumber patents in China (Figure 5.21). Consequently, in formulating the National Plan 2006–2020 for the Development of Science and Technology in the medium and long term, innovation capability in the business sector has been given more weight, through instruments such as special tax arrangements for company spending on R&D or the public procurement of technology. But a situation of this kind cannot be easily changed in a short time.

But supply-side policy is still important in China's policy agenda. For example, mega-projects have been selected as powerful ways of narrowing the gap with the developed world. Such projects include large aircraft, the next-generation internet and next-generation telecommunications.

Domestic vs global. Since China's opening to the world, FDI has become a new force in the Chinese innovation system. A debate is ongoing on the role of FDI in innovation in China. Some have argued that FDI and multinationals provide many spill-overs for innovation in China (Liu, 2008). Others have claimed that no spill-over takes place (Lu, 2005).

In this open process, one big question is whether, if there is no protection of infant industry, companies in developing countries can compete with large multinationals. Liu (2008) demonstrated that the large domestic market can provide good leverage or a comparative advantage in competing with foreign companies. He also observed that the most dynamic industries can also be the candidate industries for companies in developing countries to catch up. But this cannot be done automatically; it needs a special S&T and innovation policy to make it happen.

At the same time, how can a developing country use standards or other tools to promote local technology? In China, frustration emerged when some companies tried to launch local standards for some technology, such as wireless

Figure 5.21. Most Prolific Countries in SCI Papers and USPTO Patents, 2003

Country	No of Papers	Country	No of Patents
US	7512	US	5228
Japan	4431	Japan	926
People's R China	4417	Germany	684
Germany	3099	Canada	244
France	1900	France	183
South Korea	1592	South Korea	84
United Kingdom	1520	Netherlands	81
Russia	1293	United Kingdom	78
Italy	1015	Taiwan	77
India	830	Israel	68
Spain	727	Switzerland	56
Taiwan	706	Australia	53
Canada	690	Sweden	39
Poland	515	Italy	31
Switzerland	498	Belgium	28
Netherlands	492	Denmark	23
Brazil	455	Singapore	20
Sweden	435	Finland	17
Australia	434	Ireland	10
Singapore	372	Austria	8
Israel	347	People's R China	8

Source: Ronald N. Kostoff, Jesse A. Stump et al., The structure and infrastructure of the global nanotechnology, Journal of Nanoparticle Research (2006) 8: 301–321.

access technology; the Chinese effort was criticised by some multinationals in the area. There will therefore be more conflicts of this kind when developing countries stand up on the global stage.

Centralisation vs decentralisation. Decentralisation has so far been an ongoing trend in China. It gives regional government more autonomy to allocate resources for innovation. In this way, innovation in China is more diversified across regions.

Coastal areas such as Guangdong, Shanghai or Zhejiang have enjoyed faster economic growth. Western regions usually lag behind. At the same time, regions have developed their own model of innovation. For example, Shanghai performs well in terms of innovation capability in large companies; Beijing has an advantage in terms of high-tech industry clusters, while Zhejiang is good at traditional industry clusters.

The decentralisation of S&T and innovation policy is therefore a very powerful tool for regional and national economic growth. But the side-effect is a growing regional gap between innovative regions and regions that are lagging behind.

Although much progress has been made in China, many challenges face it in the future.

1. Science itself in China is too strongly driven by practical goals, and this has made research in China short-sighted. Scientists cannot do work that takes more than five years to accomplish. Science is increasingly subordinate to the political and economic agenda.

2. In the technology policy area, companies are the weakest part of the system. They have not yet acquired the capability to re-innovate based on imported technology. So "Import, lag behind, import again, lag behind once more" still seems to be the pattern of technology importing. In the meantime, domestic R&D work produces few effective results. For example, the government spends huge amounts of money on developing digital machine tools, but few commercial products are put on the markets. Most companies still have to buy the technology from international suppliers.

3. In innovation policy, IPR is still a major problem. Government support usually focuses on hardware, leaving software untouched; it focuses on high-tech industry, leaving low-tech industry out. SMEs still cannot get enough support in terms of venture capital or start-up money to enter industry as they wish. There is strong support for shielding local companies from global competition and heavy government interference in key industries to strengthen national security. But this kind of trend can easily lead to techno-nationalism. The government faces a difficult dilemma: how to work effectively to promote the competence of domestic companies and at the same time ensure that the Chinese economy is integrated into the global world.

References

Bernal, D. J. (1939). *The Social Function of Science*. London: George Routledge.
Bush, V. (1945). *Science: The endless frontier*. Washington: United States Government Printing Office.

Commission of S&T (1986). *Guideline of Chinese S&T policy*. Beijing: S&T Literature Publishing House.

Evidence Ltd (2006). *Patterns of International Collaboration: China's growing research collaboration*. Leeds: Evidence Ltd, Dec 2006.

Hu Zhijian (2005). Research of the Chinese Concept of basic research: creating a free space for it? PhD Thesis, Graduate University of Chinese Academy of Sciences.

Liu, X. (2008). *Globalization, Catch-up and Innovation*. Beijing: Chinese Science Press.

Liu, X. et al. (2006). *Chinese Report on Regional Innovation Capability* (in Chinese), Beijing: Chinese Science Press.

Liu, X. & White, S. (2001). Comparing innovation systems: a framework and application to China's transitional context. J. Research Policy (30).

Liu, X. & Lundin, N. (2006). *Globalisation of biomedical industry and the system of innovation in China*. Stockholm: SNS report.

Lu, F. & Feng, K. (2005). *The Policy Choice of Developing Indigenous IPR Chinese Automobile Industry*. Beijing: Peking University Press.

Jasanoff, S. (ed.) (1997). *Comparative science and technology policy*. UK: Cheltenham; NH: Lyme; US: E. Elgar Pub.

Kostoff, R. N., Stump, J. A. et. al. (2006). The structure and infrastructure of the global nanotechnology. In: *Journal of Nanoparticle Research* (2006) 8: 301–321.

Moe (Ministry of Education) (2005). Statistics on Science and Technology in Higher Education. Department of S&T.

Most (Ministry of Science and Technology) (2005a). *The Yellow Book on Science and Technology, Vol. 7: China Science and Technology Indicators 2004*. Beijing: Scientific and Technical Documents Publishing House.

Most (2005b). Annual Report on the State Programmes of Science and Technology Development.

Most (2006a). *China Science and Technology Development Report: 2006*. Chinese S&T Literature Press.

Most (2006b). Annual Report on the State Programmes of Science and Technology Development.

Most (2006c). *China Science and Technology Statistical Yearbook: 2006*. Beijing: Chinese Statistical Press.

Most (2007). Chinese science and technology statistics. http://www.sts.org.cn /

Most and NBS (2006). China Statistical Yearbook on high-tech technology industry: 2006. Chinese Statistical Press.

NBS (National Bureau of Statistics) (2006). China Statistics Yearbook on High-tech Technology Industry. Beijing: Chinese Statistical Press.

NDRC (1994). Industrial Policy of Automobile Industry. www.sdpc.gov.cn

NDRC (2002). Industrial Policy of Automobile Industry. www.sdpc.gov.cn

OECD (1982). Innovation Policy. Paris: OECD.

OECD (1999). Managing National Innovation Systems. Paris: OECD.

OECD (2005). Innovation Policy and Performance. Paris: OECD.

OTTB (Office for Technology Transactions of Beijing) (2007). The status quo impact and policy implication of technology transfer of R&D centers of multinationals in Beijing (working report). 2007, 6.

Rip, A. & Meulen van der (1997). The post-modern research system. In: Barre, Gibbons, Maddox, Martin, Papon (eds). *Science in Tomorrow's Europe*. Editions Economica, Paris, pp. 51–69.

Rothwell, R. & Zegveld, W. (1982). *Innovation in the small and medium-sized firm.* London: Frances Pinter.

Serger, S. & Magnus, B. (2006). China's 15-year plan for science and technology—a critical assessment. Conference paper for New Asian Dynamics in Science, Technology and Innovation, Gilleleje, Denmark (27–29 September, 2006).

Von Zedtwitz, M. (2006). Chinese multinationals: new contenders in global R&D. Conference presentation. http://goingglobal2006.vtt.fi/programme.htm

Wang, Z. et al. (2000). A historical retrospect of technology import of Chinese machinery industry. In: *Journal of Dialectics of Nature* (1).

Yu, B. et al. (2007). *Pattern of Indigenous Innovation: the Case of HPEC[R].* NSFC.

Zhou, P. & Leydesdorff, L. (2006). The emergence of China as a leading nation in science. In: *Research Policy*, 35, No 1 (Feb 2006).

Chapter 6

THE SOUTH AFRICAN INNOVATION POLICIES: POTENTIAL AND CONSTRAINT[1]

Glenda Kruss and Jo Lorentzen

1. Introduction

South Africa is one of the strongest economies in Africa and key to the economic and political development of Sub-Saharan Africa (World Bank 2007). In relation to the global arena, South Africa has been variously categorized, but the central thrust is one of considerable economic potential, with significant constraints imposed by the legacy of the past. It has generally been grouped alongside middle-income countries like Brazil and India in terms of its strong but highly uneven capacity to participate in global technological innovation in the era of a 'knowledge economy' (Albuquerque 2001, UNDP 2001). The general thrust of these analyses is to emphasize the potential of the South African national system of innovation to compete in the global knowledge economy, but that socio-economic developmental demands require critical efforts for long-term sustainability, and may become a binding constraint.

After the end of Apartheid, and with the transition to a democratic government in South Africa since 1994, there have been changes in governance, in the economy and in science, technology and innovation policy. Unlike many other countries where change has been a more gradual process, the transition was an opportunity for a dramatic break with the fragmented system of the past, towards a systematic attempt to put in place new policy, structures and mechanisms to meet democratic goals.

South Africa is distinctive in that new science and technology policies were systematically redesigned in the mould of a national innovation system (NIS) approach. Policy borrowing may be traced back to the early 1990s, with foreign donors and policy experts directly influencing the policy formulation process (IDRC 1995, Amuah 1994, Kaplan 1996 and 1999). At that point, reportedly no other developing country had explicitly made the concept of a national system of innovation the anchor of its innovative endeavours. Although it rapidly gained prominence in policy circles, especially in the OECD, the NIS academic and research literature was only just emerging at the time (Freeman 1988, Lundvall 1992, Nelson 1993). But along with the associated policy practice it focused on advanced economies, and had yet to advance testable propositions and policy recommendations for the developing world.

As a consequence, the policy that was adopted did not adequately take into account the historical and contextual conditions of South Africa as a latecomer society (Lorentzen 2009a). Kruss (2007) claims that another problem is insufficient consideration of the complex segmentation within the higher education system that impacts on scientific and research capacity. The lack of maturity of government systems charged with implementing new policy imposes further limitations on the potential and intended impact.

In order to demonstrate these claims, Section 2 describes the evolving policy texts that underlay South Africa's NIS, and outlines the structure of the NIS, as well as key implementing mechanisms initiated by government to stimulate innovation. Section 3 goes on to present data that show in detail how well the country is doing in relation to the objectives contained in the policies, discussing three of the 'binding constraints' on implementation that reflect the specificities of the South African context.

2. Policy Foundations of the South African National Innovation System

2.1 Policy Formulation Strongly Influenced by Global Trends

The second half of the 1990s was a decisive period in the elaboration of the NIS. Local academics and policymakers, together with foreign experts, endeavoured to create a science and technology system that would correspond to the goals of the new political dispensation. The policy vision drew heavily on the emerging conceptual models of the developed economies. It was directly informed by theoretical trends such as the promotion of 'mode 2' knowledge in line with the global debate initiated by Gibbons et al (1994), and by the explicit adoption of a national system of innovation approach.

This effort culminated in the formulation of a policy White Paper on Science & Technology: Preparing for the 21st Century (DACST 1996). The goal articulated in this document was to achieve an improved and sustainable quality of life for South African citizens in the context of a competitive global economy through the "establishment of an efficient, well co-ordinated and integrated system of technological and social innovation [...], [t]he development of a culture within which the advancement of knowledge is valued as an important component of national development" and "[i]mproved support for all kinds of innovation which is fundamental to sustainable economic growth, employment creation, equity through redress and social development" (DACST 1996). These goals were elaborated in the broader context of the government's macro-economic strategy. The intention was that they should be put into effect through the creation of an enabling policy environment of regulatory and funding steering mechanisms.

The primary vision articulated in the White Paper on Science and Technology (1996) was the setting up of a national system of innovation based on the core principles of partnerships, co-ordination, problem-solving and multi-disciplinary knowledge production (DACST 1996: 3) The NIS was defined as 'the means through which a country seeks to create, acquire, diffuse and put into practice new knowledge that will help that country and its people achieve their individual and collective goals' (DACST 1996: 15).

The concept of a national system of innovation is loosely defined, of course, and has come to have multiple interpretations and incarnations (Sharif 2006). Important insights into the South African mediation of the approach can be gleaned from the reflections of three of the key institutional actors in the policy formulation process, in the form of a paper promoting the NIS as an approach to science and technology policy for wider adoption in NEPAD and the African Union (Paterson, Adam and Mullin 2003). With the hindsight of almost a decade, their argument began with the claim that, while the approach was originally used in developed economies, it has been developed in transitional economies with major developmental challenges, like South Africa, China and developing countries in Latin America and the Middle East. The emphasis was that instead of focusing on research or dedicated institutions as in the past, the NIS framework is a metaphor that leads policy-makers to focus on 'the harmonious and aligned interaction of all elements and linkages in the system to ensure effective and sustainable outcomes and impacts' (2003: 1). Decisions on policies to strengthen the NIS should be based on an understanding of the resources available and the current conditions within the NIS. The claim of these authors was that 'the NSI approach has proved robust and of ongoing value in scripting a consistent and coherent set of interventions that build the system as a whole' (2003: 17). Such was the reading of the concept that purportedly informed the drafting of the White Paper and the evolution of science and technology policy in South Africa.

The White Paper recognised that the promotion of technological change as a central tenet of national policy would be a challenge. Yet it recognised that failures in markets for technology required government to provide the public goods, including the sharing of risks, without which the attainment of global competitiveness and higher employment would remain elusive. It emphasised the importance of resources and access to technology as well as the capacities to absorb technological change, and underlined the importance of ongoing scientific research for such basic issues as the provision of clean drinking water, electricity, housing, and water-borne sewerage. The focus was on policies and initiatives of government and not on the private sector or any other constituents of the NIS.

2.2 Developing Strategic Policy

Government subsequently undertook foresight exercises and drew up technology roadmaps to gain a better understanding of salient developments in what were considered crucial technologies (DACST 1999). The three technology platforms identified as crucial focal points for development at that time – namely ICT, biotechnology and new materials development, an indication of the strong global influence and policy borrowing – were not based on existing research or technology strengths.

The second foundational policy text to be formulated was the National Research and Development Strategy (NRDS, DST 2002; for a critical review, see Kaplan 2004). It reflected on problematic conditions that were current at that time. Thus, the strategy document expressed concern at the disinvestments from R&D on the part of the private sector, too little funding for R&D, an ageing and shrinking scientific workforce, an inappropriate intellectual property system, and a lack of coordination within the NIS itself. It proposed that lessons be learned from international experiences in order to inform local policy practice, especially in the areas of technological change, human capital, and government coordination.

The policy text optimistically lent credence to the belief that innovation would directly impact on quality of life through improvements, for example, in the health sector. The existence of a technological solution and its wide application to a societal problem, such as diseases of poverty like tuberculosis, is not a given. The critical question in the context of a late-developing country like South Africa is whether the innovation system can carry through the required innovation effectively and to the benefit of the entire population. The NRDS further subscribed to the view that growth is intimately linked to technology and innovation missions. It therefore called for an investment target of one per cent of gross expenditure on R&D as a share of GDP and proposed a number of technology platforms for priority government funding. Prominent among these were biotechnology, ICT and advanced manufacturing, technology for and from the natural resource sectors, and technology for poverty reduction.

These two documents – the 1997 White Paper and the 2002 NRDS – were the two single most important policy statements regarding the NIS in its first decade. While the former provided the system's spirit, the latter began to describe the 'letter' of the system, i.e. the structures, mechanisms and capabilities that needed to be put in place. However, both tended largely to provide frameworks and visions to transform the old fragmented apartheid science system into the new system of innovation. Policy documents lacked substantive provisions that were sufficiently informed by an analysis of current conditions in government, universities and public research institutes, and particularly in firms as the major drivers of innovation.

To some extent this optimism was merely a question of policies needing to mature over time, through research, dialogue and consultation. Yet, analysts have noted a degree of over-optimism in policy-making, and a lack of realism in analysing what it is possible to achieve in the South African system (Van Renssen 2006). The political will and policy intent are strongly present, but - as we will argue - the capacity to implement and roll out programmes on a large scale may not exist to a sufficient degree, and may not adequately address the fault lines that permeate South African society and tend to reinforce inequality of opportunity.

2.3 Shifting Macro-Economic Policy

The extent to which early policy formulation was not sufficiently reflexive is evident in a shift from 2003 onwards, when the presidency introduced a discourse of 'two economies' and 'two nations'. This signalled a recognition that, until that point, most interventions had focused on the 'first world' economy, while the acknowledgement of the 'second economy' made it possible to target interventions to address poverty and unemployment (Mbeki 2003, Mbeki 2004, Mbeki 2005). A review of government policy achievements to date was initiated in 2004, a decade after transition. In early 2006, government launched a new strategy, the Accelerated and Shared Growth Initiative for South Africa (AsgiSA 2006), which aimed to raise the growth rate at the same time as halving poverty and unemployment. The intention was to have a dedicated strategy to address the 'binding constraints' on economic growth, job creation and decreasing poverty, under the direct leadership of the Deputy President. Six main constraints were identified for intervention: they are macro-economic policy, improving infrastructure, developing specific sector and industrial strategies, improving skills and education, growing the second economy and strengthening public administration (AsgiSA 2006).

In the light of such macro-policy review and shifts, toward the middle of the current decade, government started to firm up plans that were relevant to the further development of the NIS. In 2006 the Department of Trade and Industry published a document entitled 'A National Industrial Policy Framework' (NIPF, DTI 2006). The reasoning behind this framework was that South Africa's economy needed to undergo fundamental restructuring in order to wean itself off its reliance on global commodity demand and the domestic consumption boom. Particular attention was paid to the relatively poor performance of non-traditional tradables, which include low-skill intensive activities and thus lend themselves to addressing the country's high unemployment problem. The NIPF acknowledged the importance of the knowledge economy and thus, implicitly, of the NIS. It emphasized the need to go beyond technology importation and foreign direct investment (FDI) towards increasing innovation and development of domestic technologies. Its vision for the industrial trajectory of South Africa focused on manufactured products other than mineral processing and tradable services, including selected non-traditional agricultural and mining activities. More specifically, this included natural-resource-based sectors, medium technology sectors (including downstream mineral beneficiation), advanced manufacturing sectors, labour intensive sectors, and the tradable services sector.

Although the document acknowledged the importance of focusing on a few interventions, the list of priority areas makes it clear that policy support was de facto to be spread out among a fairly large number of sectors.

2.4 A Revised Science and Technology Strategy

In 2007, in a similar but totally unrelated move, DST proposed a Ten-Year Plan to promote a knowledge-based economy (DST 2007). Its authors were concerned about the failure of the NIS to commercialise the results of scientific research. The focus was on ambitious longer-term objectives related to frontier science. These included

- 'being among the global top ten in terms of the pharmaceutical, nutraceutical, flavour, fragrance and bio-pesticide industries
- deploying satellites that provide a range of scientific, security and specialised services for the government, the public and the private sector
- achieving a 25 percent share of the global fuel cell market with novel platinum group metal (PGM) catalysts
- development of a fuel cell programme for transport and domestic use
- initial capability in the production of hydrogen by water splitting
- being a world leader in climate science and the response to climate change
- having met the 2014 Millennium Development Goals to halve poverty' (DST 2007, 5).

Figure 6.1. Innovation Towards a Knowledge-Based Economy: Targets for Transformation

Indicator	Measure	Current	2018
SA positioned as knowledge-based economy	Growth attributable to technical progress	10% in 2002	30%
	GDP derived from knowledge-based industries		>50%
	Share of workforce employed in knowledge-based jobs		>50%
	Share of firms using technology to innovate		>50%
	GERD/GDP	0.87 in 2004; 2008 target is 1%	2%
	Share of global research outputs	0.5% in 2002	1%
	Share of high- and medium-tech exports/services	30% in 2002	55%
	South African originated US patents	100 in 2002	250
Research and technology enablers	Matriculants with university exemption in maths and science	3.4% in 2002	9%
	Share of SET tertiary students		30%
	PhD graduates per year	963 in 2002	2,200
	Gross availability of SET graduates	235,438 in 2002	450,000
	Full-time equivalent researchers	8,708 in 2002	20,000
	Researchers per 1,000 people employed		5%

Source: DST 2007, 9.

Such an ambitious strategy presupposed major interventions in the form of increased R&D investments by both the private and the public sectors. DST claimed that, due to the massive scope, the outcome would not only be a larger share of global markets in key emerging technologies, but would also include spin-offs in terms of scientific, engineering, and management capacity. Ambitious indicators that would allow government to measure success both ex post and during the process were elaborated. For example, the strategy aimed at tripling the share of economic growth attributable to technical progress to 30 per cent, and at doubling R&D spending as a percentage of GDP (to two per cent), the global share of research outputs (to one per cent), and the number of SET graduates (to 450,000 per year; see Figure 6.1).

Analysis of the NIS had identified a central weakness – namely insufficient prioritization. With a limited pool of available resources, one unintended consequence was that the scale of activity in many cases was too small to achieve policy goals or have an effective impact (OECD 2007). The Ten Year Plan reflected an attempt to prioritise and focus, but in a very specific manner, introducing what it called the "5 grand challenges" which simultaneously promoted specific outcomes and extended the research agenda. These challenges lay in the area of

- the farmer-to-pharma value chain to strengthen the bio-economy
- space science and technology
- energy security
- global change with a focus on climate change
- human and social dynamics.

To bridge the innovation chasm – this is the term locally used for the discrepancy between scientific endeavour and technological development – and address problems of funding, the Plan proposed the establishment of a co-ordinating Technology Innovation Agency (TIA) which would liaise between the formal knowledge base and the real economy, support technology-based activities, provide an intellectual property platform, stimulate investment and facilitate the development of human capital.

While the White Paper and the NRDS can be seen as founding documents of South Africa's NIS, the NIPF and the Ten-Year Plan are hallmarks of a system that is growing, is increasingly reflexive and is attempting to come to terms with how to put its vision into practice, in the face of unintended consequences of implementation to date. They demonstrate that the NIS is evolving. Viewed on their individual merit, they show the commitment of government to pursue growth through innovation and to allow as many people as possible to benefit from the results.

Each document is testimony to the efforts being made by individual government departments to elaborate how the demands of the knowledge economy affect the way in which they should operate, both in the short term and in the medium and longer term. However, a serious concern stems from the fact that these processes have taken place along parallel lines, with little inter-departmental coordination or consultation. This leads to a proliferation of activities for government, for which it may not have the capacity or resources to deliver. At the time of writing, the two departments were engaged in discussions about the articulation between the Ten-Year Plan and the NIPF, but whether this would lead to a re-evaluation of focus and a higher level of coordination is uncertain. Despite a formal commitment to coordination as a mechanism of governance, there is little cross-departmental consultation in key areas of policy formulation, resulting in low levels of interaction across government departments. Section 3 will consider the impact this lack of coordination has on the processes of implementation.

2.5 Structure and Functions of the NIS[2]

Figure 6.2 depicts the main institutional actors and their roles in the NIS. DST has direct line management responsibility for science and technology

Figure 6.2. Overall Structure of NIS

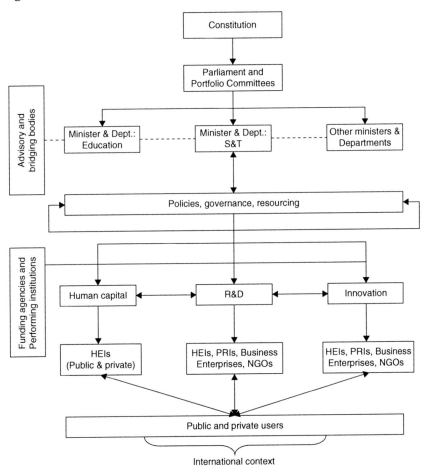

Note: The International context impacts directly and indirectly on all elements of the structure. HEI: Higher education institutions; PRIs: public research institutions; NGOs: non-governmental organisations.
Source: NACI 2006, Figure 3.

and is in charge of the resourcing and management of public research institutions. The Department of Education and the higher education institutions are responsible for providing high-level human resources and for generating new knowledge. A number of other government departments fund and perform R&D. They include the Departments of Trade and Industry, Minerals and Energy, Environmental Affairs and Tourism, Agriculture, Water Affairs and Forestry, and Health. The business sector, including the semi-state bodies, is where knowledge is transformed into new products and services. Finally, non-governmental organisations undertake R&D primarily in areas of public interest.

These actors share four functions between them. First, there is policy formulation and advice. This resides with government departments; overall coordination of S&T lies with DST. In addition, there are advisory bodies, such as the Council on Higher Education (CHE) and the National Advisory Council on Innovation (NACI). Second, a large number of agencies and bodies, such as the National Research Foundation (NRF) and the Medical Research Council (MRC), are responsible for funding. This can be either directed to specific projects or, via open calls, in support of self-initiated research. In the past few years, the share of open calls and directed funding has risen in importance compared to performance-based block funding. Third, performance is delivered by higher education institutions, public research institutions such as the science councils, and the business sector. Fourth, there is the pursuit of international S&T relations and networks, which is the responsibility of all actors. In addition to ensuring South Africa's integration into international knowledge flows, this was originally aimed at overcoming the isolation of the country's scientific community during the 1970s and 1980s.

2.6 Mechanisms for Building the NIS and Fostering Innovation

At transition in 1994, the science system was fragmented, highly uneven and inequitable. Since then, government departments have designed a range of meso- and micro-level mechanisms and incentivisation programmes with the aim of implementing policy, by promoting performance, linkages and interaction across the institutional actors of the NIS. The main thrusts of intended implementation mechanisms are described here, highlighting the wide range of multiple and potentially competing priorities described above, as well as the priority accorded to promoting 'big science', high technology capability, and research at the 'technological frontier', in building the NIS.

2.7 Enhancing Technology Missions and Platforms

The technology missions identified as focal points for development in the 1990s were not all areas of historically strong technological expertise and innovation capability. A range of programmes targeting funding and development of capacity in the strategic scientific research areas on which these technologies depend was initiated to stimulate development of SET and of the industrial sectors. As policy has evolved to focus on the five areas of 'grand challenge' over the next ten years, new mechanisms are being elaborated and initiated. One example will suffice here to illustrate the interlocking range of meso- and micro-level mechanisms intended to change structures, institutions and capabilities.

Strategic interventions in relation to growing a Biotechnology technology platform were most coherent to date, as they were initiated at an early stage. The goals of the White Paper and the technology foresight studies informed the development of a substantive National Biotechnology Strategy (2001), and are manifest in the establishment and funding of Biotechnology Regional Innovation Centres (BRICs) located in three provinces, to promote R&D, provide entrepreneurial services, technology platforms, intellectual property management, and business incubation. These consortia were aimed at facilitating collaboration between universities and companies in the mature biotechnology sector and the bioeconomy. Support structures such as a National Bioinformatics Network and a Biotechnology Advisory Committee were initiated by DST and the National Advisory Council on Innovation (NACI). The Department of Trade and Industry (DTI) established a national biotechnology incubator, EgoliBio, to support small companies and develop capacity. The sector is currently under review, but early research has suggested that it is growing slowly, and that there are currently far more research groups than firms (eGoli 2003, Walwyn 2003, Motari et al 2004).

2.8 Renewing the R&D and Academic Labour Forces

The need to reproduce the scientific, R&D and academic workforce has been a key policy focus, particularly in order to ensure that the distribution of scientists and technologists reflects national demographic patterns in South Africa. In its most recent strategic plan (2005), the National Research Foundation proposed to increase the scale and quality of the PhD degree as the key vehicle for enhancing the national system of innovation. The 'seamless approach' adopted was designed to co-ordinate funding and capacity development programmes to intervene from school level to the point of commercialisation of knowledge, from student bursaries to incentive systems for academics to centres of excellence and research chairs, and to foster international scientific collaboration.

2.9 Enhancing the R&D Institutional Infrastructure

South Africa has a number of public research institutions or science councils, most notably the Council for Scientific and Industrial Research (CSIR) and the Medical Research Council; moreover, the NRF hosts and manages National Research Facilities that are aligned with priority missions, such as space science. As publicly funded research institutions they are subject to greater public accountability in setting strategic research directions. Science councils are charged with expanding their international activities, in areas of strategic importance, and with creating internationally visible centres of excellence to open up opportunities for international collaboration. A National Equipment Programme was set up to provide funding to renew the equipment infrastructure for research and technology development, informed by a National Research and Technology Infrastructure Strategy (2004).

2.10 Enhancing Technology Transfer and Innovation

Government's role in the diffusion of both domestic and imported technologies was identified as critical, particularly to stimulating diffusion among SMMEs. Central to technology diffusion is the presence in firms of a workforce that is able to absorb new technologies, to optimise transfer of technological capacity to firms, and the creation of locally-based expertise, or 'doing, using and learning' modes of innovation. DST has tended to focus on promoting 'big science' rather than on these other more tacit modes of innovation that relate to firms rather than research institutions. Prior to the formulation of the National Industrial Strategy, DTI's response was to support direct state intervention through a co-ordinated package of investment and export incentives, as well as measures aimed at exploiting externalities, supply chain linkages and agglomeration economies in order to create labour-absorbing industrial growth. These incentives emphasized government intervention in technology promotion and innovation support, by enhancing technology transfer capacities within local firms.

2.11 Enhancing collaboration and networks

Linkages between higher education, business, and science councils were identified as critical to addressing issues such as diffusion of best practice technology, making full use of ICT and the social sciences, and avoiding problems such as duplication, fragmentation, and lack of coordination within the national system of innovation. At an early stage, DST identified a critical enabling role for government in encouraging innovation within the private sector. It established the Innovation Fund, the purpose of which was to provide financial incentives for longer-term, large innovation research projects with cross-sectoral collaborative consortia composed of researchers from the higher education sector, government science councils, the private sector, or civil society.

The main focus of the DTI's earlier policy framework was on attempting to overcome a range of weaknesses in past trade and industry performance. One mechanism was the introduction of the 'Technology and Human Resources for Industry Programme' (THRIP), which aimed to facilitate the increased participation of higher education and science council researchers and students in industrial innovation, technological adaptation and commercialisation. THRIP operated by matching the funds invested in innovation research by private companies. The Support Programme for Industrial Innovation (SPII) supported innovation of products or processes in private sector firms, providing incentives in the form of matching grants.

Together, these funding initiatives have been important in creating awareness in firms, universities and science councils of the benefits of interaction, and in fostering a number of university-industry linkages that have yielded postgraduate students, publications, patents, new processes and artefacts in priority sectors (HSRC 2003, Letseka 2004, Kruss 2006).

2.12 Intellectual Property Rights Framework

A key condition for enhancing collaboration, technology transfer and diffusion is an adequate framework of Intellectual Property Rights. The national legislative framework was influenced by British and European legislation and for the most part is in compliance with international treaties and conventions. Wolson (2003) argued that one problem was the understanding and management of intellectual property rights on the part of the scientific and R&D labour force. Clarity was lacking and different practices prevailed in relation to the ownership of research funded by higher education institutions, government and the private sector; this created a degree of confusion and disadvantage to institutions and, ultimately, to the national system of innovation in general. A proposed new consolidated national framework aimed at protecting IPR derived from publicly funded research, along the lines of the Bayh-Dole Act (2007), has given rise to concern about its suitability in South African conditions. The framework may be based on unrealistic expectations, over-estimating the potential for revenue-generation. The possibility of over-regulation could discourage firms from research collaboration with universities or licensing new technologies developed in universities, and thus act as a constraint on innovation (Wolson 2007).

3. Goals Against Performance

This description of intended strategic and funding mechanisms does not try to provide a systematic examination of the extent to which they have been implemented, or the ways in which they have succeeded - or not, as the case may be. In this section, we consider data and analysis that begin to evaluate the extent to which performance reflects the attainment of policy goals set over the past ten years.

3.1 Social and Economic Development

In general, African economies have been growing steadily in 2004–2007, driven by internal factors such as competent macro-economic management and by external factors such as higher commodity prices (The Presidency 2007: 68). Despite this growth, very few African economies are on track to achieve the Millennium Development Goals by 2015. They also continue to be marginal players in world trade, with less than three per cent of global exports. Despite the strength of its economy on the continent, South Africa faces many of the same challenges in terms of lags in social development, poverty, and HIV/AIDS and other diseases. Also, the good growth performance relies in large measure on the high global demand for commodities exported by African economies, which is an unreliable source. There is little evidence of the diversification which would increase total factor productivity. In fact, much like Africa at large, South Africa mostly exports low-growth products into below-average growing markets (Edwards and Alves 2006). Since South Africa relies on foreign capital inflows to finance its burgeoning balance of payments deficit, any deterioration in the global economy would have serious consequences for the country, as attested by recent trends in 2008 and 2009.

In South Africa, growth has averaged over 4.5 per cent since 2004. The country is not a prime destination for inward direct investment, but gross fixed capital has been growing at close to 20 per cent. Exports account for just under one third of GDP. In 2004/05 expenditure on R&D reached 0.87 per cent of GDP and is thus on track to achieve the one per cent threshold in 2008 (DST 2004 and 2006). Gross domestic expenditure on R&D likewise increased from R7 499.6 million in 2001/2 to R12 010 million in 2004/5. South Africa remained significantly below the OECD average of 2.26 percent of GDP, in the company of European countries such as Hungary (0.88) and Portugal (0.78 in 2003), and of Brazil (0.95 for 2003) and India (0.84 for 2003) (IMD 2005).

Government claimed that the Growth, Employment and Redistribution (GEAR) macro-economic policy had paid dividends, evident in the fact that real GDP growth -which had been 3.2 in 1994, fell to 0.5 in 1998 and then rose

Figure 6.3. Socioeconomic Indicators

Indicator	2000	2001	2002	2003	2004	2005	2006
GDP growth (%)	4.2	2.7	3.7	3.1	4.8	5.1	5.0
Real per capita GDP growth (%)	2.1	0.8	1.9	1.5	3.4	3.7	3.6
Foreign direct investment (R billion)	4.280	85.763	12.153	1.275	−3.566	33.854	−47.350
Gross fixed capital formation (% of GDP)	15.1	14.8	15.4	16.0	16.3	17.3	19.2
Expenditure on R&D (% of GDP)	2000/02: 0.73			2003/04: 0.81		2004/05: 0.87	
Exports/GDP (%)	27.0	28.7	31.9	27.5	26.3	27.9	30.8
Unemployment (%, narrow/broad definition)		29.4/40.6	30.4/41.8	28.0/41.8	26.2/41.0	26.7/38.8	25.5/37.3
Total income (%, poorest 10%/richest 10%)	0.6/55.3	0.6/55.2	0.6/53.5	0.6/56.3	0.7/55.4	0.6/55.5	0.6/55.9
Gini coefficient	0.682	0.635	0.670	0.686	0.678	0.683	0.685
Life expectancy		54.6	53.8	53.0	52.3	51.9	50.7
Households not in formal dwelling (%)		16.4	12.7	12.5	11.3	15.9	
Households without access to water infrastructure (%)	17.2	13.2	10.0	9.3	8.1	6.7	6.0
Households with access to sanitation (%)	57.6	59.2	62.5	64.1	66.1	69.1	70.7
Households with access to electricity (%)	61.1	69.0	75.9	76.5	74.6	74.7	73.7
Matriculants with mathematics higher passes	19,327	19,504	20,528	23,412	24,143	26,383	33,112
Adult literacy rate (%)			70.7	72.6	73.3	74.2	
Graduating SET students	25.7	25.2	26.7	26.9	27.0	27.8	

Source: Presidency n.d.

steadily to reach 5.0 per cent in 2006 (Presidency 2007). An IMF report confirmed the strong economic growth from 2003, arguing that the economy was experiencing its longest expansion on record (IMF 2007: 5). Following the early 'sluggish' growth, the benefits of the macro-economic policy and structural reforms were reflected in more expansionary budgets that prioritised social spending and redistribution. The benefit of macroeconomic stabilization created the space to treble social grant expenditure, and improve social development through pro-poor spending (World Bank 2007).

However, by 2008, the Harvard Group – an international government advisory panel – argued that insufficient attention had been devoted to the structural obstacles to sustainable growth and equitable development. Employment has increased in line with increased growth rates, but concern about the rate of labour absorption, particularly of young people, remains. More than a third (broad definition) or a quarter (narrow definition) of the population remains unemployed. In the face of the expansion of the welfare state, poverty continues to be an issue, and inequality even more so. The total population stood at 47.9 million in mid-2007, 79.7 per cent of whom are classified as African, 9.1 per cent as White, 8.8 as Coloured, and 2.1 per cent as Indian/Asian (Statistics SA 2007). The GINI coefficient has risen over the past ten years, to its current level of 0.685. The distribution of the richest and poorest continues to be defined along racial lines. More than half of the black population is poor, and 95 per cent of the poor are black. There is also evidence to suggest widening inequality within race groups and a decline of inequality between race groups, reflecting the growth of the middle classes (Presidency 2007: 24). Inequality leads to, and is evident in, unequal access to quality public education and health services, and thus inequality of outcomes in education and health. Due mainly to the HIV/AIDS epidemic, mortality is on the rise. In 2007, life expectancy was down to 50 years. There continue to be backlogs in housing, potable water provision, sanitation, and electricity. Inequality is also spatially concentrated, with economic wealth, research and innovation activity concentrated mainly in the Gauteng province, followed by the Western Cape and the Kwa ZuluNatal provinces (DST 2005, Lorentzen 2009b).

The number of high-school graduates with qualifications in mathematics is on the rise, albeit at a lower rate than hoped for. Almost three quarters of the population are literate. More than one in four higher education students graduate in science, engineering, and technology subjects (NACI 2006, Presidency n.d., see Figure 6.3).

In sum, although there have been improvements, much has still to be addressed. Innovation has so far done little to tackle mass unemployment, persistent poverty and widespread inequality (ECA/AU 2007). This inequality is critical in interpreting the development trajectory of the South African national system of innovation. The legacy of deep-seated cultural, ideological and social divisions, coupled with a deep-seated lack of capacity and expertise on the part of a large proportion of the population, continue to impact in complex ways on what is possible.

3.2 The NIS in Review – A "Work in Progress"

Over the years the South African NIS has been the subject of a variety of reviews. Kahn (2006) gives a largely descriptive account of the system from its origins in the early 19th century. Mani (2004) praised the sophistication of innovation policy formulation and criticised the gap between policy and implementation. In his view, no public policy mechanism has effectively addressed the shortage of skills in the country. Similarly, Kraak (2007) argued that, while policies were largely aware of the requirements and challenges of the knowledge society, implementation had largely failed to keep up. Rooks and Oerlemans (2005) probed what they called the 'X-effectiveness of the NSI', by which they meant the degree to which relevant institutions achieved their organisational goals.

The most in-depth exercise was the issuing, by South Africa's National Advisory Council on Innovation (NACI 2006), of a background report for an upcoming OECD country review of the NIS which was tabled the following year (OECD 2007). To date these two reports are the most detailed assessments available of the structure and the operation of the NIS.

One of the merits of the NACI background report is that it did not confine itself to narrow S&T issues. Taking as its point of departure the ambitious promise of a "better life for all" made in the White Paper, it examined the NIS from the perspective of how well it contributes to the accomplishment of overall development of the country. For example, it mentioned the government goal of halving poverty and unemployment by 2014, the need to increase labour absorption especially in the rural areas and to find alternative employment for the thousands of miners who had lost their jobs over the previous decade. According to the report, the most serious weaknesses of the system lie in: the shortage of skills, which holds back firm innovation and to which the response of the education system has been inadequate; a rigid (venture) capital market for research and innovation; underdelivery of tasks set in the NRDS, especially in the area of S&T for poverty reduction; some inconsistency and inefficiency of effort; and a relative decline in performance compared to other countries. Among its strengths it counts primarily the solidity of the policy framework. In its own words, there are many strong features of the NSI, and the country can be justifiably proud of its achievements in the areas of innovation, novel technologies, the management of R&D and national systems, and the generation of knowledge through R&D. However, it is unfortunate that the benefits of a life enriched by economic progress and technology are restricted to so few. Some would characterise South Africa as two countries, one rich and developed, the other poor and undeveloped; the challenge for the NSI is to extend the privilege of development to the entire country (NACI 2006, 87).

The OECD review report (OECD 2007) argued that there was relatively too much focus on the role of public institutions performing R&D and an under-appreciation of the role of innovation that is not primarily linked to formal R&D at all, including indigenous knowledge, and activities in the informal economy, along with the role of non-R&D capabilities in the areas of engineering, design, and related management and technical functions. It criticised the fact that key tenets of the NRDS – such as the Technology and Innovation for Poverty Reduction Programme or the idea to marry resource-based industries to the knowledge economy (see also Lorentzen 2008) – had not been implemented at all. In contrast, other programmes that were not initially identified as strategic priorities had been supported by extensive funding, such as the development of Pebble Bed Nuclear Reactor technology. Clearly, it is easier to design and implement a biotechnology strategy, for example, given that there are many international exemplars. On the other hand, there have been few, if any, ready-made experiences of how to use innovation to address poverty, least of all from the advanced economies which provided the policy exemplars from which South Africa initially borrowed.

The report criticised the fact that too many national resources had been devoted to stimulating high-technology industries – a key example of the relatively unreflective borrowing of certain policies. It pointed out that the country should also build on existing strengths, such as the technological competencies of large firms whose benefits should be disseminated to smaller firms through policies that supported both internal and external human capital formation and knowledge development. This did not rely on R&D alone, but prominently included the "products" resulting from design, engineering and associated management activities. In other words, the OECD recommended that R&D should be important, but not the exclusive focus of policy, as has tended to be the case.

The report further noted a relatively unique feature of the South African economy, namely a high share of business R&D in total R&D combined with a heavily resource-based structure of the economy. Due to their links with the manufacturing sector, the resource-based industries are much more important than the percentage of GDP for which they account (roughly 10 per cent) would indicate. This suggested that knowledge intensification of resource-based activities along the Scandinavian model should be high on the agenda, rather than the declared intention to diversify the economy away from its commodity base (cf. Lorentzen 2008). Finally, the report criticised the fact that not enough attention had been paid to what is likely to be the principal channel of technology, namely FDI and other forms of technology import. Such foreign knowledge dynamically interacts with domestic innovation and is thus key to stage-based processes of technological advance.

3.3 Constraints on Policy

There is general agreement in these reviews that there are significant 'binding constraints' which should inform a more reflexive and contextually grounded process of elaboration and implementation of strategic policy. The Ten Year Plan formulated in 2007 attempted to take some of these constraints into account, but it is worth highlighting some of the major systemic conditions that are likely to create ongoing barriers to realising the evolving policy visions. In this section, we consider these barriers in relation to the three key NIS actors: universities, government and firms.

3.4 Insufficient Analysis of Firms as Sites of Innovation

In a country like South Africa, one would expect a more thorough knowledge base of the dynamics of technological upgrading at the micro-level in specific economic sectors, in order to inform policy directions and mechanisms. National technological capability is rooted in the innovation system, including the externalities and synergies that result from the manner in which learning happens and business is done, and from the relevant knowledge and skills that reside in related institutions (Lall 2000). Institutions are a key part of the context within which technological learning takes place. They influence productivity and, thus, economic growth. The key issue is how they influence interactions between economic agents and what difference this makes to the effectiveness of economic activity (Nelson 2005, Nelson and Nelson 2002). What such systems achieve depends at the macro-level on the success with which policy addresses market failures that are due to the respective incentive regimes, factor markets, and institutions.

Here, governments have a range of complementary assets and institutions at their disposal. The range of South African innovation programmes and funding mechanisms was described above in Section 1, but it is clear that they focus primarily on R&D and science institutions, rather than on firms. There is little evidence in policy of any analysis of the sort of benefits that accrue to local innovators and the consequences for growth and job creation. In cases where uncertainty prevents investment in greater technological specialisation, government must provide the public goods that reduce transaction costs. This must be accommodated by an appropriability regime that treads the fine line between stimulating innovative activity and allowing for wide dissemination of the results (Chesbrough, Birkinshaw, and Teubal 2006). The role technology can play in reducing poverty can only be properly understood (and, thus, supported) in the context of incentive regimes and how these interact with the strategic agendas of firms.

There are a small but significant number of such sectoral studies that view the innovation system as a problem, both in traditional and in more advanced activities (see for instance Aylward and Turpin 2003, Seaden and Manseau 2001, Lorentzen 2005, Pogue 2008, Rasiah 2006, Paterson et al. 2008, Sawers, Pretorius, and Oerlemans 2008). In addition, there is an increasing body of scholarship on linkages between firms and other NIS actors, especially in the higher education sector (Klerck 2005, Kruss 2006, Lubango and Pouris 2007). On the whole, however, there is insufficient micro-based knowledge, and extensive research is required to inform government policy activity and the innovation community in this regard (Lorentzen 2009a).

3.5 Human Resources, Skills and Higher Education

A widely recognised 'binding constraint' on implementation is directly linked to the levels of human resources required to achieve policy goals and change in South Africa.

Historically low levels of education for the majority of the population are proving to be a major constraint on economic growth, and on the development of a national system of innovation. The schooling system, shaped by the legacy of apartheid-era curricula and under-resourcing, does not produce enough graduates in mathematics and science to enrol in higher education science, technology and engineering programmes (HSRC 2003, Reddy 2006). In turn, this means that the intermediate and high level engineering skills required in order to work on expanded infrastructure development projects or on innovation in firms are not available on a sufficient scale, which acts as a constraint on economic growth.

In order for innovative activity to expand throughout the economy, an expansion of the university research system is required, particularly in relation to producing research-capable human resources. However, there are indications that it may not be possible to sustain university R&D at current levels, let alone expand the system significantly (OECD 2007). The OECD report attributed this primarily to the constraints in the 'human resources pipeline' and, secondly, to constraints on the reproduction of the academic labour force itself – issues that have received considerable attention from researchers over the last few years (HRD Review 2003, COHORT 2004, Koen 2006 and 2007). While the NRF may propose the PhD as a driver of innovation and provide funding incentives, there may not be sufficient capacity across the university system to produce these science, engineering and technology doctoral graduates in greater numbers, nor are there systematic attempts to train or recruit graduates internationally.

Levels of research and technology development capacity are extremely low at some of the new comprehensive universities created from formerly historically disadvantaged universities, and also at some of the new universities of technology, particularly those located in isolated rural areas, in the provinces with the lowest levels of development in South Africa. National efforts to promote research capacity described in Section 1 above have yet to show significant effects.

Kruss (2007) argues that the highly differentiated and segmented national university system itself acts as a major constraint on the extent to which higher education plays a role in the NIS. The higher education landscape in 2007 consisted of 22 universities and universities of technology, emerging from a process of government mandated mergers and restructuring aimed at creating new organisational forms that can potentially transform the system inherited from the past (Ministry of Education 2002, Council on Higher Education 2004). Universities and technikons were established in South Africa during specific periods to meet specific purposes, and these origins have continued to shape their differential and unequal nature and capacity to interact within the NIS.

A high degree of segmentation between types of university in the national system can discourage researchers from undertaking a wide variety of types of research and from moving between different kinds of university, without loss of reputation (Whitley 2003). This can slow down the rate of transfer of knowledge and skills between the different types of university in South Africa, so that some types of universities focus on cutting-edge frontier science, but in isolation from other types of universities that may have strengths in technological development. There are generally low levels of teaching and research collaboration between universities, whether of the same or different types, even those in close regional proximity to one another. That is not to say that such knowledge intensive collaboration does not exist at all, or that there are no mechanisms that successfully attempt to foster it, such as the THRIP and Innovation Fund schemes described above. However, the scale of such collaboration remains limited. In university systems with low segmentation, knowledge and skills flow more easily between different types of university, and the development of joint projects, collaboration and adaptation to new knowledge can be better facilitated. Higher education policy incentives need to promote greater collaboration and less segmentation across the system, so as to strengthen research and innovative capacity.

3.6 Lack of Maturity in New Governance and Administration Systems

A further 'binding constraint' on achieving government's goals that has been inherited from the past is a lack of maturity in the new systems of governance, and in administration (ASGISA 2006). The presidency was formally committed to building a system of state steering and regulation that recognized the need for 'joined-up' solutions to economic and social problems. This was manifested in cabinet clusters that cut across government line departments to develop coordinated multi-sectoral strategic responses (Kraak 2007). Building a national system of innovation requires coordinated and integrated solutions between the policies of multiple government departments, but we have seen above how policy formulation occurred in parallel unconnected processes.

Immediately after 1994, the task was to merge multiple racially defined government departments to achieve a single unified system. For example, in education, there were 19 racially defined departments dealing with schooling in different areas of the country for distinct racial groups. Concomitantly, there was contestation within government departments between technically experienced officials from the old order, and politically experienced new officials, who generally lacked technical and managerial experience. Currently, the high turnover and high vacancy rate in key posts in some key departments are resulting in inefficiencies, loss of institutional memory and inaction. New government systems are not yet mature, and the extent to which the commitment to coordination has permeated beyond the senior departmental levels and down to the administrative level is highly uneven.

The capacity of government departments to implement strategic programmes and to disburse allocated budgets is uneven. A key challenge is 'to raise institutional capacity by a sufficient degree to ensure that earmarked funds are spent productively' (The Economist Intelligence Unit 2007b: 5). The lack of continuity and lack of interactive capability (Von Tunzelmann 2007) on the part of key government actors translates into a systemic lack of coordination within and between government departments, and a potential mismatch of priorities and misalignment in the national system of innovation.

3. Conclusion

South Africa has a strong, progressive and comprehensive foundation of science, technology and innovation policy. Since 1994 there have been considerable gains in developing a national system of innovation. There is evidence that policy is maturing and evolving, despite initial policy borrowing that did not sufficiently reflect the conditions of a latecomer society. The challenge is to identify more appropriate policy means to address key 'binding constraints' that are the legacy of the past. The extent to which policy-making is sufficiently coordinated across government, and the extent to which it is sufficiently informed by analysis of the conditions in local firms, sectors and higher education, and the interaction between them, remain critical issues for policy expansion and the elaboration of incentives to steer the NIS in the desired directions. This is particularly the case if policy mechanisms are to effectively promote a NIS that addresses persistent poverty and widespread equality at the same time as growing capacity at the technological frontier.

References

Albuquerque, E. 2001. Scientific Infrastructure and Catching-up process: notes about a relationship illustrated by Science and technology statistics. RBE 55(4): 545–556.

Amuah, I. 1994. Science and technology policy for the new South Africa: a rational perspective on using science and technology to leverage national economic development. Pretoria. *Foundation for Research Development Report Series* No. 5.

Augusto, Geri. 2002. Context, Co-presence and "Compossibilities": Bioprospecting between Endogenous Knowledge and Science in *South Africa*. *International Journal of Biotechnology* 4, nos2–3: 239.

Aylward. D.; Turpin, T. 2003. New Wine in Old Bottles: A Case Study of Innovation Territories in "New World" Wine Production. *International Journal of Innovation Management* 4, n.4: 501–25.

Barben, D. 2007. Changing Regimes of Science and Politics: Comparative and Transnational Perspectives for a World in Transition. *Science and Public Policy* 34, no.1: 55–69.

Blankley, W.; Kahn, M. 2005. The History of Research and Experimental Development Measurement in South Africa and Some Current Perspectives. *South African Journal of Science* 101 (March/April): 151–56.

Chesbrough, H., Birkinshaw, J.; Teubal. M. 2006. Introduction to the research policy 20th anniversary special issue of the publication of "Profiting from Innovation" by David Teece. *Research Policy* 35: 1091–99.

Cohort (Committee of Heads of Research and Technology) (2004), Securing tomorrow today. Policy report for Colloquium on Ten Years of Democracy and Higher Education Change, November. Pretoria: Council on Higher Education.

Council On Higher Education (2004), *South African Higher Education in the First Decade of Democracy*. Pretoria: Council on Higher Education.

DACST (Department of Arts, Culture, Science and Technology, South Africa). 1996. White Paper on Science & Technology: Preparing for the 21st Century. Pretoria.

DACST (Department of Arts Culture, Science and Technology, South Africa). 1999. National Research and Technology Foresight Synthesis Report. Pretoria: DST.

DST (Department of Science and Technology, South Africa). 2001. A National Biotechnology Strategy for South Africa. 20 August.

DST (Department of Science and Technology, South Africa). 2002. South Africa's Research and Development Strategy.

DST (Department of Science and Technology, South Africa). 2005. Regional Contributions to the South African Technology Achievement Index. Unit for Local Innovation, Government Sectoral Programmes and Coordination.

DST (Department of Science and Technology, South Africa). 2006. National survey of research and experimental development 2005/6. High-level key results. Pretoria: DST.

DST (Department of Science and Technology, South Africa). 2007a. Innovation Towards a Knowledge-Based Economy: Ten-Year Plan for South Africa (2008–2018). Draft Document for Discussion, 10 July. Pretoria.

DST (Department of Science and Technology, South Africa).2007b. Science, Engineering and Technology Human Capital Strategy. 2008–2028. Draft.

DTI (Department of Trade and Industry, South Africa). 2007. A National Industrial Policy Framework. Pretoria.

ECA/AU (Economic Commission for Africa/African Union). 2007. *Economic Report on Africa 2007: Accelerating Africa's Development through Diversification.* Addis Ababa: United Nations Economic Commission for Africa.

The Economist Intelligence Unit. 2007b. Monthly Report. South Africa. London: *The Economist Intelligence Unit.* November.

Lawrence, E.; Alves, P. 2006. South Africa's Export Performance: Determinants of Export Supply. *South African Journal of Economics* 74, no.9: 473–500.

Egolibio. 2003. National Biotech Survey. Johannesburg: EgoliBio Life Sciences Incubator and Department of Science and Technology.

Freeman, C. 1988. Japan: A New National System of Innovation? In *Technical Change and Economic Theory,* eds Giovanni Dosi, Christopher Freeman, Richard Nelson, Gerald Silverberg, and Luc Soete, 330–48. London: Pinter.

Gibbons, M.; Limoges, C.; Nowotny., H; Schwartzman, S., Scott, P. and TROW, M. 1994. *The new production of knowledge: the dynamics of science and research in contemporary societies.* California and London: Sage.

HSRC. 2003a. Government Incentivisation of Higher Education-Industry Research Partnerships in South Africa. An Audit of THRIP and the Innovation Fund. Working partnerships: Higher education, industry and innovation series. HSRC Publishers. Cape Town.

HSRC. 2003b. Human Resources Development. Education, Employment and Skills in South Africa. Pretoria: HSRC Press and East Lansing: Michigan State University Press.

IDRC. 1995. Building a new South Africa. Volume 3. Science and technology policy. A report from the Mission on Science and Technology Policy for a Democratic South Africa. Ottawa: IDRC.

International Monetary Fund. 2007. South Africa. Staff Report for the 2007 Article IV consultation. Country Report No. 07/274. July.

Kahn, M. 2006. The South African National System of Innovation: From Constructed Crisis to Constructed Advantage? *Science and Public Policy* 33, no.2: 125–36.

Kahn, M.; Blankley, W. 2005. The changing face of South Africa's national system of innovation, 1991–2001. *Industry and Higher Education.* 19 (2): 121–130.

Kaplan, D. 1996. Science and technology in a democratic South Africa: new challenges and policy directions. Science, Technology and Society.

Kaplan, D. 1999. On the literature of the economics of technological change. Science and technology policy in South Africa. *South African Journal of Economics.* 67, no 4: 473–485.

Kaplan, D. 2004. South Africa's National Research and Development Strategy: A Review. *Science Technology & Society* 9: 273–94.

Klerck, G. 2005. Competition and Cooperation in South Africa's Biotechnology Sector. *Industry & Higher Education* (April): 169–78.

Koen, C. 2006. Higher education and work. Setting a new research agenda. *ESSD Occasional Paper* 1. Cape Town: Human Sciences Research Council.

Koen, C. 2007. Post-graduate retention and success: A South African case study. Cape Town: HSRC Press.

Kraak, A. 2007. *Knowledge Circulation and the Knowledge Economy: Opportunities and Constraints in the South African Context.* HSRC, Cape Town [mimeo].

Kruss, G. (ed). 2006. *Creating Knowledge Networks: Working Partnerships in Higher Education, Industry and Innovation.* Cape Town: HSRC Press.

Lall, S. 2000. Technological Change and Industrialization in the Asian Newly Industrializing Economies: Achievements and Challenges. In *Technology, Learning, & Innovation: Experiences of Newly Industrializing Economies.* Eds Linsu Kim and Richard Nelson, 13–68. Cambridge: Cambridge University Press.

Lall, S.; Pietrobelli, C. 2002. *Failing to Compete: Technology Development and Technology Systems in Africa.* Cheltenham: Elgar.

Letseka, M. 2005. Government incentivisation of partnerships in South Africa: an audit of THRIP and Innovation Fund. *Industry and Higher Education.* 19 (2): 161–168.

Lorentzen, J. 2005. The Absorptive Capacities of South African Automotive Component Suppliers. *World Development* 33, no.7: 1153–82.

Lorentzen, J., ed. 2008. *Resource Intensity, Knowledge, and Development: Insights from Africa and South America.* Pretoria: HSRC Press.

Lorentzen, J. 2009a. Learning by Firms: The Black Box of South Africa's Innovation System. *Science and Public Policy* 36, no.1: 33–45.

Lorentzen, J. 2009b. The Geography of Innovation in South Africa – A First Cut. International Journal of Technological Learning, *Innovation and Development* 2, no.3: 210–29.

Lubango, L. M.; Pouris, A. 2007. Industry Work Experience and Inventive Capacity of South African Academic Researchers. *Technovation* 27: 788–96.

Lundvall, B.-Å. (ed). 1992. National Systems of Innovation. London: Pinter.

Mani, S. 2004. Government, Innovation, and Technology Policy: An International Comparative Analysis. *International Journal of Technology and Globalisation* 1, n.1: 29–44.

Mbeki, T. 2003. Address of the President of South Africa to the National Council of Provinces. Parliament, Cape Town: The Presidency. 11 February.

Mbeki, T. 2004, Address of the President of South Africa, at the Final Joint Sitting of the Second Democratic Parliament. Cape Town: The presidency. 21 May.

Mbeki, T. 2005. Address of the President of South Africa at the Second Joint Sitting of the Third Democratic Parliament. Cape Town: The Presidency. 11 February.

Ministry Of Education, South Africa. 2002. Transformation and restructuring: A new institutional landscape for higher education. *Government Gazette* No. 23549. 21 June. Pretoria: Government Printers.

Motari, M.; Quach, U; Thorsteindottir, H.; Martin, D; Daar, A; Singer, P.(2004) South Africa: blazing a train for African biotechnology. *Nature Biotechnology* 22, Supplement 37–41.

NACI (National Advisory Council on Innovation). 2006. The South African National System of Innovation: Background Report to the OECD Country Review. Pretoria.

Nelson, R. R. 2006. *Economic Development from the Perspective of Evolutionary Economic Theory.* Columbia University [mimeo].

Nelson, R. R. 2005. Making Sense of Institutions as a Factor Shaping Economic Performance. Chap. In *Technology, Institutions, and Economic Growth.* Cambridge, MA: Harvard University Press.

Nelson, R. R. (ed) 1993 *National Innovation Systems: A Comparative Study.* Oxford: Oxford University Press.

Nelson, .R. R.; Nelson, K. 2002. Technology, Institutions, and Innovation Systems. *Research Policy* 31: 265–72.

OECD. 2007. Review of the [sic] South Africa's Innovation Policy. 26–27 March. DSTI/STP(2007)12. Paris.

Paterson, A.; Adam, R.; Mullin, J. 2003. The relevance of the national system of innovation approach to mainstreaming science and technology for development in NEPAD and the AU. Discussion paper. October 2003.

Paterson, A. Mariette Visser, Jacques du Toit, and Jo Lorentzen. 2008. National Skills Survey 2007. Pretoria: HSRC.

Pogue, T. E. 2008. Missed Opportunities? An Indicative Technology from South Africa's Mining Sector. In *Resource Intensity, Knowledge, and Development: Insights from Africa and South America*, ed. Jo Lorentzen. Pretoria: HSRC Press.

Policy Coordination And Advisory Services (Pcas). 2003. Towards a Ten Year Review: Synthesis report on implementation of government programmes. Discussion Document. Pretoria: Office of the Presidency. October.

Pouris, A. 2005. Technological Performance Judged by American Patents Awarded to South African Inventors. *South African Journal of Science* 101 (May/June): 221–24.

Presidency. Republic Of South Africa. N.d. Development Indicators. Mid-Term Review. Pretoria.

Rasiah, R. 2006. Ownership, Technological Intensities, and Economic Performance in South Africa. *International Journal of Technology Management* 36, nos1–3: 166–89.

Reddy, V. (ed). 2006. Marking Matric. Colloquium proceedings. Cape Town: HSRC Press.

Rooks, G.; Oerlemans. L. 2005. South Africa: A Rising Star? Assessing the X-effectiveness of South Africa's National System of Innovation. *European Planning Studies* 13, n.8: 1205–26.

Sawers, J. L; Pretorius, M. W; Oerlemans, Leon A.G. 2008. Safeguarding SMEs Dynamic Capabilities in Technology Innovative SME-Large Company Partnerships in South Africa. *Technovation* 28: 171–82.

Sharif, N. 2006. Emergence and Development of the national systems of innovation concept. *Research Policy*. 35 (5): 745–766.

Teece, D. J. 2000. Firm Capabilities and Economic Development: Implications for the Newly Industrializing Economies. In *Technology, Learning, & Innovation: Experiences of Newly Industrializing Economies*. Eds Linsu Kim and Richard Nelson, 105–28. Cambridge: Cambridge University Press.

United Nations Development Programme (Undp). 2001. Human Development Report 2001. Making new technologies work for human development. New York: UNDP.

Vandana, C.; Kolavalli, S. 2006. Technology, Adaptation, and Exports – How Some Developing Countries Got It Right. In *Technology, Adaptation, and Exports*, ed. Vandana Chandra, 1–47. Washington, DC: World Bank.

Van Renssen, S. 2006. Innovation in South Africa: too much, too soon? *SciDevNet*.12 May 2006.

Viotti, Eduardo B. 2002. National Learning Systems. A New Approach on Technological Change in Late Industrializing Economies and Evidences from the Cases of Brazil and South Korea. *Technological Forecasting & Social Change* 69: 653–80.

Von Tunzelmann, N. 2007. Approaching network alignment. U-Know contribution to the State-of-the-Art. U-Know Consortium. Deliverable D3 for Understanding the relationship between knowledge and competitiveness in the enlarging European Union.

Walwyn, D. 2003. *Biotechnologists*. In *HSRC*. Ed. Human Resources Development Review 2003. Cape Town: HSRC Press.

Whitley, R. 2003. Competition and pluralism in the public sciences: the impact of institutional frameworks on the organization of academic science. *Research Policy*. 32: 1015–1029.

Wolson, R. 2003. Intellectual property management in South African higher education institutions: some policy issues. Research report. Proceedings of of the CHE colloquium: Building relationships between higher educaiton and the private and public sectors and contributing to their high-level personpower and knowledge needs. Sandton 27 and 28 June 2002. Pretoria: Council on Higher Education.

Wolson, R 2007. The role of technology transfer offices in building the South African biotechnology sector: an assessment of policies, practices and impact. *Journal of Technology Transfer*. 32: 343–365.

World Bank. 2007. South Africa and the World Bank Group. Joint Country Partnership Strategy 2008 to 2012. Presentation. Johannesburg. 30 October.

NOTES

Preface

1 Communication from the Commission to the Council and the European Parliament, COM(2008) 588 final of 24 September 2008.
2 The workshop was co-funded by the European Commission's Directorate-General for Research, Directorate for International Cooperation.
3 Globelics (the Global Network for the Economics of Learning, Innovation and Competence Building Systems) is a global network of scholars who apply the concept of 'Learning, Innovation and Competence Building System' (Lics) as their analytical framework. The network is focusing especially on strengthening Lics in countries in the South. For further information, see the Globelics website: http://www.globelics.org/

Foreword: The Brics Countries and Europe

1 To illustrate, for the 2009 annual conference to take place in Dakar, Senegal received around 450 full papers from scholars who wanted to attend the conference. Of these, 200 papers were selected for presentation.
2 The application of the Washington consensus had mainly negative consequences for domestic innovation capacity in Latin America and Africa while the opening of the economies in East Asia combined with export-oriented strategies resulted in acceleration of economic growth (Wade 2004). In the latter case government steering of the opening of the economy and not least massive investments in the knowledge base were prerequisites for success (Amsden 1989). The simple truth may be that opening the economy for imports of commodities and foreign investment is useful only when you have a reasonably strong technological base. And a strong technological base cannot come exclusively via foreign direct investment; it requires active public policy (Lall 1992). Without strong domestic 'absorptive capacity', spillovers from foreign direct investment would be negligible.
3 Looking at Europe's workplaces as learning sites demonstrates dramatic differences between the north/west and the south/east of Europe. Upgrading the weakest countries would also stimulate innovation and economic performance (Arundel et al. 2007). It would be the most direct way towards strengthening competitiveness and at the same time promoting social cohesion.

1. Science, Technology and Innovation Policies in the Brics Countries: An Introduction

1 See www.globelics.org

2 See www. redesist.ie.ufrj.br

3 This is also true in Latin American countries, where it is being applied and understood in close connection with the basic conceptual ideas of the structuralism approach developed in the region since the 1950s under the influence of the Economic Commission for Latin America and the Caribbean. Since the mid-1990s, the work of RedeSist has been using such a dual frame of reference.

4 See for instance Mytelka & Farinelli, 2003; Freeman, 2003; Chesnais & Sauviat, 2003.

5 It is worth noting that the statistical data used in this introduction, as well as those utilised in most analyses of the BRICS, are those produced by international agencies. The BRICS project is aware that there are imperfections, inadequacies and gaps that make comparability more difficult. Specific research on appropriate indicators is essential to better represent what is happening in these countries. It should be stressed that addressing these inadequacies constitutes an important objective of the BRICS project.

6 These figures are underestimated as, for reasons of national security, a large part of government expenditure in this area is not published.

7 This figure is from The Economist (2009b) and is based on a report published by HSBC, ranking 17 countries by the green elements of their stimulus package. Just for comparison, according to the study, India is investing nothing under its $ 13.7 billion stimulus plan in such ventures and Japan allocated only 2.6 per cent (US$ 12 billion).

8 The effectiveness of such incentives in inducing firms to invest in innovation activities has been hotly debated. In a synthesis of this debate an extensive evaluation of Australian innovation policy concluded that 'firms should be barely receptive to subsidies directed at R&D alone, any more than people buying cars would respond to a reasonable subsidy on the tyres' (Productivity Commission, 2007, p. 35).

2. Achievements and Shortcomings of Brazil's Innovation Policies

1 The concept of National System of Innovation adopted here is a broad one (Freeman 1987 and Lundvall 1992).

2 This was totally different from what happened in Spanish America. The first university in Latin America was founded in Santo Domingo, in 1538, soon after the conquest of the New World. Its objective was to train religious and political leaders. In less than a century, 12 universities were set up by the Spanish in North and South America (such as the University of Cordoba in Argentina, in 1613) (Buarque 2003).

3 This was only exceeded by three East Asian NICs, South Korea (18.99 per cent), Singapore (11.41 per cent) and Indonesia (10.20 per cent).

4 Even if difficulties in financing were observed and the targets were not totally fulfilled, there is no doubt that the II PND's investments represented "an effort of capital accumulation and a diversification of the industrial structure towards heavy industry, without precedent in the history of Brazilian industrialisation" (Tavares and Lessa 1984: 6).

5 The resulting industrial structure was not so different from that of most OECD economies at the time: in 1980, the three most developed economies had roughly two

thirds of their industrial production originating from these sectors: 64.4 per cent for the US, 64.5 per cent for Japan and 69.8 per cent for West Germany (OECD 1984a).

6 The bulk of FUNTEC's support for scientific and technological development in its earliest period (1964–1971) was directed towards the R&D infrastructure: 76 per cent of financial resources was addressed to human resources (postgraduate programmes) and 19 per cent to the research projects of public research institutes.

7 FINEP was designated as the executive secretariat of the FNDCT, with responsibility for channelling its financial resources. The fund was the main financial instrument of the newly established Basic Plan for Science and Technology.

8 Several empirical evaluations confirm this assertion (Cassiolato 1992); Ferraz (1989) showed that in 1982 the technology expenditure of the Brazilian manufacturing sector represented 0.15 per cent of the operational revenues of industry and compared with similar figures of 1.5 per cent for the US and 2.5 per cent for Japan.

9 The number of ADTEN's operations ranged from two in 1973 to 81 in 1977 (Bielchowsky & Nunes 1978) and the total value of loans granted grew from US$ 1.8 million in 1973 to US$ 45.4 million in 1978 (Cassiolato et al. 1981). Although most borrowers (almost 90 per cent) were private firms, the reaction of entrepreneurs was, as Erber (1980: 420) pointed out, even if positive, cautious. State-owned enterprises, particularly in electric power projects, accounted for about half the total value of loans to firms and over 70 per cent of the total value of projects.

10 See Ferraz (1989) for a detailed discussion of this issue. Cassiolato (1980) found evidence of significant degrees of technological heterogeneity and differences in production costs and productivity levels with prices and rates of profits dictated by the least efficient firms for Brazilian production of sugar and alcohol during the 1970s.

11 For a review of Brazilian industrial policies from the 1950s to the 1970s, with special reference to the lack of mechanisms for technological development, see Suzigan (1988), who explicitly concluded: "the inefficiency and lack of competitiveness of Brazilian industry resulted from the absence of a strategy for scientific and technological development as part of the industrialisation policies implemented from the 1950s".

12 The main areas supported by this project were: chemistry and chemical engineering, biotechnology, geosciences and mineral technology, instrumentation, science education, and science planning and management. The project supported specific fields of knowledge but also addressed some general deficiencies of the National Innovation System, such as metrology, basic industrial technology, information science, chemical reagents and research consumables.

13 For an analysis of the industrial policy implemented at the beginning of the 1990s, see Guimarães (1996) and Erber & Cassiolato (1997).

14 The plan explicitly stated: "The industry and foreign trade policy has the purpose of enhancing efficiency in producing and trading goods and services, by means of the modernisation and restructuring of industry and, thus, helping to improve the quality of life of the Brazilian population".

15 Law No 9.532 of 1997 (published on 10 December 1997).

16 Non-reimbursable financing was granted to S&T institutions with firms paying their counterpart.

17 The guidelines for industry, technology and foreign trade policy (PITCE) were issued in November 2003 and officially announced by the Ministry of Development, Industry and Foreign Trade in March 2004. In line with the idea of spreading the pro-innovation discourse throughout the ministries, the guidelines were jointly formulated by several agencies of the Federal Government.

18 The objectives were: consolidating, improving and modernising the national system of science, technology and innovation, by expanding the national science and technology base; creating an environment favourable to innovation in the country, strengthening the industry, technology and foreign trade policy, encouraging the business sector to invest in research, development and innovation activities; integrating all regions in the national efforts to build capabilities in science, technology and innovation; developing a broad basis of support and engagement within society with regard to the industry, technology and foreign trade policy; transforming S,T&I into a strategic element within Brazilian policy for social and economic development (BRASIL 2006, p. 12).

19 As explicitly stated in the official policy document: "the lines of action to be considered by the Federal Government for the implementation of the industry, technology and foreign trade policy are: ... Technological innovation and development ... Along with the above actions, it is necessary to concentrate efforts on some knowledge-intensive areas ...- these are strategic choices in activities that: account for significant shares of international investments in research and development; ... are directly related to innovation in processes, products and modes of use ... (BRASIL 2003, p. 27).

20 In order to solve this problem of coordination the Executive established the Brazilian Agency for Industrial Development (ABDI) almost one year after the launch of the PITCE guidelines. However, the solution to the problem of coordination proved unfeasible, since the ABDI is an autonomous social service which, therefore, does not have any legal power over bodies belonging to the public administration. See Suzigan & Furtado (2006).

21 In Portuguese "Lei do Bem". This legislation provided several incentives and made changes to the legal framework in an attempt to foster private investment.

22 Budget allocations for grants, coordinated by the Ministry of Science and Technology and implemented by FINEP, started being provided in 2005.

23 Bill No 1631/07, governing operation of the National Fund for Scientific and Technological Development (FNDCT), was sent to the National Congress in 2007 and was still under examination at the end of 2008.

24 The criticism of using tax incentives persisted, as well as problems regarding the creation of contingency reserves for the sectoral funds. The resources of the sectoral funds for 2007 remained relatively stable compared to 2006, both as a percentage of GDP and as a percentage of the total budget of the Ministry of Science and Technology. The resources available for interest rate subsidies remained stable between the two years, representing around 0.01 per cent of the total budget of the Federal Government.

25 Note also the debates on the impact of macroeconomic policy and the innovation policy adopted for the production system, especially on manufacturing industry. For a discussion of this issue, see: Erber (2001), Fanelli and Frenkel (1996) and Ferraz et al. (2003 and 2003a), among others.

26 See, for instance, Sagasti (1978) and Guimarães (2006).

27 The economic history of Brazil over the last 50 years features two periods of steep acceleration of FDI flows. They have different origins and followed different patterns. In the first period, Brazilian FDI inflows represented around 5% of total world FDI, with a significant acceleration in the second half of the decade. Brazil was, however, a very large recipient of FDI flows to the developing world. During the 1970s the relative share of FDI inflows to Brazil in total FDI inflows to the developing world fluctuated around 25% and reached a peak of 50% in 1974. In the 1980s, with the crisis, both in absolute and relative terms FDI inflows to Brazil were significantly reduced. The foreign capital that flew to Brazil during this period was basically greenfield investment in manufacturing

activities. In this period FDI contributed to the consolidation of the Brazilian industrialisation process and supplemented the blocks of investments under the second National Development Plan that concentrated on industrial inputs — the chemical industry, steel, metallurgy, etc.

28 However, in this second period the relative size of FDI inflows to Brazil as related to total FDI inflows in the developing world was significantly smaller. With the upsurge of China, Brazil's share reached a peak of 15 per cent of FDI to developing countries in 1998, but never went much above 5 per cent during the period analysed.

29 RedeSist empirically investigated approximately 80 local innovation systems in Brazil from the late 1990s onwards. In practically all of these cases evidence was found in that direction. See www.redesist.ie.ufrj.br

3. Prospective Agenda for Science and Technology and Innovation Policies in Russia

1 Ministry for Economic Development. Concept for Long-Term Development Until 2020, 2008. A draft version is available online: http://www.economy.gov.ru/wps/wcm/myconnect/economylib/mert/welcome/pressservice/eventschronicle/doc12179496481 41 (In Russian).

2 See the official document 'Basic Policies of the Russian Federation in the Sphere of Scientific and Technological Development for the Period Ending 2010 and Further Prospects', Commission by the President of the Russian Federation No PR–578, 30.03.2002. (In Russian).

3 See the Federal Law On Autonomous Institutions, 03.11.2006 No 174–FZ. (In Russian).

4 See the Federal Law On Changes to the Selected Legal Statements of the Russian Federation Concerning the Integration of Education and Science, 01.12.2007, No 308–FZ. (In Russian).

5 See the Government Statement 'On Government Support Measures for the Education Institutions Implementing Innovation Education Programmes', 14.02.2006, No 89. (In Russian).

6 The draft Statement of the Ministry for Science and Education 'On performance evaluation of R&D organisations' (2008) is available online: www.mon.gov.ru/work/nti/dok/gsn/post04.doc (in Russian).

7 Federal Law No 70–FZ, 07.04.1999.

8 See the Resolution of the President of the Russian Federation 'On Conferment of Science City Status on Obninsk City, Kaluga Region', 06.06.2000, No 821. (In Russian).

9 See the Resolution of the President of the Russian Federation 'On Conferment of Science City Status on Dubna City, Moscow Region', 20.12.2001, No 1472. (In Russian).

10 More than 70 per cent of science cities incorporate innovation-oriented higher education institutions.

11 See the Federal Law 'On Special Economic Zones in the Russian Federation', 22.07.2005, No 116–FZ. (In Russian).

12 See Government Statement No 838–R. 07.06.2006. (In Russian).

13 See the Federal Law On the Russian Corporation for Nanotechnology, 12.07.2007, No 139–FZ. (In Russian).

14 See the Government Statement 'Science and Education Manpower for Innovative Russia', 20.07.2008, No 568. (In Russian).

4. Science, Technology and Innovation Policies in India: Achievements and Limits

1 The Indian Council of Medical Research (ICMR) was set up as early as 1911, followed by the Indian Council of Agricultural Research (ICAR) in 1929 and the Council of Scientific and Industrial Research (CSIR) in 1942.

2 Starting in the mid-eighties, the government undertook these reforms at a fairly good speed for a period of six to seven years. The Indian corporate sector was freed from the government controls over capacity regulation, which began in the late seventies, reservation of markets and access to foreign exchange. Capacity controls were removed, particularly in the sectors of importance to big business. Selectively, several industrial segments were de-reserved and de-licensed for the benefit of their entry. The Monopolies and Restrictive Trade Practices Act was diluted to facilitate expansion and diversification of large firms or firms belonging to big business groups. In the case of foreign investment regulation, automatic approval, or exemption from case-by-case approval, was granted for equity investment up to 51 per cent and for foreign technology agreements in identified high-priority industries. The Foreign Exchange Regulation Act was amended, so that companies with foreign equity exceeding 40 per cent of their total assets were treated on a par with foreign companies. However, foreign-controlled companies were restrained from direct access to Indian markets. Foreign-controlled companies were allowed entry if they fulfilled the obligations of furthering exports from India or of bringing highly monopolised technologies to the country.

3 This clearly suggests that the advocates of external liberalisation were incorrect when they suggested that the liberalisation of technology imports would allow large firms to broaden and deepen technology imports to a significant level and benefit major innovations leading to more exports from these firms. It is also clear that at the moment the country has fewer bargaining chips to persuade foreign licensors to part with the technology packages that would allow domestic firms to become export-competitive on the basis of imported know-how in high-tech manufacturing. This can work to some extent in the case of low-technology manufacturing and in the services sector where factors other than knowledge *per se* provide a competitive advantage to domestic firms.

4 Examples of CSIR-MNC tie-ups include DuPont for identification of molecules and drugs, Park Davis for supply of medicinal plants, Abbot Labs for synthesis of organic molecules and General Electric Company for intermediates for polycarbonates. Prominent instances of R&D feeding into foreign monopolies include General Electric, Texas Instruments, CISCO, ASTRA-Zeneca and Indal works for Alcan. Ciba-Giegy has a tie-up with Hoechst and winds up R&D operations after screening natural products.

5 Plan funding for the development of higher education has not increased in proportion to the increase in the funds allocated to education. The allocation during the ninth plan was less than 8 per cent. Over the period 1990-97 the share of expenditure on higher education out of total expenditure on education by both central and State government declined successively from 14.7% to 11.5%. The decline was greater in the central sector – from 32.2% to 15.7%. Expenditure on higher education as a percentage of GNP has fallen considerably. It is less than half of the 1981 level.

6. The South African Innovation Policies: Potential and Constraint

1 This chapter draws on Lorentzen (2009).
2 This section relies on NACI 2006, Section 3.2.

Lightning Source UK Ltd.
Milton Keynes UK
27 August 2010

158998UK00001BA/1/P